GCSE OCR Gateway Additional Science Foundation Revision Guide

This book is for anyone doing **GCSE OCR Gateway Additional Science** at foundation level. It covers everything you'll need for your year 11 exams.

GCSE Science is all about **understanding how science works**. And not only that — understanding it well enough to be able to **question** what you hear on TV and read in the papers.

But you can't do that without a fair chunk of **background knowledge**. Hmm, tricky.

Happily this CGP book includes all the **science facts** you need to learn, and shows you how they work in the **real world**. And in true CGP style, we've explained it all as **clearly and concisely** as possible.

It's also got some daft bits in to try and make the whole experience at least vaguely entertaining for you.

What CGP is all about

Our sole aim here at CGP is to produce the highest quality books — carefully written, immaculately presented and dangerously close to being funny.

Then we work our socks off to get them out to you — at the cheapest possible prices.

Contents

Module B4 — It's a Green World

Module C4 — The Periodic Table

Module P4 — Radiation for Life

Published by CGP

From original material by Richard Parsons.

Editors:
Katie Braid, Joe Brazier, Katherine Craig, Emma Elder, Felicity Inkpen,
Edmund Robinson, Helen Ronan, Hayley Thompson, Julie Wakeling, Dawn Wright.

Contributors:
Mike Bossart, Lucy Muncaster

ISBN: 978 1 84762 753 7

With thanks to Ian Francis, David Hickinson, Julie Jackson, Ann Shires, Jamie Sinclair, Jane Towle and Karen Wells for the proofreading.

With thanks to Jan Greenway, Laura Jakubowski and Laura Stoney for the copyright research.

With thanks to Science Photo Library for permission to use the image used on page 10.

Data used to draw graph on page 15, source developed by the National Center for Health Statistics in collaboration with the National Center for Chronic Disease Prevention and Health Promotion (2000). http://www.cdc.gov/growthcharts

Data used to construct stopping distance diagram on page 51 from the Highway Code.

Groovy website: www.cgpbooks.co.uk

Printed by Elanders Ltd, Newcastle upon Tyne.
Jolly bits of clipart from CorelDRAW®

The Scientific Process

For your exams and your controlled assessment you need to know about how the world of science works.

Science is All About Testing a Hypothesis

'Controlled assessment' is the scary name for the piece of coursework you have to do. See page 8 for more.

Scientists make an observation

1) Scientists observe (look at) something they don't understand — e.g. an illness that a person has.
2) Then they come up with a possible explanation for what they've observed.
3) This explanation is called a hypothesis.

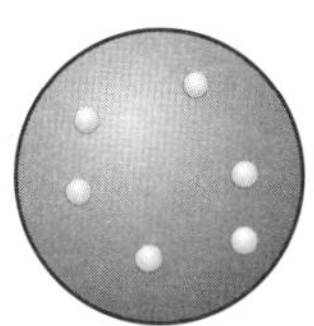

About 100 years ago, we thought atoms looked like this.

They test their hypothesis

1) Next, they test whether the hypothesis might be right or not.
2) They begin by making a prediction — a statement based on the hypothesis that can be tested by carrying out experiments.
3) Then they collect evidence (data from experiments) to test their prediction.
4) If their prediction is right, this shows that their hypothesis might be right too.
5) This doesn't mean the hypothesis is true though — other predictions might turn out to be wrong.

Then we thought they looked like this.

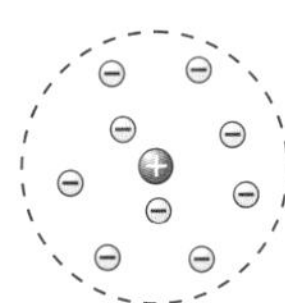

Other scientists test the hypothesis too

1) Once a scientist has come up with and tested a hypothesis, they'll show their work to other scientists to be checked. This is called the peer review process.
2) They then show their work to everyone by printing it in journals (science magazines) and talking about it at conferences (meetings).
3) Other scientists then try to repeat the results of the original experiment. They also carry out their own experiments to collect more evidence.

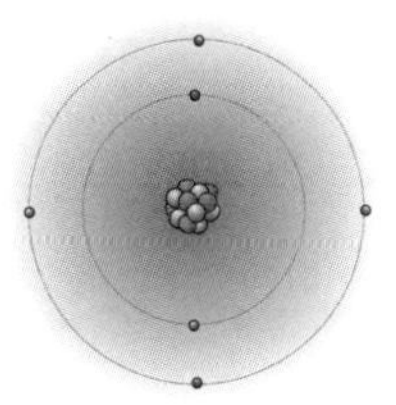

And then we thought they looked like this.

The hypothesis is accepted or changed

1) If all the experiments back up the hypothesis, scientists start to have a lot of trust in it.
2) But, if someone does an experiment and the results don't fit with the hypothesis then scientists must:
   a) change the hypothesis, OR
   b) come up with a completely new hypothesis.

You expect me to believe that — then show me the evidence...

If scientists think something is true, they need to find evidence to convince others. This is all part of testing a hypothesis. The hypothesis might survive these tests, but it might not. It's how science moves on.

Scientific Information and Development

In everyday life (and in your exams unfortunately) you'll come across lots of scientific information.

Scientific Ideas Change as New Evidence is Found

1) Scientific explanations are provisional — they only explain the evidence that's currently available.
2) New evidence may come up that can't be explained.
3) Scientific explanations are more convincing when there's a lot of evidence to support them.
4) But scientific explanations never become fact. As new evidence is found, hypotheses can change or be replaced.

Different Scientists Can Have Different Explanations

1) Different scientists might come up with different explanations for the same evidence.
2) More predictions and experiments would help to work out which explanation is the most convincing.
3) You might be given some scientific evidence and some explanations.
   You need to be able to say whether the evidence does or doesn't support the explanations.
4) This is easy — just look to see whether it's a sensible explanation to make from the evidence, or whether the explanation just doesn't fit with the evidence at all.

Scientific Information Can't Always be Trusted

1) When you're given some scientific information, don't just believe it straight away.
2) You need to think about whether there's any evidence to support it.

- Someone might give scientific information without any evidence to back it up.
- This might be because there's no evidence to support what they're saying.
- Information that isn't backed up with any evidence could just be an opinion — you've got no way of telling whether it's true or not.

Society Affects the Development of Science

1) The question of whether we should or shouldn't use new scientific developments can't be answered by experiments — there is no "right" or "wrong" answer.
2) The best we can do is get a consensus from society — a decision that most people are more or less happy to live by.
3) Science can give more information to help people make this decision, and the decision might change over time. But in the end it's up to people and their sense of right and wrong.
4) Decisions about how science is used can also be affected by lots of other factors, e.g. economic, social and cultural issues.

It's a scientific fact that the Moon's made of cheese...

Whenever you're given any scientific information just stop for a second. Ask yourself how convincing it really is — look to see if any evidence has been used to support it. It might just be an opinion — there's a big difference.

Planning Investigations

Here's how practical investigations should be carried out — by both professional scientists and you.

To Make an Investigation a Fair Test You Have to Control the Variables

Investigations that you plan should always be a fair test.

1) In a lab experiment you usually change one thing (a variable) and measure how it affects another thing (another variable).

> EXAMPLE: you might change only the angle of a slope and measure how it affects the time taken for a toy car to travel down it.

2) Everything else that could affect the results needs to stay the same. Then you know that the thing you're changing is the only thing that's affecting the results.

> EXAMPLE continued: you need to keep the slope length the same. If you don't you won't know if any change in the time taken is caused by the change in angle, or the change in length.

3) The variable that you change is called the independent variable.
4) The variable that's measured is called the dependent variable.
5) The variables that you keep the same are called control variables.

> EXAMPLE continued:
> Independent = angle of slope
> Dependent = time taken
> Control = length of slope

The Equipment Used has to be Right for the Job

Accurate measurements are really close to the true value of what you're measuring.

1) You need to make sure you choose the right equipment.
2) For example, the measuring equipment you use has to be able to accurately measure the chemicals you're using. If you need to measure out 11 ml of a liquid, use a measuring cylinder that can measure to 1 ml, not 5 or 10 ml.
3) The smallest change a measuring instrument can measure is called its RESOLUTION. E.g. some mass balances have a resolution of 1 g and some have a resolution of 0.1 g.
4) You should also be able to explain why you've chosen each bit of kit.

Experiments Must be Safe

1) There are lots of hazards (dangers) you could be faced with during an investigation, e.g. radiation, electricity, gas, chemicals and fire.
2) You should always make sure that you think of all the hazards there might be.
3) You should also come up with ways of reducing the risks from the hazards you've spotted.
4) For example, for an experiment involving a Bunsen burner:

> Hazard:
> - Bunsen burner is a fire risk.
>
> Ways risk can be reduced:
> - Keep chemicals that can catch fire away from the Bunsen.
> - Never leave the Bunsen alone when lit.
> - Always turn on the yellow safety flame when not in use.

Hazard: revision boredom. Reduce by: using CGP books

Wow, all this even before you've started the investigation — it really does make them run more smoothly though.

Getting the Data Right

You'll want to make sure that you get the best results you possibly can. Here's a few things you can do:

Trial Runs Help Figure out the Range and Interval of Variable Values

1) A trial run is a quick version of your experiment.
2) Trial runs help you work out whether your plan is right or not — you might decide to make some changes after trying out your method.
3) They're used to figure out the range of independent variable values used (the highest and lowest value).
4) And they're used to figure out the interval (gaps) between the values too.

Slope example from previous page continued:

- You might do trial runs at 20, 40, 60 and 80°. If the time taken is too short to accurately measure at 80°, you might narrow the range to 20-60°.
- If using 20° intervals gives you a big change in time taken you might decide to use 10° intervals, e.g. 20, 30, 40, 50...

Data Should be as Reliable and Accurate as Possible

1) Reliable results are results that always come out the same every time you do the same experiment.
2) If your results are reliable they're more likely to be true. This means you can have more trust in your conclusions.
3) You can make your results more reliable by repeating the readings at least twice (so that you have at least three readings). Then you can calculate the mean (average, see next page).
4) Checking your results match with secondary sources, e.g. studies that other people have done, also makes your data more reliable.
5) You should also always make sure that your results are accurate.
6) Really accurate results are those that are really close to the true answer.
7) You can get accurate results by making sure the equipment you're using is sensitive enough (see previous page).

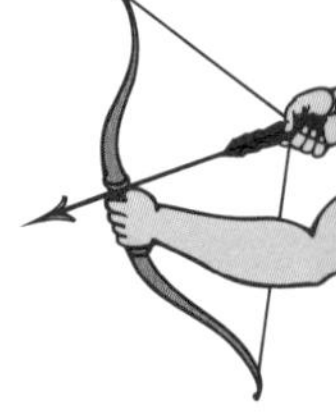

You Can Check For Mistakes Made When Collecting Data

1) When you've collected all the results for an experiment, you should have a look to see if there are any results that don't seem to fit in with the rest.
2) Most results are slightly different, but any that are totally different are called anomalous results.
3) They're caused by human errors, e.g. by a whoopsie when measuring.
4) The only way to stop them happening is by taking all your measurements as carefully as possible.
5) If you ever get any anomalous results, you should try to work out what happened.
6) If you can work out what happened (e.g. you measured something wrong) you can ignore them when processing your results.

Reliable data — it won't ever forget your birthday...

All this stuff is really important — your data will be meaningless if it's not reliable and accurate. So give this page a read through a couple of times and your data will be the envy of all the scientists in the world. Yes, all of them.

Processing, Presenting and Interpreting Data

The fun doesn't stop once you've collected your data — it then needs to be processed and presented...

Data Needs to be Organised

1) Data that's been collected needs to be organised so it can be processed later on.
2) Tables are dead useful for organising data.
3) You should always make sure that each column has a heading and that you've included the units.

Test tube	Result (ml)	Repeat 1 (ml)	Repeat 2 (ml)
A	28	37	32
B	47	51	60
C	68	72	70

Data Can be Processed Using a Bit of Maths

1) Raw data just isn't that useful. To make it useful, you have to process it in some way.
2) One of the most simple calculations you can do is the mean (average):

To calculate the mean ADD TOGETHER all the data values. Then DIVIDE by the total number of values. You usually do this to get a single value from several repeats of your experiment.

Test tube	Result (ml)	Repeat 1 (ml)	Repeat 2 (ml)	Mean (ml)
A	28	37	32	(28 + 37 + 32) ÷ 3 = 32.3
B	47	51	60	(47 + 51 + 60) ÷ 3 = 52.7
C	68	72	70	(68 + 72 + 70) ÷ 3 = 70.0

Different Types of Data Should be Presented in Different Ways

1) You need to present your data so that it's easier to see any patterns.
2) Different types of investigations give you different types of data, so you'll always have to choose what the best way to present your data is.

Pie charts can be used to present the same sort of data as bar charts. They're mostly used when the data is in percentages or fractions.

Bar Charts

1) If the independent variable comes in clear categories (e.g. blood types, metals) you should use a bar chart to display the data.
2) You also use them if the independent variable can be counted in chunks, where there are no in-between values. For example, number of people (because you can't have half a person).
3) There are some golden rules you need to follow for drawing bar charts:

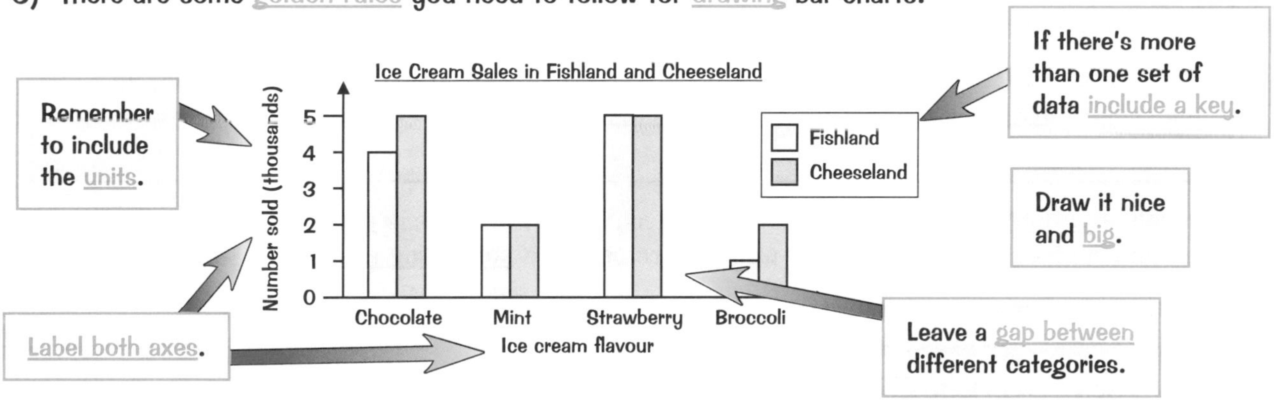

Processing, Presenting and Interpreting Data

Line Graphs

If the independent variable can have any value within a range, (e.g. length, volume, temperature) you should use a line graph to display the data.

Remember to include the units.

The dependent variable (the thing you measure) goes on the y-axis (the vertical one).

The independent variable (the thing you change) goes on the x-axis (the horizontal one).

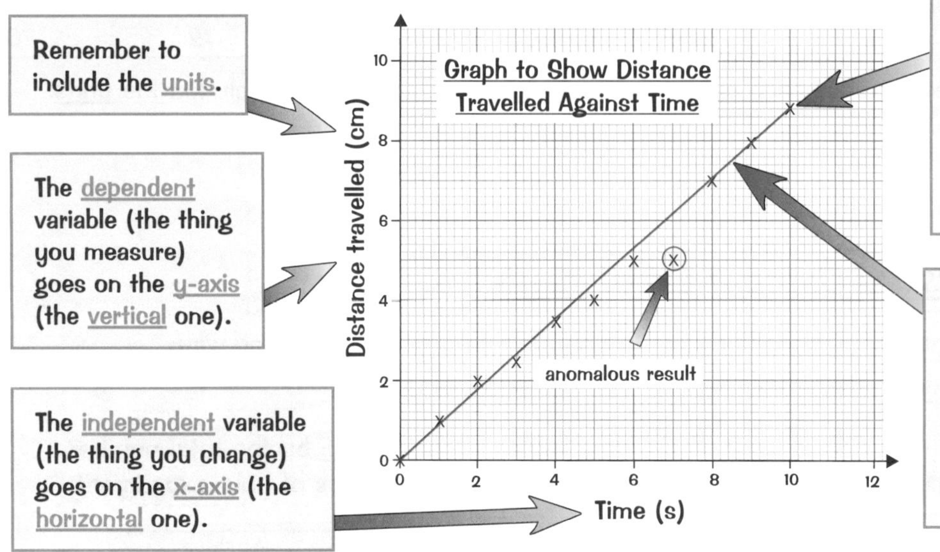

When plotting points, use a sharp pencil and make a neat little cross (don't do blobs).

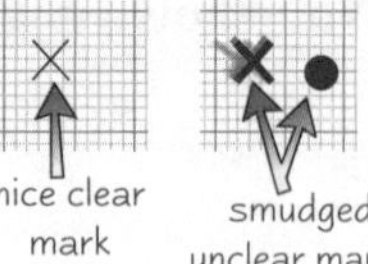

Don't join the dots up. You should draw a line of best fit (or a curve of best fit). Try to draw the line through or as near to as many points as possible, ignoring anomalous results.

You can use line graphs to process data a bit more.
For example, if 'time' is on the x-axis, you can calculate the gradient (slope) of the line to find the rate of reaction:

1) Gradient = y ÷ x
2) You can calculate the gradient of the whole line or a section of it.
3) The rate would be in cm^3/s (cubic centimetres of gas per second).

Volume of gas (cm^3)
Time (s)

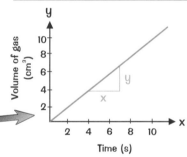

Line Graphs Can Show Patterns in Data

1) When you're carrying out an investigation it's not enough to just present your data — you've also got to find any patterns in the data.
2) Line graphs are great for showing patterns in data.

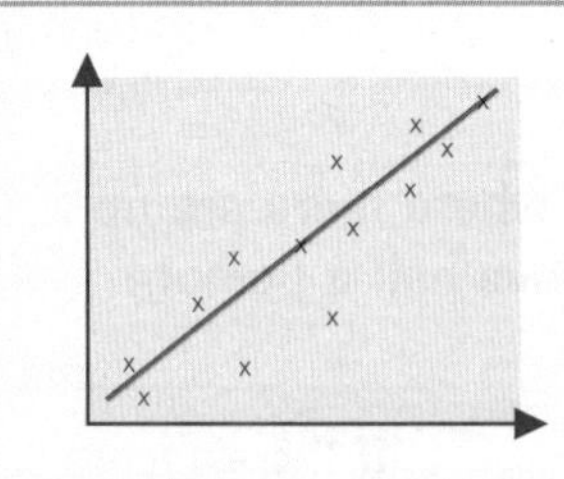

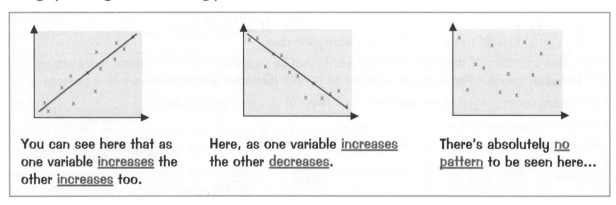

You can see here that as one variable increases the other increases too.

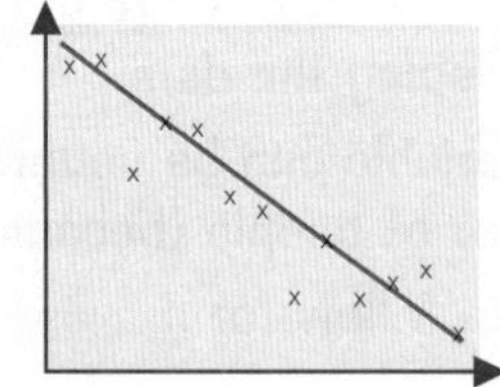

Here, as one variable increases the other decreases.

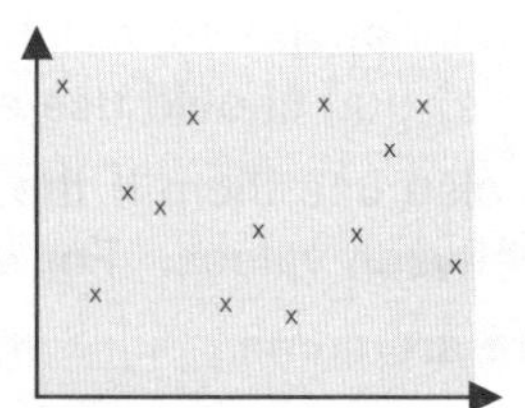

There's absolutely no pattern to be seen here...

3) If there's a pattern between two variables, it doesn't mean that one is causing the other to change. It just means they're related in some way. There could be something else causing the change.

As age of man increases, length of nose hair also increases...

Process, present, interpret... data's like a difficult child — it needs a lot of attention. Go on, make it happy.

Concluding and Evaluating

At the end of an investigation, the conclusion and evaluation are waiting. Don't worry, they won't bite.

A Conclusion is a Summary of What You've Learnt

1) Once you've collected, presented and analysed your data, you need to come to a conclusion.
2) You just have to look at your data and say what pattern you see.

EXAMPLE: The table on the right shows how effective two washing powders were at removing stains when used at 30 °C.

Washing powder	% of stained area removed on average
A	60
B	80
No powder	10

CONCLUSION: Powder B is more effective at removing stains than powder A at 30 °C.

3) You also need to use the data that's been collected to justify the conclusion (back it up).

EXAMPLE continued: Powder B removed 20% more of the stained area than powder A on average.

4) It's important that the conclusion matches the data it's based on — it shouldn't say anything that the data doesn't show.

EXAMPLE continued: You can't conclude that powder B will remove more of the stained area than powder A at any other temperature than 30 °C — the results might be totally different.

5) You should also use your own scientific knowledge (the stuff you've learnt in class) to try to explain the conclusion.

Evaluation — Describe How it Could be Improved

In an evaluation you look back over the whole investigation.

1) You should comment on the method — was the equipment suitable? Was it a fair test?
2) Comment on the quality of the results — were they reliable and accurate?
3) Were there any anomalous results — if there were none then say so.
4) If there were any anomalous results, try to explain them — were they caused by errors in measurement? Were there any other variables that could have affected the results?
5) When you look back at your investigation like this, you'll be able to say how sure you are that your conclusion is right.
6) Then you can suggest any changes that would improve the quality of the results. For example, you might suggest changing the way you controlled a variable, or changing the interval of values you measured.
7) This would mean you could be more sure about your conclusion.
8) When you suggest an improvement to the investigation, always say why you think this would make the results better.

Evaluation — in my next study I will make sure I don't burn the lab down...

I know it doesn't seem very nice, but writing about where you went wrong is an important skill. It shows you've got a really good understanding of what the investigation was about. It's difficult for me — I'm always right.

Controlled Assessment

You'll probably carry out a few investigations as you go through the course. But at some point you'll have to do the one that counts... the controlled assessment. Here's a bit about it...

There are Three Parts to the Controlled Assessment

1 Research and Collecting Secondary Data

For Part 1 you'll be given some material to introduce the task and a research question. You need to:

1) Carry out research and collect secondary data (data that other people have collected).
2) Show that you thought about all the different sources you could have used (e.g. books, the Internet) and chose the best ones. You also need to explain why you chose those sources.
3) Write a full list (bibliography) of all the sources you used.
4) Present all the data you collected in the best way, e.g. using tables.

2 Planning and Collecting Primary Data

For Part 2 you'll be given some more information to get your head around. Read this through and then:

1) Come up with a hypothesis based on the information you've been given.
2) Plan an experiment to test your hypothesis. Think about:
   - What equipment you're going to use (and why that equipment is right for the job).
   - What measurements you're going to take of the dependent variable.
   - How you're going to make sure your results are accurate and reliable.
   - What range of values and interval you will use for the independent variable.
   - What variables you're going to control (and how you're going to do it).
   - How many times you're going to repeat the experiment.
3) Say what the risks of the experiment will be and how you'll reduce them.
4) Carry out the experiment to collect primary data.
5) Present all the data you collected in the best way, e.g. using tables.

Don't forget to explain all the choices you made when planning the experiment.

3 Analysis and Evaluation

For Part 3 you'll have to complete a question paper. It'll ask you to do things like:

1) Process (e.g. using a bit of maths) and present (e.g. using graphs) both the primary and secondary data you collected in Part 1 and Part 2.
2) Analyse and interpret the data to find any patterns.
3) Compare your primary and secondary data to look for similarities and differences.
4) Write a conclusion based on all the data you collected.
   Make sure you back it up with your own scientific knowledge.
5) Say whether the data supports your hypothesis or not.
6) Evaluate the methods you used to collect the data and the quality of the data that was collected.
7) Say how sure you are about your conclusion.
8) Make suggestions for how the investigation could be improved. You'll also need to say why your suggestions would be an improvement.

Read this through and your assessment will be well under control...

You could use this page like a tick list for the controlled assessment — to make sure you don't forget anything.

Cells

Biology's all about living stuff. And all living stuff is made up of cells. So let's make a start with cells...

Learn These Animal Cell Structures...

The following cell structures are found in most animal cells:

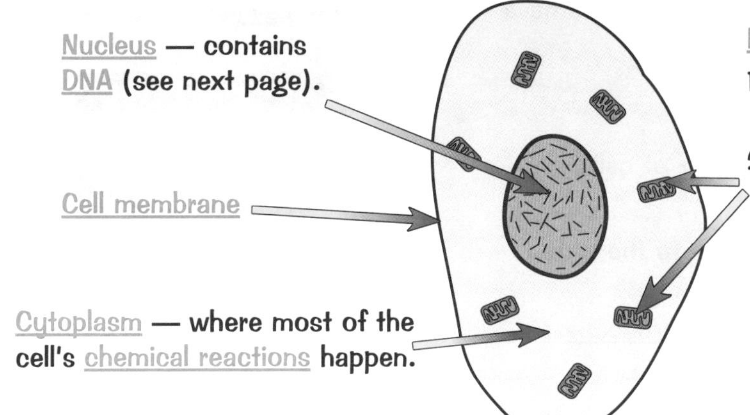
Nucleus — contains
DNA (see next page).
Cell membrane
Cytoplasm — where most of the
cell's chemical reactions happen.

Mitochondria — where respiration takes place.

1) Respiration provides energy for life processes (see page 17).
2) Cells that need lots of energy contain lots of mitochondria, e.g.
   - liver cells — which need lots of energy to carry out important chemical reactions.
   - muscle cells — which need energy to contract (and cause movement).

...And These Plant Cell Structures Too

Plant cells usually have all the structures that animal cells have, plus a few extra:

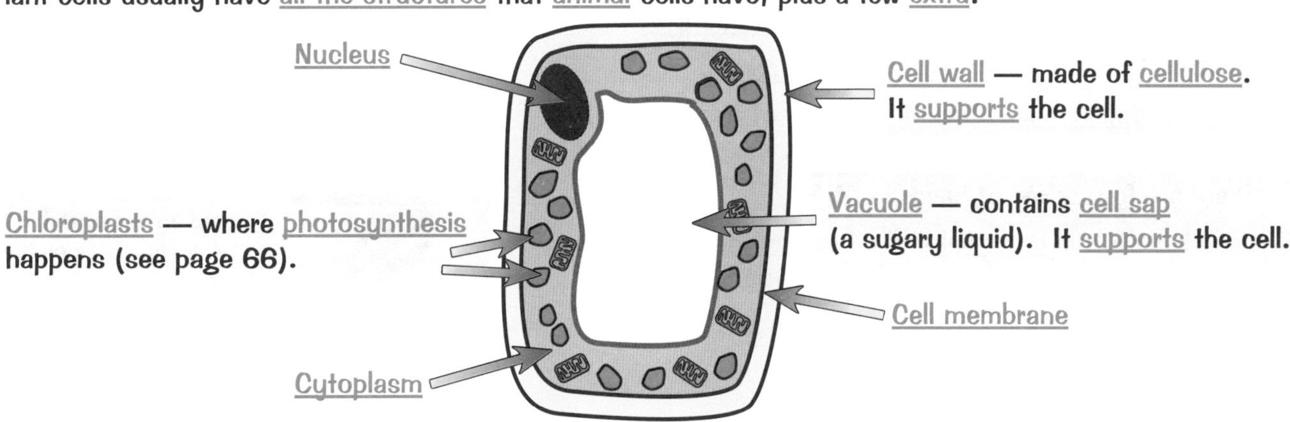
Nucleus
Chloroplasts — where photosynthesis
happens (see page 66).
Cytoplasm
Cell wall — made of cellulose.
It supports the cell.
Vacuole — contains cell sap
(a sugary liquid). It supports the cell.
Cell membrane

Bacterial Cells Are A Bit Different

Bacterial cells are smaller and simpler than plant and animal cells...

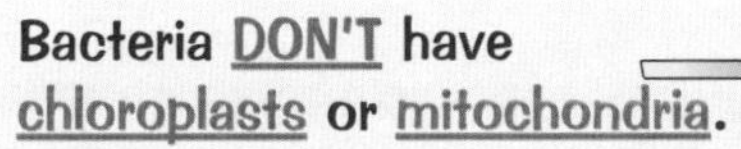
Bacteria DON'T have
chloroplasts or mitochondria.

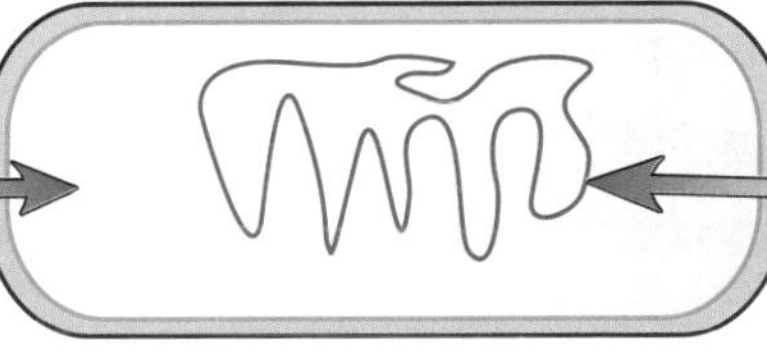

Bacterial cells DON'T have a 'true' (proper) nucleus — their DNA just floats about in the cytoplasm.

Cell structures — become a property developer...

You need to know what makes bacterial cells that bit different from plant and animal cells — it's mainly that they don't have anything interesting like a nucleus, chloroplasts or mitochondria.

Cells and DNA

You can look at a cell using a microscope — but not at it's DNA. Scientists had to use other ways to figure out what DNA looks like — and they only did it recently.

You Need to Know How to Make a Stained Slide of Onion Cells

You can look at onion cells under a microscope, but first you have to put them on a slide.
Here's how you do it.

1) First you have to cut up an onion.
2) Then, using tweezers, remove the slimy skin between the onion layers — this is a single layer of cells.
3) Add the skin to a microscope slide.
4) Add a drop of iodine solution or methylene blue to the slide. These are dyes that will stain cell structures.
5) Add a cover slip and place the slide under the microscope.
6) With a bit of luck it'll look something like the picture.

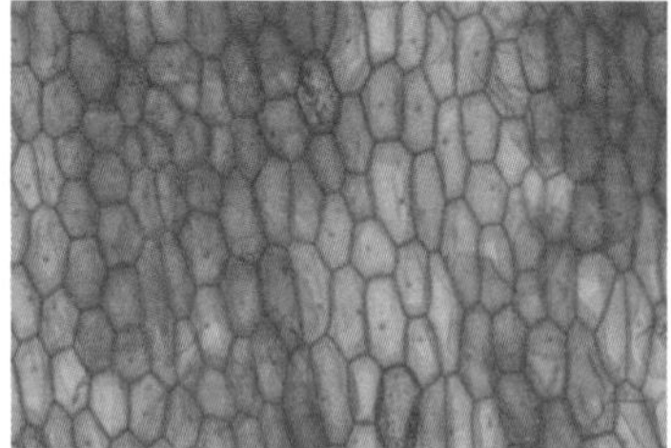

SIDNEY MOULDS / SCIENCE PHOTO LIBRARY

Onion cells under a microscope.

The Cell Nucleus Contains Chromosomes

1) Chromosomes are long molecules of coiled up DNA.
2) The DNA contains short sections called genes.
3) DNA is a double helix (a spiral made up of two strands).
4) It's made from chemicals called bases. There are four different bases in DNA.
5) Each base forms cross links to a base on the other strand. This keeps the two strands held tightly together.

A DNA Double Helix

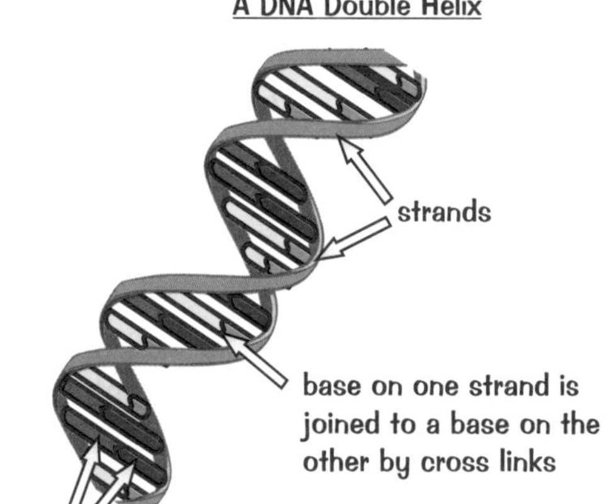
strands
base on one strand is joined to a base on the other by cross links
bases

Watson and Crick Were The First to Work Out the Structure of DNA

1) Watson and Crick were the first scientists to build a model showing what DNA looks like.
2) They used data from other scientists to help them understand the structure of the molecule. This included:
   - Data from X-rays showing that DNA is a double helix formed from two chains wound together.
   - Other data showing that the bases are found in pairs.

Q: What do DNA and a game of rounders have in common...?

Answer: four bases, and don't you forget it. Scientists spent years and years trying to work out the structure of DNA. When Watson and Crick finally cracked it, it became the scientific discovery of the twentieth century.

Protein Synthesis and Mutations

Now you know what genes are, you need to know what they do...

Proteins are Made by Reading the Genetic Code

See previous page for more on genes and bases.

1) Genes contain a set of coded instructions about how to make different proteins.
2) These instructions are called the genetic code.
3) Different types of cells make different proteins. So do different organisms.
4) Each individual gene has a different sequence of bases. This allows it to code for a particular protein.
5) By controlling the production of proteins, the genetic code controls a cell's activities. It also controls some of an organism's characteristics, e.g. eye colour.

A Copy of a Gene is Needed to Make a Protein

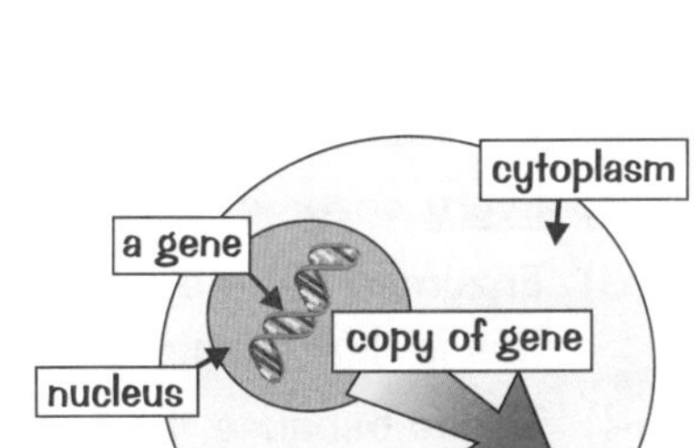
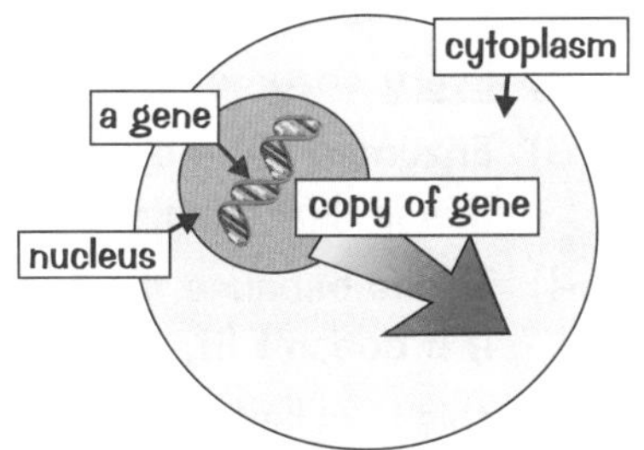

1) The code in genes is needed to make proteins.
2) Proteins are made in the cell cytoplasm.
3) Genes are found in the cell nucleus and can't move out because they're too big. So the cell needs to get the code from the gene to the cytoplasm.
4) This is done by copying the gene. The copy carries the code between the gene and the cytoplasm.

Proteins Have Lots of Different Functions

1) Proteins are long chains of amino acids.
2) Cells need proteins to grow and to repair damage — but proteins have loads of other functions too. You need to know four of them:
   - ENZYMES — see next page.
   - CARRIER MOLECULES — e.g. haemoglobin (found in red blood cells) transports oxygen round the body.
   - HORMONES — e.g. insulin controls the blood sugar level.
   - STRUCTURAL PROTEINS — e.g. collagen strengthens certain tissues.

Mutations Are Changes to Genes

1) Gene mutations can cause different proteins to be made.
2) Producing the wrong protein can be a bit of a disaster — so many mutations are harmful.
3) Some mutations are beneficial (helpful) though. E.g. they might produce a new protein that works better than the old one.
4) Some mutations don't have any effect. They don't change the protein that is made at all.
5) Mutations can happen spontaneously (by chance).
6) Mutations happen more often if you're exposed to harmful radiation or certain chemicals.

And I thought the aliens were in control...

... but it turns out that genes are really where it's at. It's a tricky page so make sure you revise it carefully.

Enzymes

Enzymes are handy little things — they speed up chemical reactions in your body.

Enzymes Control Cell Reactions

1) Enzymes are proteins that act as BIOLOGICAL CATALYSTS.
2) This means that they catalyse (speed up) the chemical reactions in living cells.
3) Reactions catalysed by enzymes include respiration, photosynthesis and protein synthesis. So remember:

ENZYMES are BIOLOGICAL CATALYSTS that SPEED UP CHEMICAL REACTIONS in cells.

Enzymes are Very Specific

1) The substance that changes in a chemical reaction is called the substrate.
2) Every enzyme has an active site — the part where it joins on to its substrate to catalyse the reaction.
3) Enzymes are really picky — they usually only work with one substrate. The posh way of saying this is that enzymes have a HIGH SPECIFICITY for their substrate.
4) This is because the substrate has to be the right shape to fit into the active site. If it doesn't fit, the enzyme won't catalyse the reaction.
5) This is called the 'lock and key mechanism' — the substrate (key) needs to fit the enzyme (lock).

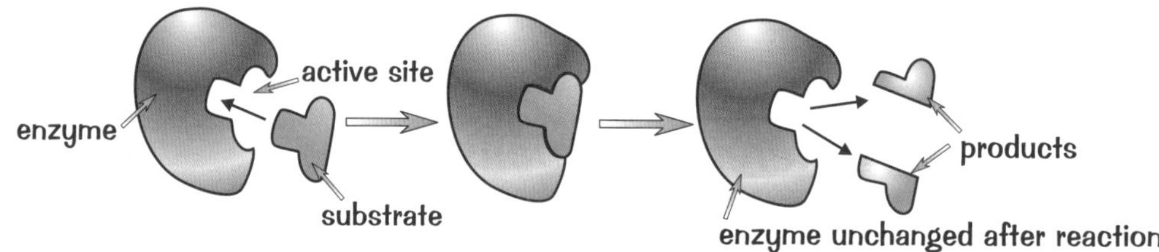

Enzymes Have an Optimum Temperature and pH

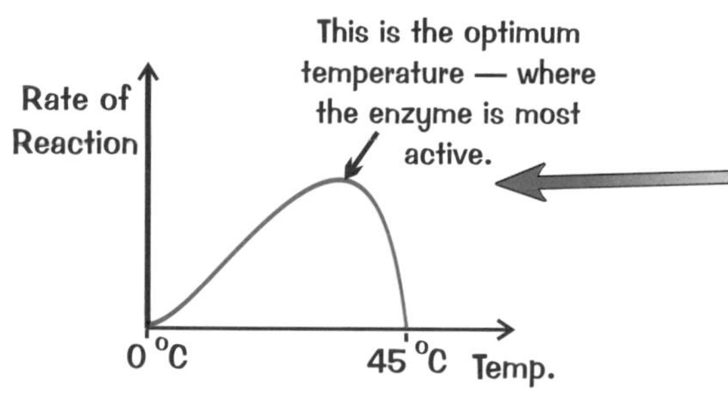

1) Changing the temperature changes the rate of an enzyme-catalysed reaction.
2) A higher temperature increases the rate at first. If it gets too hot the rate rapidly decreases.
3) Each enzyme has its own optimum temperature. This is the temperature at which the enzyme works best.

1) The pH also has an effect on enzymes.
2) Like with temperature, all enzymes have an optimum pH that they work best at.
3) If the pH is too high or too low, the enzyme won't work very well and the rate of reaction will be slow.

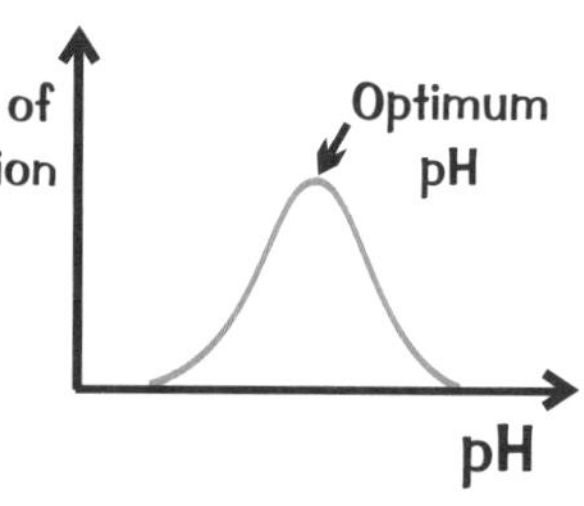

If only enzymes could speed up revision...

Enzymes aren't just useful for controlling chemical reactions in the body — we even put them in things like biological washing powders to speed up the breakdown of nasty stains (like tomato ketchup).

Cell Division and Differentiation

Cell division — pretty important if you're planning on being bigger than a bacteria. Which I am, one day.

New Cells are Produced by Cell Division

1) Cells divide so that organisms can:
   - Grow — to get bigger.
   - Replace worn out cells — e.g. our red blood cells are replaced every 120 days.
   - Repair damaged tissue — like cuts and bruises.
2) These new cells are produced by a type of cell division called 'MITOSIS'. The parent cell splits to form two new genetically identical cells (i.e. two cells with the same DNA).
3) Every time a cell divides, the chromosomes need to be copied, so that each new cell still has the full amount of DNA.
4) So before cell division the DNA replicates (copies itself).
5) Mitosis also allows some organisms to reproduce asexually. This is where one parent produces offspring that are genetically identical to itself.

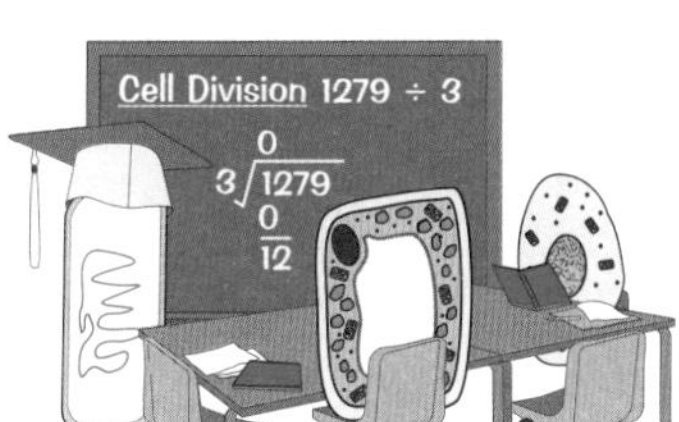

Cells Differentiate to Become Specialised

1) Most cells in your body are SPECIALISED for a particular job. For example, white blood cells are brilliant at fighting invaders but can't carry oxygen, like red blood cells (see page 19).
2) DIFFERENTIATION is the process by which a cell changes to become specialised for its job.

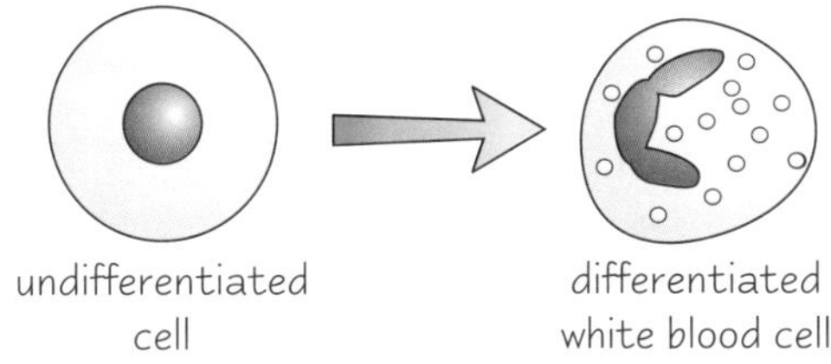

Stem Cells Can Turn into Different Types of Cells

1) Some cells are undifferentiated. They can develop into different types of cell, tissues and organs depending on what instructions they're given.
2) Undifferentiated cells are called STEM CELLS.
3) Stem cells are found in early human embryos.
4) Scientists can extract stem cells from embryos and grow them.
5) They think they may be able to use the stem cells to treat medical conditions, e.g. by growing stem cells into nerve cells to repair damaged nerves.
6) This is called stem cell therapy.

Some people are against stem cell research. They feel that human embryos shouldn't be used for experiments since each one is a potential human life. Others think that helping patients who are suffering is more important than the rights of embryos.

Right — now that I have your undivided attention...

There are some crazy words on this page — mitosis, stem cells, differentiated, specialised... it's enough to make your head spin. But worry not. There's no problem in the world that can't be solved with flash cards.

Growth and Multi-cellular Organisms

Most growth involves cell division and cell specialisation (see previous page).
Different organisms grow in different ways though...

Plants and Animals Grow in Different Ways

You need to know the differences between plant and animal growth...

ANIMALS	PLANTS
Grow when they're young and stop when they get to a particular size (full growth).	Grow continuously (throughout their lives).
• All growth happens by cell division. • All parts of the animal grow.	• Growth in height is by cell enlargement (cells getting longer). • Growth by cell division only happens in certain parts of the plant. These are the meristems (at the tips of the shoots and roots).
The ability to differentiate is lost at an early stage.	Lots of plant cells don't ever lose the ability to differentiate.

Being Multi-cellular Has Some Important Advantages

1) Simple organisms are often unicellular — this means they only have one cell, e.g. bacteria.
2) More complex organisms are usually multi-cellular — this means they have lots of cells, e.g. humans.
3) There are some big advantages in being multi-cellular...

- Being multi-cellular means you can be BIGGER.
- Being multi-cellular allows your cells to DIFFERENTIATE (see page 13). Instead of being just one cell that has to do everything, you can have different types of cells that do different jobs.
- This means multi-cellular organisms can also be more COMPLEX. E.g. they can have specialised organ systems.

Ha! Puny bacteria —
I'm more complex than you!
Are not!

My supermarket is multi-cellular — it sells loads of things...

If this page hasn't got your pulse racing with excitement, I really don't know what will. Growth is actually pretty darn important. Just imagine, if you hadn't grown up you'd still be a tiny wee thing in nappies. So hurrah for growth. In fact, it's so brilliant, you really need another page on it...

Growth

Growth is an increase in size or mass. But you need to know a lot more than that...

There are Different Methods for Measuring Growth

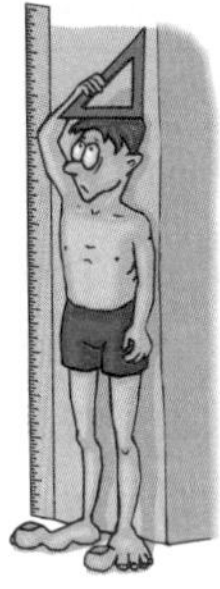

1) Growth can be measured as an increase in:
   - Height
   - Wet mass (the weight of the organism when it's alive)
   - Dry mass (the weight of the organism when it's dead and has been dried out)
2) The best way to measure growth in plants and animals is to measure changes in dry mass.

Human Growth has Different Phases

1) Humans go through five main phases of growth:

PHASE	DESCRIPTION
Infancy	Roughly the first two years of life. Rapid growth.
Childhood	Period between infancy and puberty. Steady growth.
Adolescence	Being a teenager. Begins with puberty and continues until growth stops. Rapid growth.
Maturity/adulthood	Period between adolescence and old age. No growth.
Old age	Between age 65 and death.

Puberty is when the body develops sexual characteristics, e.g. pubic hair.

2) Humans grow fastest JUST AFTER BIRTH and during ADOLESCENCE.
3) Growth stops when a person reaches adulthood.
4) The graph on the right is an example of a typical human growth curve.

5) It shows how weight increases for boys between the ages of 2 and 20.
6) When the line is steeper, growth is faster (e.g. during adolescence).

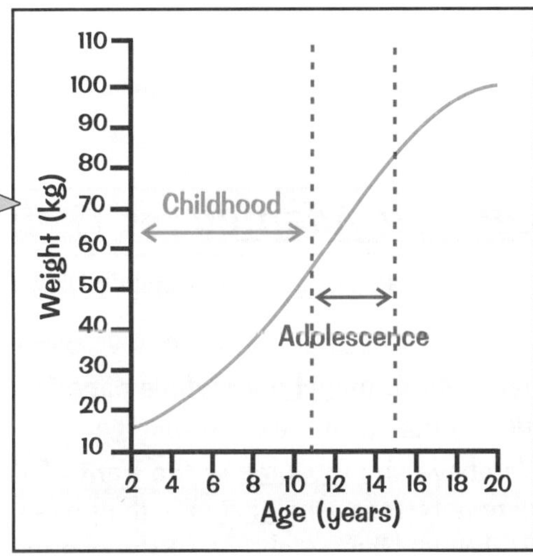

I'm growing rather sick of this topic...

Listen, you think you're sick of reading these lame jokes? Just think how I feel, having to make them up.

Sexual Reproduction

People can look very similar to their mum and dad, often a good mix of the two. Here's why.

Meiosis is Another Type of Cell Division — It Creates Gametes

1) Gametes are the sex cells — eggs and sperm.
2) They're formed by MEIOSIS in the ovaries and testes.
3) The body cells of mammals are diploid. This means that each body cell has two copies of each chromosome in its nucleus.
4) The chromosome copies are found in matching pairs.
5) Gametes have half the number of chromosomes as body cells — this means they're haploid. They only have one copy of each chromosome from each pair.
6) This is so that when the egg and the sperm combine, they'll form a cell with the diploid number of chromosomes (see below).

Sexual Reproduction Involves Fertilisation

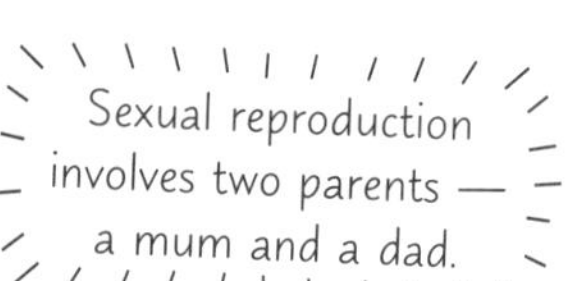

Sexual reproduction involves two parents — a mum and a dad.

1) Sexual reproduction produces a unique individual. It involves fertilisation.
2) Fertilisation is when two gametes (a sperm and an egg) combine.
3) This forms a diploid cell called a zygote.
4) The zygote gets half its chromosomes from its mum and half from its dad. So it gets half its genes from each parent.
5) The combination of genes on its chromosomes will control the zygote's characteristics.
6) This creates genetic variation.

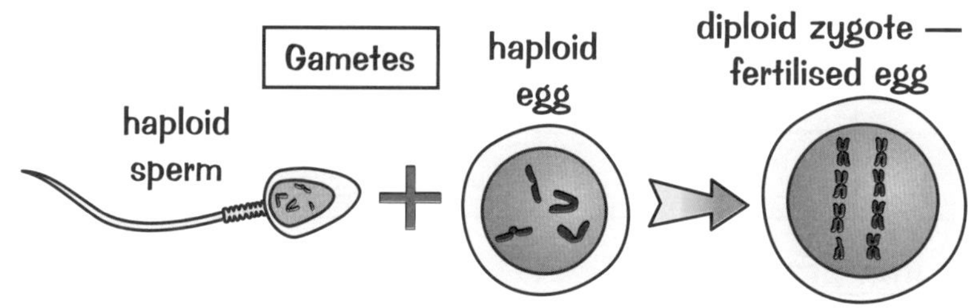

Sperm Cells are Adapted for Their Function

A sperm's function is to transport the male's DNA to the female's egg.

1) Sperm are made in large numbers to increase the chance of fertilisation.
2) Sperm have lots of mitochondria (see page 9) to provide the energy to swim to the egg.
3) Sperm also have an acrosome at the front of the 'head'. The acrosome releases the enzymes they need to digest their way through the membrane of the egg cell.

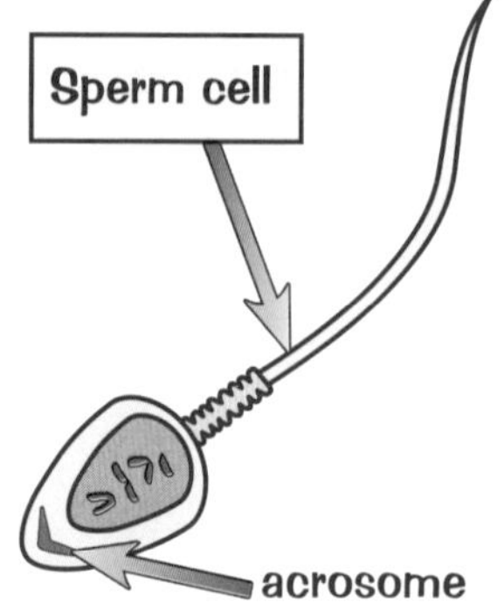

No sniggering in the back, please...

For many kids in year seven, the mere sight of a sperm is enough to make them giggle. Those of them that don't think it's an innocent tadpole, anyway. But that's not the case for you lot. We hope.

Respiration

You need energy to keep your body going. Energy comes from food, and it's released by respiration.

Respiration is NOT "Breathing In and Out"

1) Respiration goes on in every cell in your body.
2) It's the process of RELEASING ENERGY from GLUCOSE.
3) This energy is needed for all life processes in plants and animals. It's used to do things like:
   - contract muscles
   - control body temperature (in mammals only)
   - build up larger molecules (like in protein synthesis)

4) There are two types of respiration, AEROBIC and ANAEROBIC.

Aerobic Respiration Needs Plenty of Oxygen

1) Aerobic respiration happens when there's plenty of oxygen available.
2) It's the best way to release energy from glucose.
3) This is the type of respiration that you're using most of the time.
4) You need to learn the word and chemical equations for aerobic respiration:

$$\text{glucose} + \text{oxygen} \rightarrow \text{carbon dioxide} + \text{water} \quad (+\text{ENERGY})$$
$$C_6H_{12}O_6 + 6O_2 \rightarrow 6CO_2 + 6H_2O \quad (+\text{ENERGY})$$

5) As your rate of respiration increases, two things happen:
   - You use more oxygen (your oxygen consumption increases).
   - You make more carbon dioxide (your carbon dioxide production increases).

Anaerobic Respiration Doesn't Use Oxygen At All

1) When you exercise hard, your body can't supply enough oxygen to your muscles for aerobic respiration. So your muscles have to start respiring anaerobically as well.
2) Anaerobic respiration takes place without oxygen.
3) It produces lactic acid.
4) It also releases much less energy per glucose molecule than aerobic respiration.
5) You need to learn the word equation:

$$\text{Glucose} \rightarrow \text{Lactic Acid} \quad (+\text{ENERGY})$$

6) Lactic acid builds up in the muscles, which gets painful and makes your muscles fatigued (tired).
7) The advantage is that at least you can keep on using your muscles.

I reckon aerobics classes should be called anaerobics instead...

You might get a question in the exam asking you to use data from experiments to compare respiration rates — just remember, increased oxygen consumption (or carbon dioxide production) means an increased respiration rate.

Respiration and Exercise

I'm not going to lie to you — that is an equation you can see below.
But it's not as bad as it looks. Really.

The Respiratory Quotient Shows the Type of Respiration Being Used

1) The respiratory quotient (RQ) can tell you whether someone is respiring aerobically or anaerobically.
2) You can calculate it using this equation:

$$RQ = \frac{\text{Amount of } CO_2 \text{ produced}}{\text{Amount of } O_2 \text{ used}}$$

3) The RQ is usually between 0.7 and 1 — this means that the person is respiring aerobically.
4) If the RQ value is greater than 1 then the person is short of oxygen and is respiring anaerobically too.

Exercising Increases Breathing Rate and Heart Rate

1) When you exercise, your breathing rate increases. So does your heart rate.
2) This is so oxygen and glucose can be delivered to the muscles more quickly.
3) It also helps to remove carbon dioxide from the body more quickly.
4) You can find out your heart rate by measuring your pulse rate.

- You take someone's pulse by placing two fingers on their wrist and counting the number of pulses you feel in a minute.
- Each pulse is one heart beat.

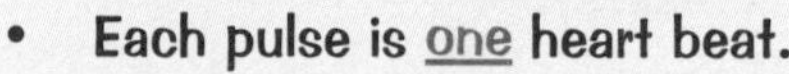

- Your resting pulse rate should be something like 70 beats/min.

5) Pulse rate remains high after you stop exercising to help you recover.
6) You're recovery time is the time it takes for your pulse rate to go back to normal.

You can test this in an experiment:

1) Measure your pulse rate at rest.
2) Run about for 3 minutes.
3) Measure your pulse rate every two minutes till it's back to normal.
4) The time it takes for your pulse to return to normal is your recovery time.

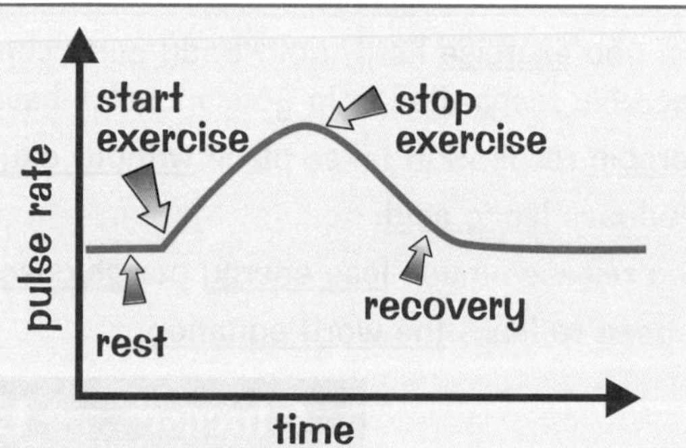

7) If you're fit your recovery time is faster than if you're unfit.

Don't stop respirin' — hold on to that feelin' (of being alive)...

Phew, I'm glad that's over. Learning about exercise is almost as tiring as actually exercising.
Make sure you know how to measure your recovery time and work out an RQ value for the exam.

Functions of the Blood

Blood is very useful stuff — it's a big transport system for moving things around the body. Amazing.

Plasma is the Liquid Bit of Blood

Plasma is a pale yellow liquid which carries just about everything that needs transporting around your body:

1) Red blood cells, white blood cells, and platelets (see below).
2) Water.
3) Digested food products (like glucose and amino acids) from the gut to all the body cells.
4) Waste products, e.g. carbon dioxide and urea — these need to be removed from the body.
5) Hormones — these act like chemical messengers.
6) Antibodies — these are proteins produced by the white blood cells (see below).

Red Blood Cells Carry Oxygen

Red blood cells transport oxygen from the lungs to all the cells in the body.
The structure of a red blood cell is adapted to its function (job):

Biconcave is just a posh way to say they look a bit like doughnuts (see diagram below).

1) Red blood cells are small and have a biconcave shape. This gives them a large surface area for absorbing oxygen.
2) Being small also means they can easily pass through the tiny capillaries (see next page).
3) They contain haemoglobin, which combines with oxygen.
4) Red blood cells don't have a nucleus — this frees up space for more haemoglobin, so they can carry more oxygen.

White Blood Cells are Used to Fight Disease

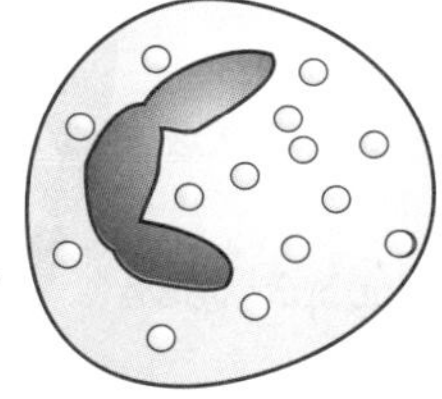

1) White blood cells defend the body against disease.
2) They produce antibodies (molecules that fight disease-causing microorganisms).

Platelets Help Blood Clot

1) Platelets are small fragments of cells.
2) They help the blood to clot (clump together) at a wound.

It's all blood, sweat and tears — kind of...

The average human body contains about six and a half pints of blood altogether. Every single drop contains millions of red blood cells — all of them perfectly designed for carrying plenty of oxygen to where it's needed.

Blood Vessels and the Heart

The blood has to get around the body somehow — which is what the blood vessels are for. But blood doesn't just move around the body on it's own, of course. It needs a pump.

Blood Vessels Carry Blood Around the Body

There are three different types of blood vessel:

1) ARTERIES — these carry the blood away from the heart.
2) CAPILLARIES — these are involved in the exchange of materials at the tissues.
3) VEINS — these carry the blood to the heart.

Blood is under higher pressure in the arteries than in the veins.

The Heart Pumps Blood Around the Body

1) The right side of the heart pumps blood to the lungs.
2) The left side of the heart pumps blood to the rest of the body.

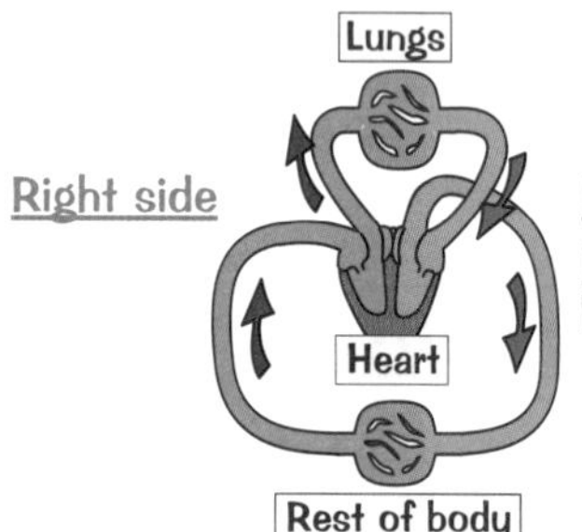

Learn This Diagram of the Heart with All Its Labels

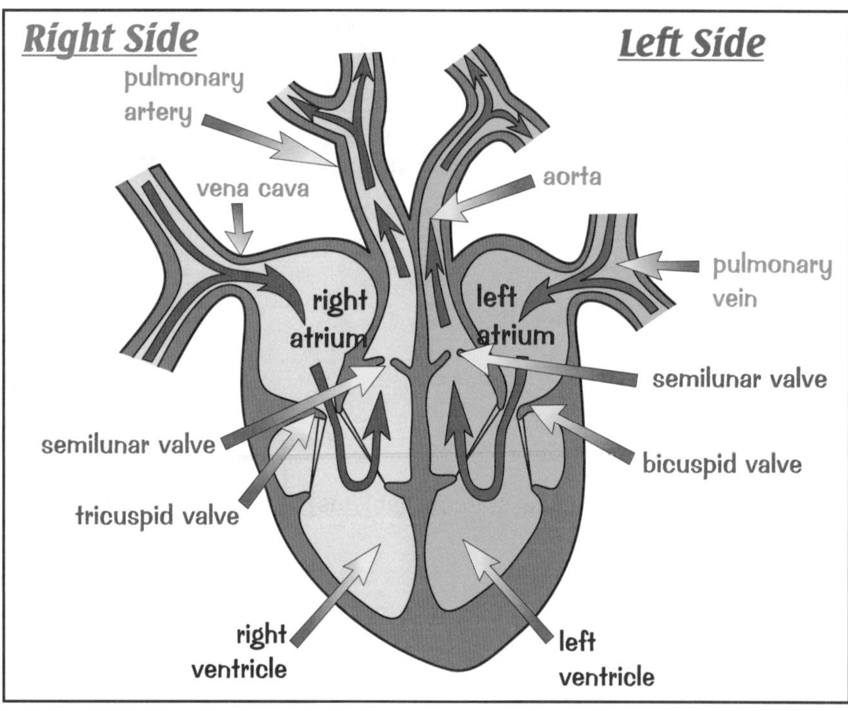

1) The right atrium of the heart receives blood from the body. (The plural of atrium is atria.)
2) The right ventricle pumps blood to the lungs.
3) The left atrium receives blood from the lungs.
4) The left ventricle pumps blood out round the whole body.
5) The main blood vessels that go to and from the heart are the:
   - vena cava
   - pulmonary vein
   - pulmonary artery
   - aorta
6) The left ventricle has a much thicker wall than the right ventricle. It needs more muscle because it has to pump blood around the whole body.
7) Blood flows through the heart from areas of high pressure to low pressure. E.g. When the right atrium contracts the pressure increases, pushing the blood into the right ventricle.
8) The semilunar, tricuspid and bicuspid valves prevent the backflow of blood.

Okay — let's get to the heart of the matter...

You can feel a pulse in your wrist or neck. This is the blood being pushed along by another heartbeat.

Selective Breeding

'Selective breeding' sounds like it could be a tricky topic, but it's actually dead simple. You take the best plants or animals and breed them together to get the best possible offspring. That's it.

Selective Breeding is Very Simple

1) Selective breeding is when humans decide which plants or animals are going to breed.
2) Organisms are selectively bred to develop the best characteristics, which are things like:
   - Maximum yield of meat, milk, grain etc.
   - Good health and disease resistance.

'Yield' is just means 'amount made'.

3) This is the basic process involved in selective breeding:
   - From your existing stock select the ones which have the best characteristics.
   - Breed them with each other.
   - Select the best of the offspring, and breed them together.
   - Continue this process over several generations.
4) In agriculture (farming), selective breeding can be used to improve yields.

EXAMPLE:

- A farmer might want to increase the amount of meat his cows produce.
- The farmer could select the cows and bulls with the best characteristics for producing meat, e.g. large size.
- He could breed them together.
- He could select the offspring that produce the most meat and breed them together.
- After doing this for several generations the farmer would get cows with a very high meat yield.

The Main Problem with Selective Breeding is Inbreeding

1) A selective breeding program can lead to inbreeding.
2) Inbreeding is where closely related organisms breed with each other.
3) It can lead to health problems in the population.

I use the same genes all the time too — they flatter my hips...

Selective breeding's not a new thing. People have been doing it for absolutely yonks. That's how we ended up with something like a poodle from a wolf. Somebody thought 'I really like this small, woolly, yappy, wolf — I'll breed it with this other one'. And after thousands of generations, we got poodles. Hurrah.

Genetic Engineering

Genetic engineering — it's basically just playing around with genes. Cool.
This page and the next will tell you everything you need to know.

Genes Can be Transferred Between Organisms

1) Scientists can select genes and artificially transfer them from one living organism into another.
2) This is called genetic engineering (or genetic modification).
3) Genetic engineering can produce organisms with different characteristics.
4) Genetic engineering programmes select a gene that codes for a useful characteristic in one organism and transfer it into another organism.
5) This is how plants were made that are resistant to certain diseases (see next page).

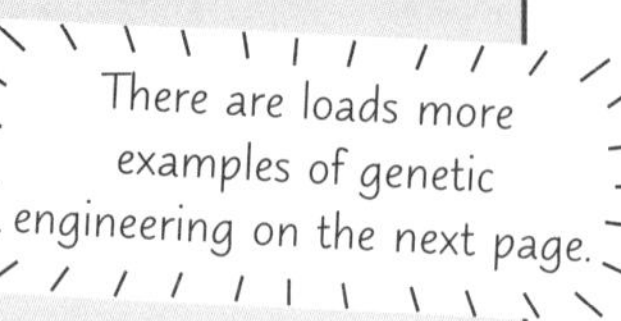

There are loads more examples of genetic engineering on the next page.

Genetic Engineering is Great — Hopefully

You need to be able to explain some of the advantages and risks involved in genetic engineering.

1) The main advantage is that you can produce organisms with new and useful features very quickly.
2) The main risk is that you might insert a gene that has unexpected harmful effects.
   - For example, genes are often inserted into bacteria so they produce useful products.
   - If these bacteria mutated and started causing disease, the new genes might make them more harmful and unpredictable.

There Are Moral and Ethical Issues Involved

All this is nice, but you need to think about the ethical issues too:

1) Some people think it's wrong to genetically engineer other organisms just for our benefit. This can be a problem in the genetic engineering of animals, if the animal suffers as a result.
2) People worry that we won't stop at engineering plants and animals. In the future, rich people might be able to decide the characteristics they want their children to have — this won't be very fair on people who can't afford it.
3) Some people think it's dangerous to carry on experimenting with genetic engineering, when we don't know what the long-term effects might be.

If only they could genetically engineer you to be better at exams...

You can do great things with genetic engineering. But some people worry that we don't know enough about it, or that someone might come along and try to combine the Prime Minister with a grapefruit. Possibly. If you get asked in the exam to identify features of plants and animals that might be selected for in a genetic engineering programme, don't panic. Just use your common sense and think about features that might actually be useful.

Examples of Genetic Engineering

Now, I'll bet you're just dying to know what genetic engineering has been used for. Well, here are a few examples. Don't you ever say I'm not good to you.

Learn These Three Examples of Genetic Engineering

VITAMIN A

1) In some parts of the world, rice is the main source of food for lots of people.
2) In these areas, people don't get enough vitamin A .
3) This is because rice doesn't contain much vitamin A.
4) Genetic engineering has allowed scientists to take a gene that controls beta-carotene production from carrot plants, and put it into rice plants.
5) Humans can then change the beta-carotene into vitamin A. Problem solved.

Nice jeans.
Thanks.

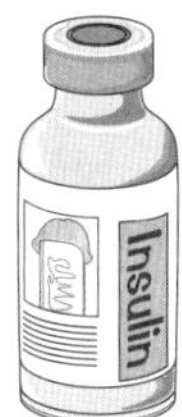
Insulin

INSULIN

1) The gene for human insulin production has been put into bacteria.
2) The bacteria are then able to make human insulin.
3) The bacteria are allowed to reproduce — so there are lots of bacteria, making lots of insulin.
4) Large amounts of insulin can then be extracted.

RESISTANCE

'Resistant to' means 'isn't harmed by'.

1) Some plants are resistant to things like herbicides (weedkillers), frost damage and disease.
2) Unfortunately, it's not always the plants we want to grow that have these features.
3) But now, thanks to genetic engineering, we can cut out the gene for resistance and stick it into useful plants such as crops. Splendid.

Other Types of Genetic Engineering Could Be Used in the Future

1) GENE THERAPY is a type of genetic engineering.
2) It involves changing a person's genes in an attempt to cure a genetic disorder.
3) Scientists haven't got it to work properly yet, but they're working on it for the future.

Jean-etic engineering — designing the perfect jeans...

Genetic engineering is the bees' knees, there's no doubt about it. It's helped us to grow more food, improve the food we already grow and even produce medicines like insulin. The amazing thing is that it's still got loads more potential — for example, in treating genetic diseases. This is cutting edge stuff.

Cloning

The first animal to be cloned was a sheep. You'd have thought we had enough sheep in the world, but apparently not. Some scientists decided we needed another one. So they made Dolly...

Cloning is Making an Exact Copy of Another Organism

1) Cloning produces genetically identical copies of an organism.
2) These copies are called clones.
3) Clones occur naturally in both plants and animals.
   Identical twins are clones of each other.
4) Cloning is an example of asexual reproduction — see page 13.

Cloning an Adult Animal is Done by Transferring a Cell Nucleus

The first mammal to be successfully cloned from an adult cell was a sheep called "Dolly".

Dolly was made using a method called nuclear transfer.
Here's how it works:

1) The nucleus of a sheep's egg cell was removed.
2) Another nucleus was inserted into the egg cell. This nucleus came from a body cell of a different sheep.
3) The egg cell became Dolly, a clone of the sheep from which the body cell came.

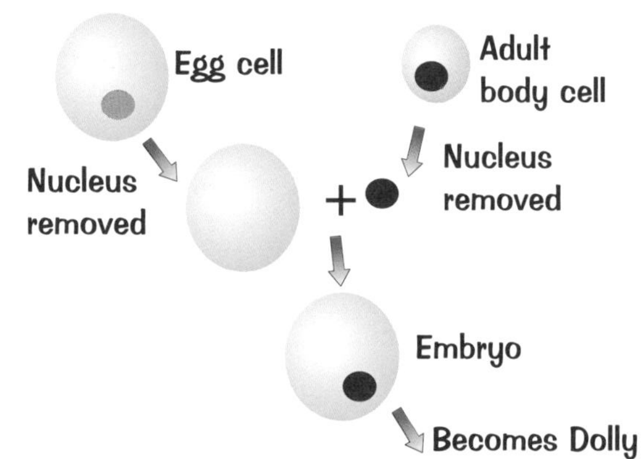

Uses of Cloning

1) Cloning allows you to produce lots of animals with useful characteristics, e.g. cows with a high milk yield.
2) Animals that can produce useful human products (e.g. hormones) could be developed by genetic engineering and then cloned.
3) Human embryos could be produced by cloning adult body cells.
   The embryos could then be used to supply stem cells for stem cell therapy (see page 13).

Cloning Humans Could be Possible — But There are Ethical Issues

1) In other mammals, pregnancies involving cloned embryos often end in miscarriage or a still birth.
2) Clones of other mammals have also been unhealthy and often die young — so human clones might too.
3) Clones might find it hard to cope mentally with the fact that they're just clones of other human beings.

A whole lamb from a single cell? Pull the udder one...

Cloning is exciting stuff. It's got loads of potential for helping to save lives — and it could pick you up some exam marks. So, learn everything on the page, cover it up, and see if you can clone it on a blank piece of paper.

Cloning Plants

Some of us may be searching for a way to clone ourselves — but plants can already do it.

Many Plants Produce Clones — All by Themselves

1) Some plants can reproduce asexually by mitosis (see page 13).
2) This means they produce clones of themselves without involving another plant...

Example 1

Strawberry plants and spider plants produce runners. These are shoots that grow over the ground and form leaves and roots of their own.

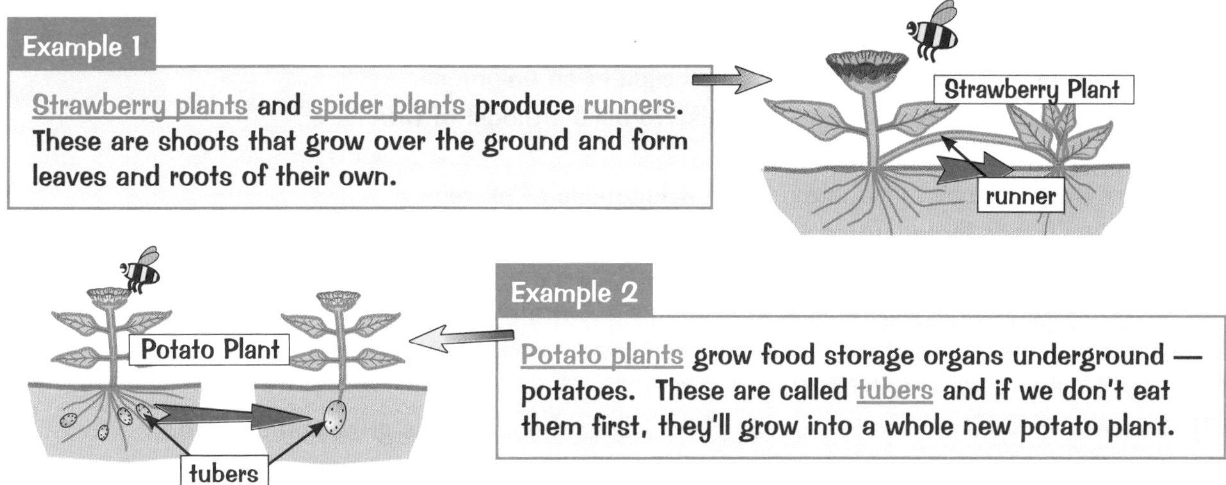
Strawberry Plant
runner
Potato Plant
tubers

Example 2

Potato plants grow food storage organs underground — potatoes. These are called tubers and if we don't eat them first, they'll grow into a whole new potato plant.

3) Plants grown from cuttings (bits of the parent plant) are also clones. Here's how to take and grow a cutting:

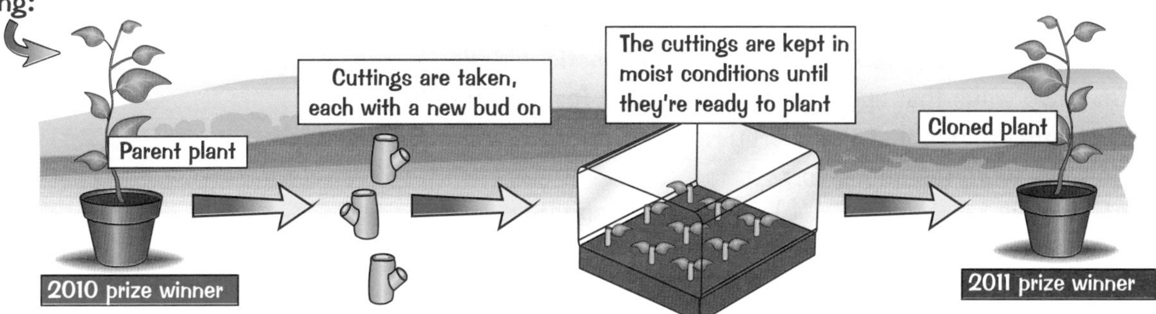
Parent plant
Cuttings are taken, each with a new bud on
The cuttings are kept in moist conditions until they're ready to plant
Cloned plant
2010 prize winner
2011 prize winner

4) A technique called tissue culture can also be used to clone plants. This is where you take a piece of tissue from a parent plant and grow it in a growth medium (a jelly containing plant nutrients).

Commercial Use of Cloned Plants Has Pros and Cons

1) You can be sure of the characteristics of the plant because it'll be genetically identical to the parent. This means you'll only get good ones, and won't waste time and money growing duds.
2) It's possible to produce lots of plants that are hard to grow from seeds.
3) BUT, if the plants suffer from a disease or start doing badly because of a change in the environment, they'll all have the same problems.
4) This is because cloning leads to a lack of genetic variation (all the plants have the same genes).

Stop cloning around — just learn it...

Plants are way better at being cloned than mammals are. That's why gardeners have been cloning plants for years using cuttings. It's dead easy — you can even try it yourself.

Revision Summary for Module B3

Here goes, folks — a beautiful page of revision questions to keep you at your desk studying hard until your parents have gone out and you can finally nip downstairs to watch TV. Think twice though before you reach for that remote control. These questions are actually pretty good — certainly more entertaining than 'Train Your Husband Like He's a Dog'. Question 14 is almost as good as an episode of 'Supernanny'. Question 4 is the corker though — like a reunion episode of 'Friends' but a lot funnier. Give the questions a go. Oh go on.

1) Why do liver and muscle cells have large numbers of mitochondria?
2) Give two ways in which bacterial cells differ from animal and plant cells.
3) Describe how you would make a stained slide of an onion cell.
4) What evidence did Watson and Crick use to build a model of DNA?
5) Where in the cell are proteins made?
6) Other than enzymes, give three different functions of proteins.
7) Give two things that increase the chance of mutation if you are exposed to them.
8) What are enzymes?
9) Why do enzymes usually only work with one substrate?
10) Name two things, other than repairing damaged tissues, that organisms use mitosis for.
11) Explain what 'differentiation' is.
12) Describe two differences in the way plant cells and animal cells grow and develop.
13) Give three advantages of being multi-cellular.
14) Give three ways that you can measure growth.
15) Humans go through two main phases of rapid growth. When do these take place?
16) Give one difference between body cells and the cells produced by meiosis.
17) Briefly outline how fertilisation results in genetic variation.
18) Give two ways that sperm cells are adapted for their function.
19) Give three things that the energy released during respiration is used for.
20) Give the word equations for:
    a) aerobic respiration b) anaerobic respiration
21) What is the formula for calculating the respiratory quotient?
22) Describe how you could measure your recovery rate.
23) Give four features of red blood cells that make them well adapted to carrying oxygen.
24) What is the function of:
    a) white blood cells b) platelets
25) Which type of blood vessel carries blood away from the heart — arteries, capillaries or veins?
26) Why does the left ventricle have a thicker wall than the right ventricle?
27) What is selective breeding?
28) Give a disadvantage of selective breeding.
29) What is genetic engineering?
30) Give one advantage and one risk of genetic engineering.
31) Describe three examples of genetic engineering being done now.
32) Describe an example of genetic engineering that might be carried out in the future.
33) Describe the method of cloning that was used to produce Dolly the sheep.
34) Give three uses of cloning animals.
35) Give an example of a plant that can produce clones naturally.
36) Suggest two advantages and two disadvantages of the commercial use of cloned plants.

Atoms, Molecules and Compounds

You should already know these basics, but just in case your memory is a bit hazy here's a refresher...

Atoms are Made up of Even Smaller Particles

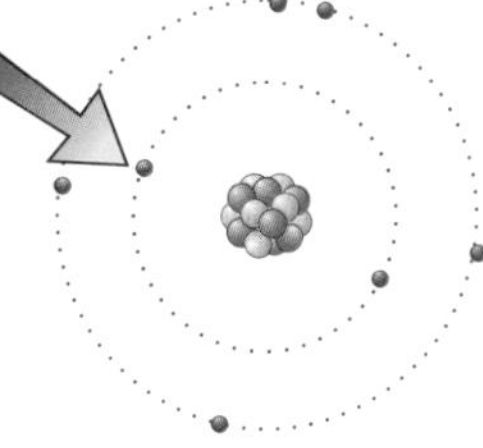

1) Atoms are really tiny — they're too small to see.
2) They're made up of even smaller particles.
3) Electrons are one type of particle found in atoms. They're negatively (–) charged.

Atoms can Gain and Lose Electrons

1) Sometimes an atom loses or gains one or more electrons and this gives it a charge.
2) Charged atoms are known as ions.
3) Positive ions (+) are formed if atoms lose electrons.
4) Negative ions (–) are formed if atoms gain electrons.

Atoms can Join Together to Make Molecules

1) An element is a substance that has only one type of atom — so oxygen is an element.
2) When one or more atoms are joined together you get molecules or compounds.
   E.g. oxygen molecules are made from two oxygen atoms joined together.

   (O) = Oxygen atom (O)(O) = Oxygen molecule

3) A compound is a substance made up of different types of atom.
   E.g. carbon dioxide molecules are made from two oxygen atoms and a carbon atom joined together.

   (O) = Oxygen atom (C) = Carbon atom  = Carbon dioxide molecule

4) Atoms join together using chemical bonds.
5) There are two main types of bonding between atoms — ionic and covalent.

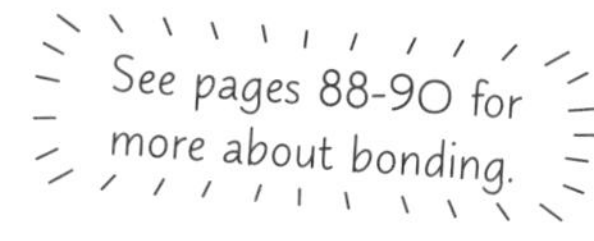
See pages 88-90 for more about bonding.

COVALENT BONDS

1) Sometimes atoms can share a pair of electrons.
2) This is called covalent bonding.

IONIC BONDS

1) Ionic bonds are made between ions (charged atoms).
2) When a positive ion meets a negative ion, they are attracted to each other.
3) This attraction is an ionic bond — it holds the ions together.

Cl

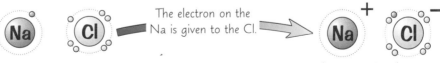

The electron on the Na is given to the Cl.

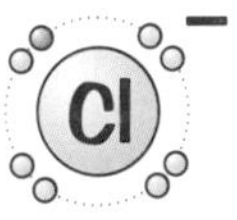

Na has a positive charge and Cl has a negative charge. They are held together by an ionic bond.

Don't panic — it's only a bunch of letters and numbers...

It's easy to tell atoms, molecules and ions apart. Atoms are shown as one letter, e.g. O or C, molecules have more than one atom, e.g. CO or H_2O and ions are shown with a charge, e.g. Na^+, H^+ or Ca^{2+}.

Atoms, Molecules and Compounds

Scientists use formulas to show different molecules. There are two types of formula you need to know about...

The Molecular Formula Tells You What Atoms There Are

1) You can tell what kind of atoms and how many there are in a substance by looking at its molecular formula.
2) The molecular formula is made up of letters and numbers. E.g. H_2O, CH_4, HCl are all molecular formulas.
3) The letters in the formula tell you the type of atoms (elements) it's made up of.
4) The little number at the bottom tells you how many of that atom there are.

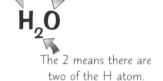

This molecule is water. The H means there is a hydrogen atom.

The O means there is an oxygen atom.

H_2O

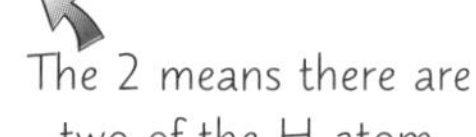

The 2 means there are
two of the H atom.

The Displayed Formula Shows How the Atoms are Arranged

1) You can draw out pictures that show the atoms and the bonds in different molecules.
2) These are called displayed formulas. For example:

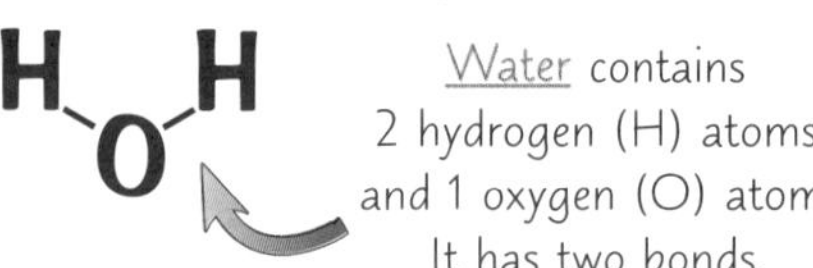

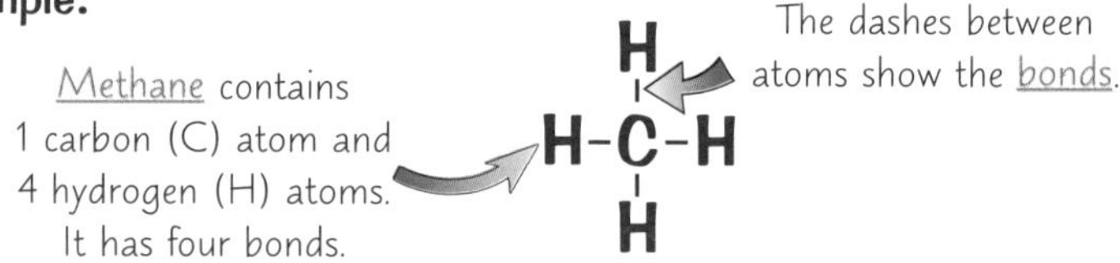

Some Formulas Have Brackets

1) Don't panic if the molecular formula has brackets in it. They're easy too. For example: $CH_3(CH_2)_2CH_3$ The 2 after the bracket means that there are 2 lots of CH_2.
2) Drawing the displayed formula of the compound is a good way to count up the number of atoms.
3) So, altogether there are 4 carbon atoms and 10 hydrogen atoms in this molecule.
4) You might need to write out the molecular formula from the displayed formula.
5) It's easy — just count up the number of each type of atom and write it as above, e.g. CH_4, H_2O.

$CH_3(CH_2)_2CH_3$

```
  H H H H
H-C-C-C-C-H
  H H H H
```

You Need to Remember Some Formulas

You'll need to learn others later, but these'll be a good start.

Carbon dioxide — CO_2 Hydrogen — H_2 Hydrochloric acid — HCl

Calcium carbonate — $CaCO_3$ Water — H_2O

Some chemicals have slightly more interesting names...

With so many chemicals around, you'd think there'd be some interesting names... And so there are. There's windowpane (C_9H_{12}). And angelic acid ($CH_3CHC(CH_3)COOH$). And the one named after Wilfred Welsh, which goes by the name of welshite ($Ca_2SbMg_4FeBe_2Si_4O_{20}$). Better than boring names like 'ethene'.

Chemical Equations

If you're going to get anywhere in chemistry you need to know about chemical equations...

Chemical Equations Show What Happens in a Reaction

1) In a chemical reaction chemicals react together to make new chemicals.
2) The chemicals that react are called reactants. The chemicals that are made are called products.
3) Scientists use equations to show what happens in chemical reactions.

Word Equations

1) In a word equation all the chemicals are written out as words — clever that.
2) If you know the reactants and the products you can write out the word equation.
3) You put the reactants on the left and the products on the right, then separate them with an arrow. For example:

These are the reactants. → methane + oxygen → carbon dioxide + water ← These are the products.

Symbol Equations

1) These are just like word equations but the chemicals are shown using molecular formulas.
2) For example, the symbol equation for the word equation above is:

$$CH_4 + 2O_2 \rightarrow CO_2 + 2H_2O$$

You may have spotted that there's a '2' in front of the O_2 and the H_2O. The reason for this is explained below...

Symbol Equations Need to be Balanced

1) You balance equations by putting numbers in front of the molecules so there are the same number of each type of atom on each side of the arrow.
2) But you can't change numbers in the molecular formulas. So changing O_2 to O_3 is a no-no.
3) Start by putting a number in front of one of the molecules to balance that type of atom. Then keep doing it until they all balance. For example:

1 $CH_4 + O_2 \rightarrow CO_2 + H_2O$

1C, 4H, 2O   1C, 2H, 3O

The equation is not balanced — there are different numbers of hydrogen and oxygen atoms on each side of the equation.

2 There aren't enough H's on the right. So, add a 2 in front of the H_2O.

$CH_4 + O_2 \rightarrow CO_2 + 2H_2O$

1C, 4H, 2O   1C, 4H, 4O

3 Now there aren't enough O's on the left. So, add a 2 in front of the O_2.

$CH_4 + 2O_2 \rightarrow CO_2 + 2H_2O$

1C, 4H, 4O   1C, 4H, 4O

Hooray. The equation is now balanced — there is the same number of each type of atom on both sides of the equation.

It's all about getting the balance right...

Balancing equations isn't as scary as it looks — you just plug numbers in until it works itself out. Get some practice in — you'll see. You can balance equations with displayed formulas in exactly the same way. Just make sure there are the same number of each type of atom on both sides — dead easy.

Energy Transfer in Reactions

Chemical reactions can either release heat energy, or take in heat energy.

In an Exothermic Reaction — Energy is Given Out

An **EXOTHERMIC REACTION** is one which **GIVES OUT ENERGY** to the surroundings.

In an Endothermic Reaction — Energy is Taken In

An **ENDOTHERMIC REACTION** is one which **TAKES IN ENERGY** from the surroundings.

Temperature Changes Help Decide If a Reaction's Exo or Endo

1) The energy given out or taken in during a reaction is usually heat energy.
2) If you see an increase in temperature the reaction is exothermic — heat is given out.
3) If you see a drop in temperature the reaction is endothermic — heat is taken in.

Bond Breaking is Endothermic... Bond Making is Exothermic

1) In a chemical reaction, old bonds are broken and new bonds are made.
2) Energy must be taken in to break old bonds — so bond breaking is an endothermic process.

BOND BREAKING - ENDOTHERMIC

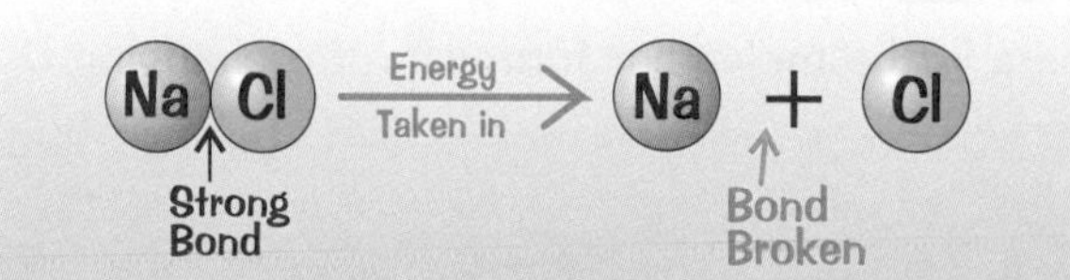

3) Energy is given out when new bonds are made — so bond making is an exothermic process.

BOND MAKING - EXOTHERMIC

Mg + O ⟶ Mg O + Energy Given out

Strong Bond Made

Chemistry in "real-world application" shocker...

When you see Stevie Gerrard hobble off the pitch and press a bag to his leg, he's using an endothermic reaction. The cold pack contains an inner bag full of water and an outer one full of ammonium nitrate. When he presses the pack the inner bag breaks and they mix together. The ammonium nitrate dissolves in the water (an endothermic reaction) and it takes in heat from Stevie's injured leg. Pretty cool, huh.

Measuring the Energy Content of Fuels

You can do experiments to compare how much energy different fuels give out.

Use Calorimetry to Work Out Energy Transferred

You can find out how much energy a fuel contains by using a calorimetric method. You just heat up some water with your fuel and then use the lovely equation below to work out the energy transferred per gram.

This Calorimetric Method Uses a Copper Calorimeter

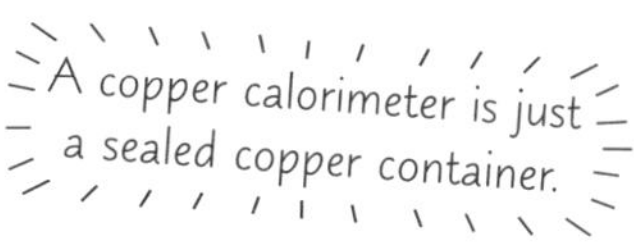

A copper calorimeter is just a sealed copper container.

1) Put some fuel into a spirit burner (or a bottled gas burner if the fuel is a gas)

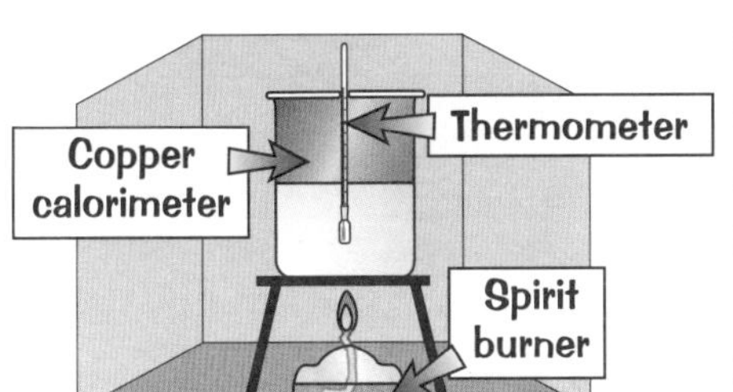

2) Weigh the burner full of fuel.
3) Measure out, say, 200 g of water into a copper calorimeter.
4) Take the temperature of the water.
5) Put the lit burner under the calorimeter. When the water temperature has risen by 20-30 °C, blow out the spirit burner.
6) Make a note of the highest temperature the water reaches.
7) Reweigh the burner and fuel.
8) The mass of fuel burned is the initial mass of fuel and burner minus the final mass of fuel and burner.

Make It a Fair Test by Keeping Conditions the Same

1) If you're comparing two fuels in an experiment, you have to repeat the method above with the second fuel.
2) For the experiment to be a fair test, everything (except the fuel used) should be the same.
3) This means that: (i) you should use the same apparatus, (ii) you should use the same amount of water each time, (iii) the water should start and finish at the same temperature each time.
4) In order for the results to be reliable you would have to repeat the experiment several times and get rid of any results which were clearly wrong (anomalous results).

Calculate the Energy Transferred Using these Equations

The amount of energy transferred to the water is given by:

ENERGY TRANSFERRED (in J) = MASS OF WATER (in g) × SPECIFIC HEAT CAPACITY OF WATER (= 4.2 J/g °C) × TEMPERATURE CHANGE (in °C)

This will always be 4.2 for water.

Which can also be written like this: **Energy transferred = $m \times c \times \Delta T$**

ΔT just means the change in the temperature.

Example: How much energy is transferred by a fuel that heats 200 g of water from 21 °C to 35 °C?

Answer: Energy transferred $= m \times c \times \Delta T$
$= 200 \times 4.2 \times (35 - 21)$
$= 11760$ J

Don't worry — you'll be given the equation in the exam.

Hope you've got the energy to revise all this...

In the exam they might give you some data from simple calorimetric experiments to compare. All you'll have to do is say which fuel releases the most energy — they'll even give you the equation. Pretty easy if you've learnt it.

Chemical Reaction Rates

The rate of a chemical reaction is how fast the reactants are changed into products.

Reactions Can Go at All Sorts of Different Rates

A chemical reaction takes place when particles collide.
The more collisions you have the faster a reaction will go.

1) One of the slowest reactions is the rusting of iron.
2) Burning is a very fast reaction.
3) An explosion is a very fast reaction that releases a lot of gaseous products.

You Can Do an Experiment to Measure the Rate of a Reaction

1) To measure the rate of a reaction you need to know how much product is formed in a certain amount of time.
2) You can do this by measuring the volume of gas given off in a reaction.
3) You'll need a flask, a gas syringe (to collect the gas) and a stopwatch to do this.
4) Once the reaction has started, measure the volume of gas given off at regular time intervals.
5) For example, measure how much gas you have after 10 seconds, 20 seconds, 30 seconds etc.

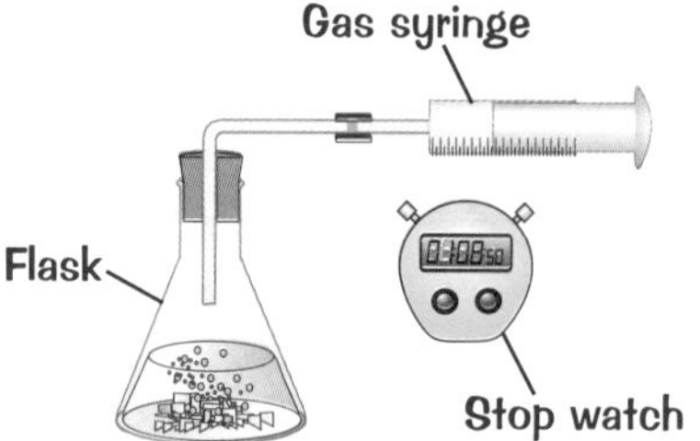

A Reaction Stops when the Limiting Reactant is Used Up

1) The limiting reactant is the reactant that's totally used up by the end of the reaction.
2) Once all of the limiting reactant is used up, the reaction can't continue and you can't get any more product.
3) There might still be some of the other reactant left at the end — we say this reactant is in excess.

> Example: When you burn magnesium in oxygen in the lab, which reactant (magnesium or oxygen) is the limiting reactant?
>
> Answer: The oxygen is all around in the air and will not run out. This means that oxygen is the reactant in excess. When there is no magnesium left the reaction will stop. This means magnesium is the limiting reactant.

4) The amount of product you get is directly proportional to the amount of limiting reactant you start with.
5) This means that if you double the amount of limiting reactant you'll get double the amount of product. If you halve the amount of limiting reactant you'll get half the amount of product.

Get a fast, furious reaction — tickle your teacher...

First off... remember that the amount of product you get depends on the amount of reactants you start with. So all the stuff about the rate of a reaction is only talking about how quickly your products form — not how much of them you get. It's an important difference — so get your head round it right now.

Collision Theory

The rate of a reaction depends on four things — temperature, concentration (or pressure for gases), whether a catalyst is used and the size of the particles. This page explains why these things affect the reaction rate.

More Collisions Increases the Rate of Reaction

Reactions happen if particles collide. The more often they collide, the faster the rate of the reaction.

1) Increasing the Temperature Increases the Rate of Reaction

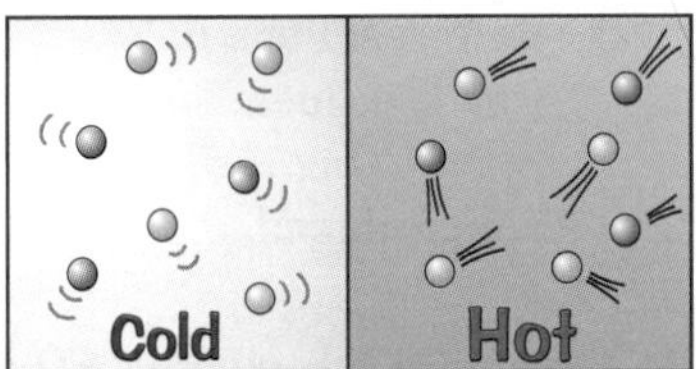

1) When the temperature is increased the particles all move quicker.
2) If they're moving quicker, they're going to collide more often.
3) Higher temperatures also means the collisions are more energetic.
4) So the rate of the reaction increases.

This means they've got more energy.

2) Increasing the Concentration or Pressure Increases the Rate of Reaction

1) If a solution is made more concentrated it means there are more particles of reactant in the same volume, so they'll collide more often.
2) In a gas, increasing the pressure means the molecules are more crowded, so there are more collisions.
3) This means the rate of reaction increases.

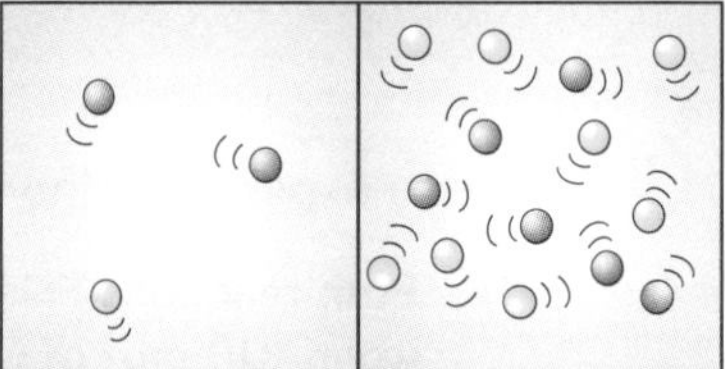

Low Concentration (Low Pressure) | High Concentration (High Pressure)

3) Using Smaller Particles Increases the Rate of Reaction

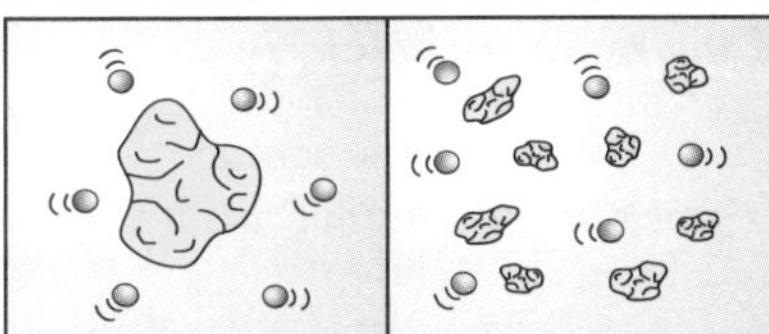

big lump = small surface area | smaller pieces = large surface area

1) If one of the reactants is a solid lump then breaking it up into smaller pieces (like a powder) will increase its surface area.
2) This means the particles of the other reactant will have more area to work on so they'll collide more often.
3) More collisions means a faster rate of reaction.

Small particles in the air burn very very fast because they have a big surface area. If there's a spark they'll EXPLODE. So factories that make fine combustible powders (powders that will easily burn), have to be careful. For example, custard powder, sulfur or flour making factories.

4) A Catalyst Increases the Rate of a Reaction

1) A catalyst is a substance which increases the speed of a reaction, without being chemically changed or used up in the reaction.
2) Because it isn't used up, you only need a tiny bit of it to catalyse large amounts of reactants.
3) Catalysts tend to be very fussy about which reactions they catalyse though — you can't just stick any old catalyst in a reaction and expect it to work.

Collision theory — it's always the other driver...

It may sound a bit weird but all this stuff is pretty much just common sense. You just have to remember that particles colliding more often = a faster rate of reaction. It's a bit like the dodgems really... If you go really fast or put more people in dodgem cars or create loads more mini-sized dodgems you'll crash more. Excellent.

Rate of Reaction Data

In the exam they might ask you to explain rate of reaction data or draw sketch graphs like these ones. Yey.

Reaction Rate Graphs Show Rate of Reaction Data

A In this experiment, 5 g of marble chips were added to hydrochloric acid. The volume of CO_2 produced was measured every 10 seconds. The results are plotted below. Line 1 is for small chips and line 2 is for large chips.

1) The steeper the slope of a graph, the faster the reaction. Reaction 1 is faster than Reaction 2.

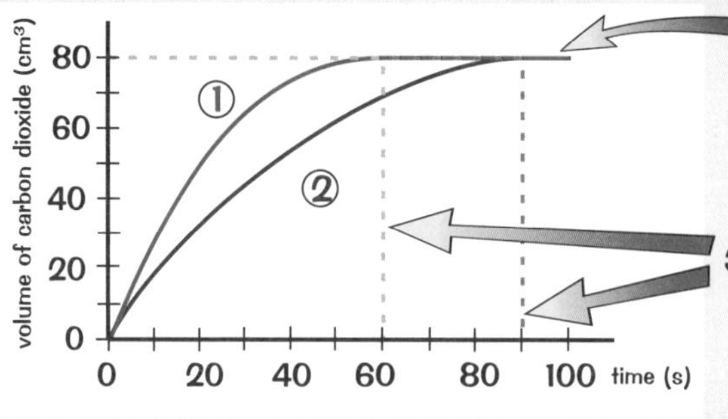

2) Both reactions finish (the line goes flat) when 80 cm³ of CO_2 are produced.

3) Reaction 1 takes about 60 s, Reaction 2 about 90 s to finish — Reaction 1 is faster.

If you use the same amount of reactants you'll end up with the same amount of products no matter what conditions you use.

B In this experiment the size of the chips is the same but two different temperatures are used.

1) Both reactions finish when 100 cm³ of CO_2 have been produced.

3) As Reaction 3 is faster it must be at a higher temperature.

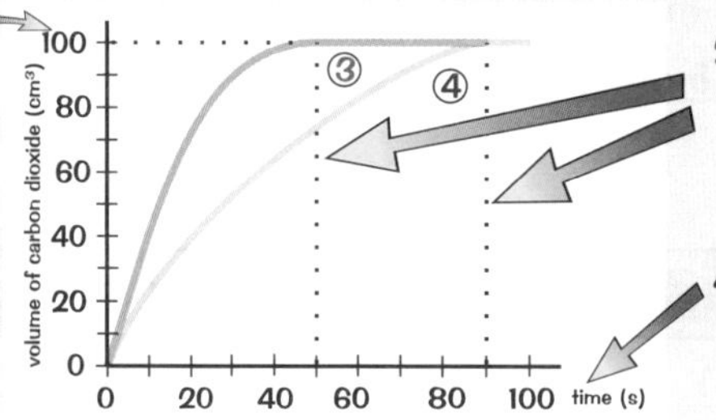

2) Reaction 3 is faster (about 50 s, compared to Reaction 4's 90 s or so). The slope of its graph is also steeper because it's a faster reaction.

4) The units on the axes are cm³ and s, so the units for the rate of the reaction are cm³/s.

The rate of reaction can also be measured in cm³/min, g/s and g/min.

C This time, a piece of magnesium has been added to hydrochloric acid. The graph shows the volume of hydrogen produced when two different concentrations of acid are used.

1) Reaction 5 is faster than Reaction 6 — its slope is steeper.

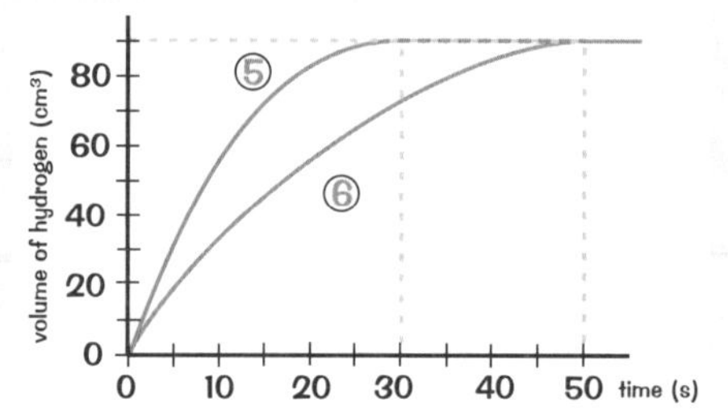

2) Since Reaction 5 is faster, it must use the more concentrated acid.

D This graph shows the effect of adding a catalyst.

1) Line 7 is the reaction with a catalyst.

2) Line 8 is the reaction without a catalyst.

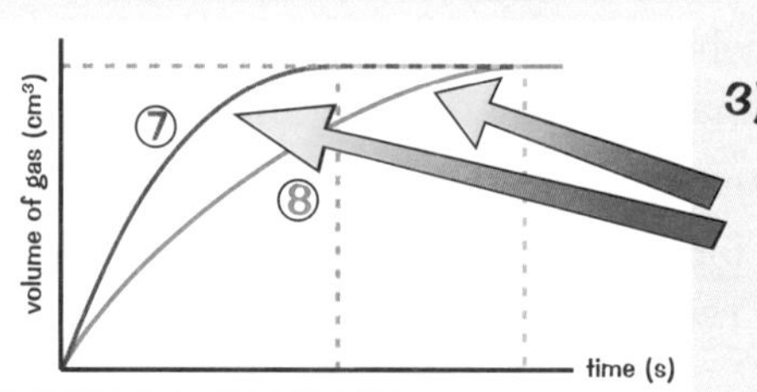

3) The graph tells you that the catalyst speeds up the reaction — line 7 is steeper than line 8 and line 7 flattens out first.

My reactions slow down when it gets hot — I get sleepy...

You can easily compare the rate of two reactions by comparing the slopes of their graphs. The steeper the slope, the faster the reaction. It's as simple as falling down a hill — the steeper the hill, the faster you'll fall.

Reacting Masses

The biggest trouble with relative atomic mass and relative formula mass is that they sound so blood-curdling. They're very important though, so take a few deep breaths, and just enjoy, as the mists slowly clear...

Relative Atomic Mass, A_r — Easy Peasy

In the periodic table, the elements all have two numbers. The bigger one is the relative atomic mass.

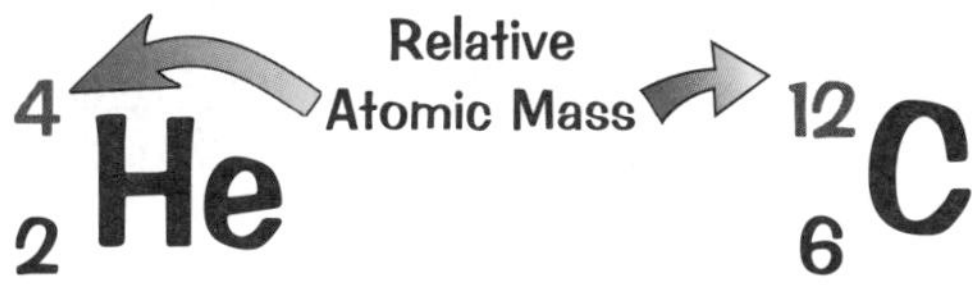

Relative Formula Mass, M_r — Also Easy Peasy

If you have a compound like $MgCl_2$ then it has a relative formula mass, M_r. This is just all the relative atomic masses added together.

Example: For $MgCl_2$...

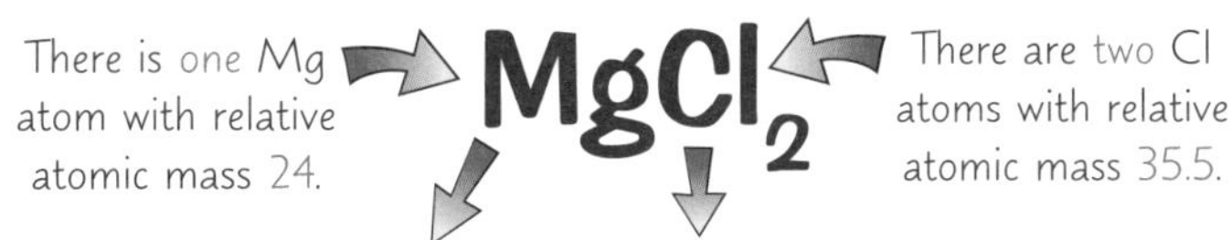

$24 + (35.5 \times 2) = 95$. So, the M_r for $MgCl_2$ is simply 95.

Compounds with Brackets in...

Example: Find the relative formula mass of calcium hydroxide, $Ca(OH)_2$.

There's one Ca atom with relative atomic mass 40. → $Ca(OH)_2$ ← There are two lots of oxygen atoms ($A_r = 16$) and two lots of hydrogen atoms ($A_r = 1$) because of the 2 outside the brackets.

So... $40 + (16 \times 2) + (1 \times 2) = 40 + 32 + 2 = 74$.
So, the relative formula mass for $Ca(OH)_2$ is 74.

In a Chemical Reaction, Mass is Always Conserved

1) In a chemical reaction, the total mass of reactants is the same as the total mass of products.
2) This is because the number of atoms at the start of a reaction is the same as the number at the end.
3) It's called 'the principle of conservation of mass'.
4) You can use symbol equations and relative formula masses to show that mass is conserved in a reaction.

Example: Use the relative formula masses given to show that mass is conserved in the reaction: $C_2H_4 + H_2 \rightarrow C_2H_6$

Method: Just add up the M_rs on the left and the M_rs on the right.

$28 + 2 \rightarrow 30$

$30 \rightarrow 30$

Mass of products = mass of reactants, so mass is conserved.

Molecule	M_r
C_2H_4	28
H_2	2
C_2H_6	30

Phew, Chemistry — scary stuff sometimes, innit...

This page is really important... You've gotta remember that in a reaction no mass is lost and no mass is gained. Otherwise you'll be messing with the first law of thermodynamics — and you wouldn't want that, would you...

Calculating Masses in Reactions

Oh no, not more calculations I hear you cry. But don't despair, they aren't as bad as they look. Honest.

You Can Use Conservation of Mass to Help With Calculations

If you can remember that the total mass of reactants used is equal to the total mass of products made (see page 35) then you can do all kinds of calculations. Like these...

Example: Magnesium (Mg) reacts with oxygen (O) to make magnesium oxide (MgO).

$$2Mg + O_2 \rightarrow 2MgO$$

48 g of Mg makes 80 g of MgO. What mass of O_2 is used in the reaction?

Method: 1) The mass of products has to equal the mass of reactants so...

Mass of Mg + Mass of O_2 = Mass of MgO

2) Now all you have to do is plug in the numbers and work out what's missing.

48 g of Mg + Mass of O_2 = 80 g of MgO

So 32 g of O_2 is used (48 + 32 = 80).

Example: Hydrogen peroxide (H_2O_2) decomposes to make water (H_2O) and oxygen (O_2).

$$2H_2O_2 \rightarrow 2H_2O + O_2$$

6.8 g of H_2O_2 makes 3.6 g of H_2O. What mass of O_2 will be made?

Method: 1) Mass of products has to equal the mass of reactants so...

Mass of H_2O_2 = Mass of H_2O + Mass of O_2

2) Plug in the numbers and work out what's missing.

6.8 g of H_2O_2 = 3.6 g of H_2O + Mass of O_2

So 3.2 g of O_2 is produced (6.8 = 3.6 + 3.2).

Something decomposes when it breaks down into more than one substance when it's heated.

If You Double the Reactant, you Double the Product

1) The mass of the reactant is directly proportional to the mass of the limiting reactant (see page 32).
2) This means that if you double the amount of limiting reactant you'll get double the amount of product.
3) In calculations, this means that what you do to one side of the equation you have to do to the other as well.
4) It's dead simple. For example...

Example: In the reaction, $2Mg + O_2 \rightarrow 2MgO$, the limiting reactant is the magnesium.
20 g of Mg makes 34 g of MgO. How much Mg would you need to make 68 g of MgO?

Method: 1) Work out how the mass of product has changed.

The amount of MgO produced has gone from 34 g to 68 g, so it's doubled (× 2).

2) Do the same to the limiting reactant.

So double the amount of Mg... 20 g × 2 = 40 g.
And there you go. 40 g of Mg will make 68 g of MgO. Easy.

Reaction mass calculations? — no worries, matey...

Calculating masses is a very useful skill to have. No, really. Like if you're trying to make medicines or fertilisers it's important not to make a mistake. All you've got to do is knuckle down and learn the examples. It's worth it.

Atom Economy

In chemical reactions you want as much of the reactants as possible to get turned into useful products. That's where atom economy comes in — it tells you exactly how good your reaction is at doing this.

"Atom Economy" — % of Reactants Changed to Useful Products

1) A lot of reactions make more than one product. For example, sodium plus water gives sodium hydroxide and hydrogen (two products).
2) Some of the products will be useful, but others will just be waste.
3) The atom economy of a reaction tells you the amount of atoms that are wasted when manufacturing (making) a chemical.
4) 100% atom economy means that all the atoms in the reactants have been turned into useful (desired) products.
5) The higher the atom economy the 'greener' the process.

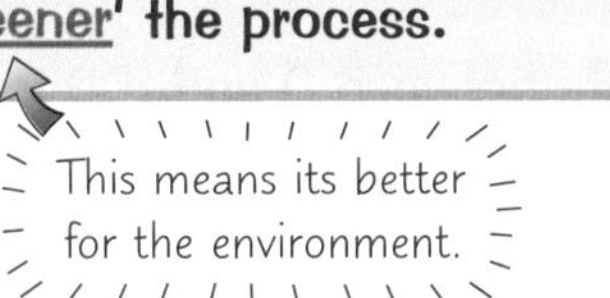
This means its better
for the environment.

Atoms

You Can Use this Equation to Calculate the Atom Economy

You need to learn this equation:

$$\text{atom economy} = \frac{M_r \text{ of desired products}}{M_r \text{ of all products}} \times 100$$

There's more on M_rs on page 35.

Here's an example:

Example: Sodium hydroxide (NaOH) reacts with hydrochloric acid (HCl) to produce sodium chloride (NaCl) and water (H_2O). Sodium chloride is the useful product in this reaction.

$$NaOH + HCl \rightarrow NaCl + H_2O$$

Calculate the atom economy of this reaction.

Molecule	M_r
NaOH	40
HCl	36.5
NaCl	58.5
H_2O	18

Method:
1) Identify the useful product — that's the sodium chloride.
2) Write down the M_r of the useful product: M_r of NaCl = 58.5
3) Calculate the M_r of all the products: M_r of NaCl + H_2O = 58.5 + 18 = 76.5
4) Use the formula to calculate the atom economy:

$$\text{atom economy} = \frac{58.5}{76.5} \times 100 = 76.5\%$$

So in this reaction, 76.5% of the starting materials are turned into useful product. That's pretty good — only 23.5% of the atoms are wasted (100 – 76.5 = 23.5%).

Atom economy — important but not the whole story...

In the real world, high atom economy isn't enough. You need to think about the percentage yield of the reaction as well. You'll get to learn all about that on the next page, but make sure you've learnt all this lovely stuff first.

Percentage Yield

The yield of a reaction is just how much product you make. Percentage yield tells you about the overall success of an experiment. It compares what you think you should get with what you actually get.

Percentage Yield Compares Actual and Predicted Yield

1) The predicted yield of a reaction is how much product you expect to get.
2) How much product you end up with is called the actual yield.
3) Percentage yield compares the predicted and actual yields.
4) You can use this formula to calculate percentage yield:

$$\text{percentage yield} = \frac{\text{actual yield (grams)}}{\text{predicted yield (grams)}} \times 100$$

Example: If actual yield is 1.2 g and predicted yield is 3.4 g, calculate the percentage yield.

$$\text{Percentage yield} = \frac{1.2}{3.4} \times 100 = 35.3\%$$

5) Percentage yield is always somewhere between 0 and 100%.
6) 100% yield means that no product has been lost.
7) 0% yield means that no product has been made.

Yields are Always Less Than 100%

In real life, you never get a 100% yield. Some product or reactant always gets lost along the way. Here's a few ways this can happen:

1) Evaporation

When you heat liquids some will evaporate off. This means you'll lose some of your product.

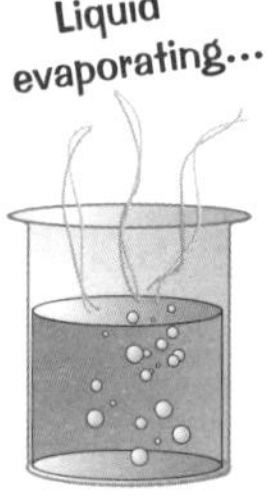

2) Not Everything Will React to Make Product

In many chemical reactions not all of the reactants react to make products.

Sometimes, no matter how hard you try, you won't be able to get all your reactant to react. Sad times.

3) Filtration

When you filter mixtures, you nearly always lose a bit of liquid or a bit of solid.

- Some liquid will stay with the solid and filter paper (as they always stay a bit wet).
- Some solid usually gets left behind when you scrape it off the filter paper — even if you're really careful.

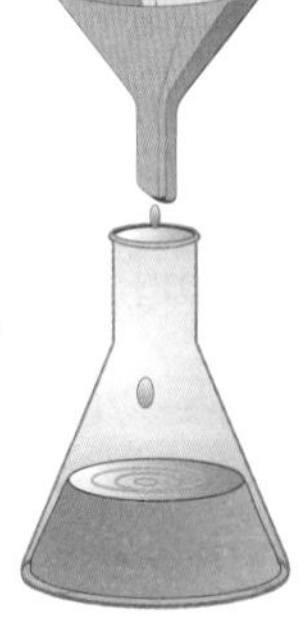

4) Transferring Liquids

You always lose a bit of liquid when you transfer it from one container to another.

Some of it always gets left behind on the inside surface of the old container.

Think about it — it's always wet when you finish.

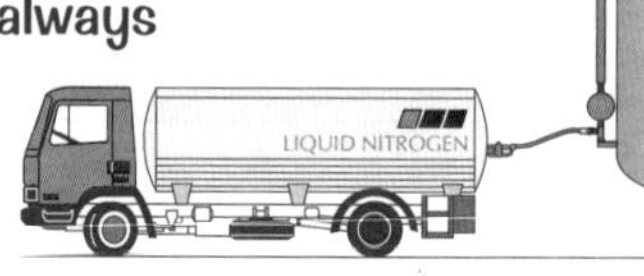

You can't always get what you want...

Unfortunately, no matter how careful you are, you're not going to get a 100% yield in any reaction. So you'll always get a little loss of product. In industry, people work very hard to keep wastage as low as possible.

Chemical Production

There are lots of ways you could manufacture drugs — it all depends on how much you want to make.

Continuous Production Runs All the Time

1) In a continuous process production never stops.
2) Chemicals that we need lots of, like ammonia, are made by continuous processes.

Daisy also makes ammonia using a continuous process.

Batch Production Only Operates at Certain Times

1) In batch processes, chemicals are made only when they're needed.
2) This means the process isn't running all the time.
3) Pharmaceutical drugs (medicines) are made by batch processes because we only need small amounts.

Several Factors Affect the Cost of Pharmaceutical Drugs

Lots of things can increase the cost of making specialist chemicals. Make sure you know these ones...

1) RESEARCH AND TESTING

Finding a drug, testing it, changing it, testing again, until it's ready. It's really important that the drugs are properly tested to make sure they're safe before they are licensed for use.

You have to get a licence from the government before you're allowed to sell a drug.

2) LABOUR COSTS

Making pharmaceutical drugs is pretty labour-intensive (it takes a lot of people). All the employees need to be paid which can cost a lot of money.

3) ENERGY COSTS

These can be very high for both continuous and batch production. For example, to get high temperatures for a reaction you need to use a lot of energy which costs money.

4) RAW MATERIALS

The raw materials for pharmaceuticals are often rare and are sometimes expensive.

CGP Lab — Testing in Progress

5) TIME TAKEN FOR DEVELOPMENT

This involves the work of lots of highly paid scientists and could take many years.

6) MARKETING

Companies spend a lot of money advertising new products to make sure that customers buy them.

I wish they'd find a drug to cure exams...

Did you know that it takes about 12 years and £900 million to make a new drug and get it onto market. Wow. That's enough money to buy an island. And one for your mum. And one for your mates... Make sure you know why medicines cost so much to make and that you know the difference between batch and continuous processes.

Chemical Production

There are loads of different ways scientists can make pharmaceutical drugs. One way is to use chemicals that come from plants. Scientists can also make the chemicals themselves but this takes waaay longer.

Raw Materials Can be Made Synthetically or Extracted

1) The raw materials used to make specialist chemicals (like pharmaceutical drugs) can be made synthetically (in the lab).
2) They can also be extracted (removed) from plants.
3) You can extract a chemical from a plant using these steps:
   - Crush the plant to release the chemical.
   - Boil it in a suitable solvent — this will dissolve the chemical.
   - Use chromatography to separate out the chemical you want.

Crush

Boil to dissolve in a suitable solvent

CHROMATOGRAPHY

Separate by chromatography

Spots of different chemicals move up the plate at different speeds

Dissolved substance

Solvent

1) Chromatography is a used to separate chemicals.
2) One type used to extract plant chemicals is thin layer chromatography (TLC).
3) For this you put some of the solution on a TLC plate.
4) When it's put in a solvent the solution will separate into its different chemicals.
5) Then you can just choose the one you want. Clever.

Test For Purity Using Chromatography And Boiling and Melting Points

1) It's important that pharmaceutical drugs are made as pure as possible.
2) This is so that you know exactly what dose (amount) you're taking and to make sure that the impurities don't cause dangerous side effects.
3) In the exam, you might be given data on a purity test and asked what it shows. It's fairly straightforward...

- Pure substances won't be separated by thin layer chromatography — you'll only get one blob.
- Pure substances have a specific melting point and boiling point.
- If a substance is impure, the melting point will be too low and the boiling point will be too high.

Example: Sample A and Sample B both contain the same chemical. Use the data in the table to explain which sample is pure.

Answer: Sample A is pure because it couldn't be separated by chromatography and it has a higher melting point.

	Melting Point (°C)	Separated by Chromatography?
Sample A	112	No
Sample B	109	Yes

This page is pure class...

Chromatography is pretty tricky to get your head around at first. But all you really have to know is that it is used to separate chemicals. Only one page left to go in this section. Woo hoo.

Allotropes of Carbon

Woah, scary chemistry word alert. But never fear — all it means is 'different forms'. Phew.

Diamond and Graphite are Allotropes of Carbon

1) An allotrope is a different structural form of the same element in the same physical state (e.g. both solids).
2) This just means that they're made of the same stuff but built differently.
3) Diamond and graphite are both allotropes of carbon.
4) They both have giant molecular structures. This is because carbon can form lots of bonds with itself.

Diamond is Used in Jewellery and Cutting Tools

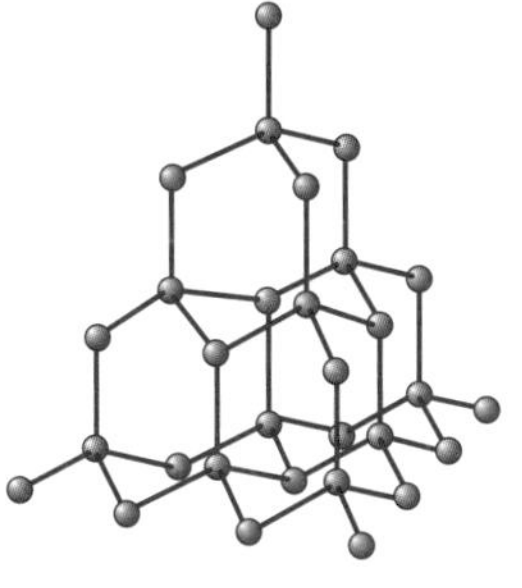

1) Diamonds are lustrous (shiny), clear and colourless. Ideal for jewellery.
2) Diamond is also really hard and has a very high melting point. This makes diamonds ideal as cutting tools.
3) It's also insoluble in water (it won't dissolve) and doesn't conduct electricity.

Graphite Makes the Lead of Your Pencil

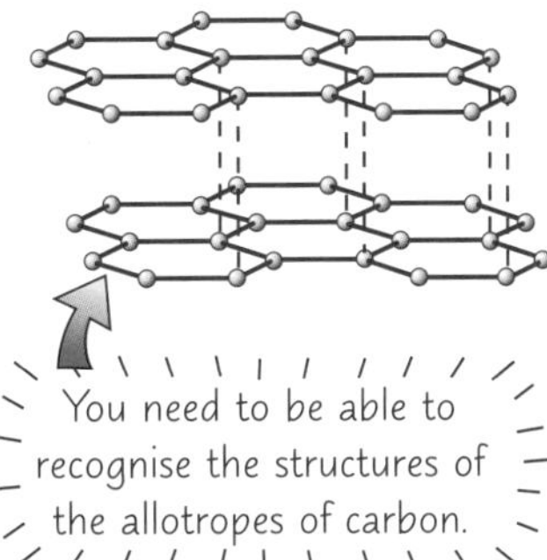

You need to be able to recognise the structures of the allotropes of carbon.

1) Graphite is black and opaque (you can't see through it), but still kind of lustrous.
2) The layers of graphite are slippery and can be rubbed off onto paper to leave a black mark — that's how a pencil works.
3) This also makes graphite ideal as a lubricating material — it makes things slippy.
4) Graphite is also insoluble in water and it conducts electricity.

Fullerenes are Also Allotropes of Carbon

1) Fullerenes are molecules of carbon, shaped like hollow balls or closed tubes.
2) The smallest fullerene is Buckminsterfullerene. It's made of carbon atoms joined in a ball.
3) Fullerenes can be used to 'cage' other molecules.
4) The carbon ball forms around another atom or molecule, which is then trapped inside.
5) This could be a new way of delivering a drug into the body.
6) Fullerenes can be joined together to form nanotubes — teeny tiny hollow carbon tubes:

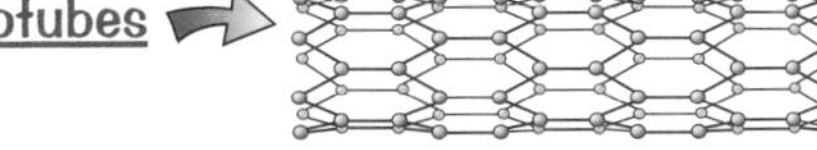

Buckminsterfullerene

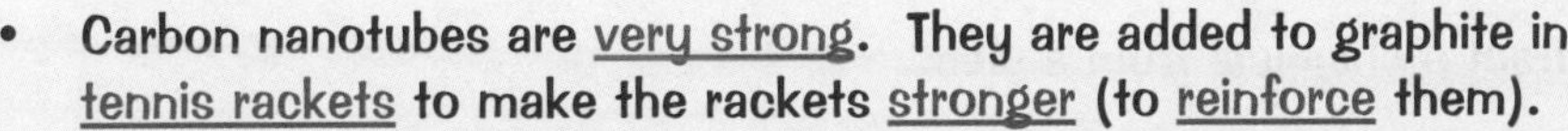

- Carbon nanotubes are very strong. They are added to graphite in tennis rackets to make the rackets stronger (to reinforce them).
- Nanotubes conduct electricity, so they can be used as semiconductors in electric circuits.

Semiconductors are materials that can conduct electricity better than insulators but not quite as well as metals.

Carbon is a girl's best friend...

Fullerenes. Confused? Just think of it as knitting teeny weeny atomic footballs, and you'll be fine...

Revision Summary for Module C3

Some more tricky questions to stress you out. The thing is though, why bother doing easy questions? These meaty monsters find out what you really know, and worse, what you really don't. Yeah, I know, it's kinda scary, but if you want to get anywhere in life you've got to face up to a bit of hardship. That's just the way it is. Take a few deep breaths and then try these.

1) What is an ionic bond?

2)* A molecule has the molecular formula $CH_3(CH_2)_4CH_3$. How many C and H atoms does it contain?

3)* A molecule has the molecular formula C_3H_8. Write down its displayed formula.

4)* Magnesium reacts with oxygen to make magnesium oxide. Write the word equation for this reaction.

5)* Balance this equation: $Na + H_2O \rightarrow NaOH + H_2$.

6) What is an endothermic reaction?

7) There is a temperature rise during a reaction. Is the reaction exothermic or endothermic?

8) Draw and label a diagram of the apparatus that could be used for a calorimetric experiment.

9) Give two things you should do to make sure a calorimetric experiment is a fair test.

10) A reaction produces a gas. How could you measure the rate of the reaction?

11) What four things affect the rate of a reaction?

12) Why do gases react faster when they're under higher pressure?

13)* The graph on the right shows two different reactions. Which reaction has the faster rate, A or B?

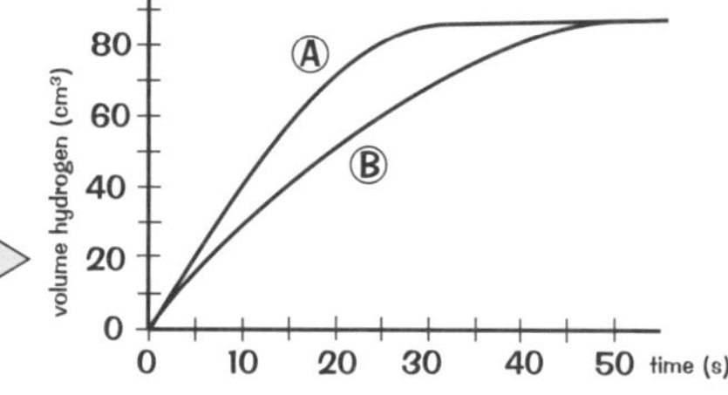

14)* Find A_r or M_r for each of these (use the periodic table inside the front cover):
a) Ca b) Ag c) CO_2 d) $MgCO_3$ e) $Al(OH)_3$
f) ZnO g) Na_2CO_3 h) sodium chloride

15)* 73 g of HCl reacts with 80 g of NaOH to make 36 g of water. What mass of NaCl will be produced?

16) Explain what 100% atom economy means.

17) Write the equation for the atom economy of a reaction.

18) What is the formula for percentage yield?

19) What is 'continuous production'?

20) Why are pharmaceutical drugs made using batch production?

21) Give three reasons why pharmaceutical drugs are expensive.

22) Describe how you would extract a chemical from a plant.

23) Explain why diamond makes a good cutting tool.

24) Explain why graphite is ideal as a lubricating material.

* Answers on page 116.

Speed and Velocity

Reckon you can speed on through this module? On your marks. Get set. Go...

Speed is Just the Distance Travelled in a Certain Time

1) To find the speed of an object, you need to measure the distance it travels (in metres or km) and the time it takes (in seconds or hours).
2) Then the speed is calculated in metres per second (m/s) or kilometres per hour (km/h).
3) The greater the speed of an object, the further it can travel in a certain time, or the less time it takes to go a certain distance.
4) If an object is speeding up (or slowing down) then you might need to find the average of its speed over the journey.
5) Average speed, distance and time are related by the formula:

$$\text{Average speed} = \frac{\text{Distance}}{\text{Time}}$$

EXAMPLE: A cat walks 2 km in 4000 seconds. Find its average speed, in metres per second.

ANSWER: 1 km = 1000 m, so 2 km = 2 × 1000 = 2000 m
Using the formula:
average speed = distance ÷ time = 2000 m ÷ 4000 s = 0.5 m/s

The Formula Looks a Bit Harder when you're Working Out Distance

This is just the same formula you used before, but messed about with a bit:

If something is 'at rest' it means the velocity is 0 m/s.

u is the speed at the start — v is the speed at the end

distance is sometimes given as the letter s

$$\text{Distance} = \frac{(u + v)}{2} \times t$$

t is the time

(You need to get pretty slick at using this formula.)

EXAMPLE: A ferret speeds up from 0 to 3 m/s in a time of 60 seconds. What distance does it cover in this time?

ANSWER: u = 0 m/s, v = 3 m/s and t = 60 s
distance = (0 + 3) ÷ 2 × 60 = 90 m

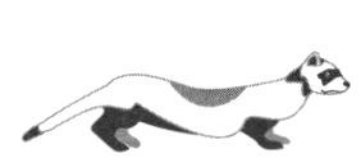

Speed is Just a Number, but Velocity Has Direction Too

mph means miles per hour.

1) The speed of an object is just how fast it's going. E.g. speed = 30 mph.
2) Sometimes it's important to know the direction too.
3) Velocity describes both the speed and direction of an object. E.g. velocity = 30 mph due north.
4) You can have negative velocities.
5) If a car travelling at 20 m/s turns around to go in the opposite direction, the speed is still 20 m/s but the velocity becomes –20 m/s.
6) If two objects are moving parallel to each other, their relative velocity is the difference in their velocities (you just subtract one from the other).

   For example, two cars are travelling at speeds of 30 m/s in opposite directions. Their relative velocity is 30 m/s – (–30 m/s) = 60 m/s.

30 m/s

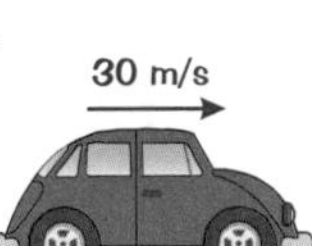

-30 m/s

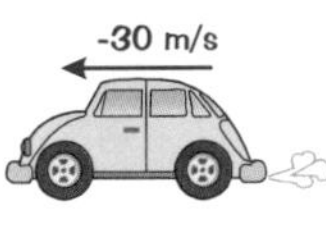

Ferret ferret ferret ferret...

You'll be given the formula in the exam. Just make sure you know how to use it.

Speed and Distance

A real-world example now — speed cameras...

Speed Cameras Measure the Speed of Cars

1) Speed cameras can be used to catch speeding drivers.
2) Lines painted on the road at a certain distance apart are used to measure the distance travelled by the car.
3) A photo of the car is taken as it passes the first line and a second photo is taken a short time later.
4) These photos can then be used to measure the distance travelled by the car in this time.

Example:
A speed camera takes two photos of a car. The photos are taken 0.5 s apart. From the lines on the road, you know the car has travelled 5 m in this time. What was the speed of the car?

Answer: Average Speed $= \frac{\text{distance}}{\text{time}} = \frac{5\text{ m}}{0.5\text{ s}} = 10\text{ m/s}$

5) In some places (like motorways) you'll find average speed cameras instead.
6) These use two separate cameras — one as you enter the speed check area and one as you leave it.
7) They record the time it takes for you to travel the known distance between the two cameras, and use that to work out your average speed over that distance.

Distance-Time Graphs

Distance-time graphs show how the movement of an object changes.

1) GRADIENT (steepness) = SPEED.
2) Flat sections are where it's stopped.
3) The steeper the gradient, the faster it's going.
4) 'Downhill' sections mean it's changed direction and is coming back toward its starting point.
5) Curves show acceleration or deceleration (see next page).
6) A steepening curve means it's speeding up (increasing gradient).
7) A levelling off curve means it's slowing down (decreasing gradient).

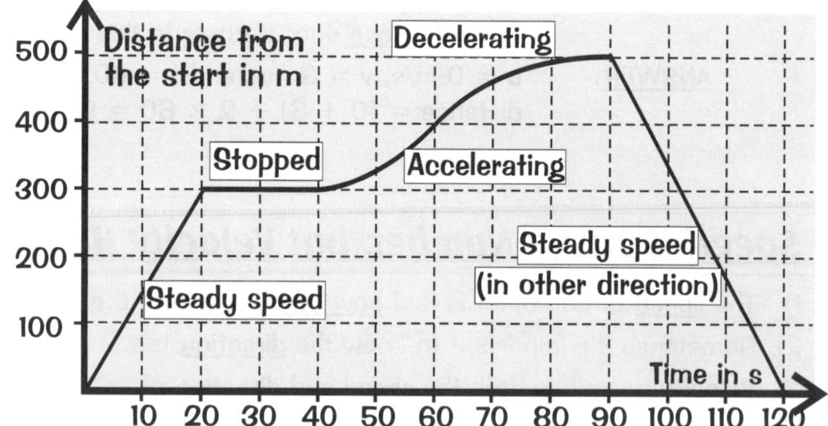

Distance-time graphs — more fun than gravel (just)...

You might have to draw graphs in an exam too, so have a peak at pages 5-6 for a bit more on how to go about it.

Speed and Acceleration

Is your revision speeding up? Then you're accelerating. Whoop - di - do.

Acceleration is How Quickly You're Speeding Up

1) Acceleration is the change in speed over a certain time.
2) An increase in speed is a positive acceleration.
3) A decrease in speed is a deceleration — a negative acceleration.
4) The bigger the change in speed in a certain time, the bigger the acceleration (or deceleration).
5) The units of acceleration (or deceleration) are m/s^2.

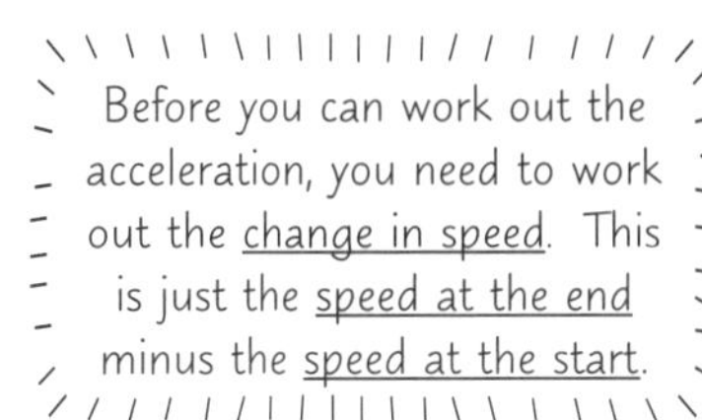

Before you can work out the acceleration, you need to work out the change in speed. This is just the speed at the end minus the speed at the start.

$$\text{Acceleration} = \frac{\text{Change in Speed}}{\text{Time Taken}}$$

EXAMPLE: A skunk accelerates from 2 m/s to 6 m/s in 5 s. Find its acceleration.

ANSWER: First, find change in speed: 6 – 2 = 4 m/s.
Then, using the formula:
acceleration = change in speed ÷ time taken
= 4 m/s ÷ 5 s = 0.8 m/s^2

Speed-Time Graphs

The lines on a speed-time graph mean different things to those on a distance-time graph:

1) GRADIENT = ACCELERATION.
2) Flat sections are where something's moving at a steady speed.
3) The steeper the gradient, the greater the acceleration or deceleration.
4) Uphill sections (/ — positive gradient) are acceleration.
5) Downhill sections (\ — negative gradient) are deceleration.
6) The area under any section of the graph is the distance travelled in that time.

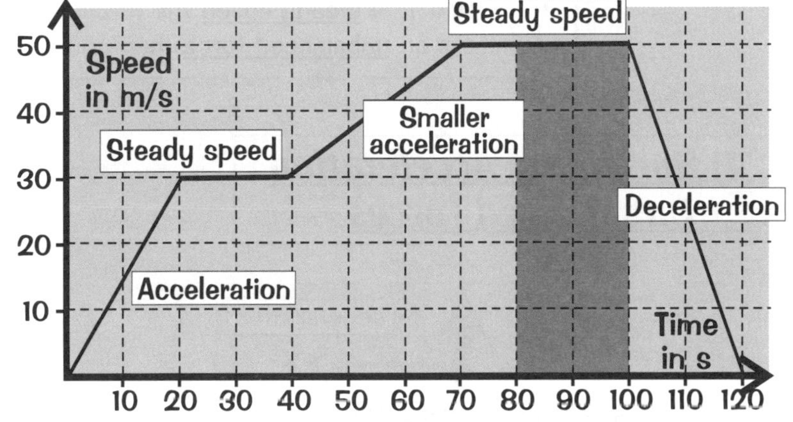

For example, the distance travelled between 80 s and 100 s is equal to the shaded area on the graph. So the distance travelled = 20 × 50 = 1000 m.

Understanding speed-time graphs — it can be a real uphill struggle...

The tricky thing about distance and speed-time graphs is that they can look pretty much the same but show totally different kinds of motion. Make sure you learn how to calculate acceleration too. And don't forget the units.

Forces

A force is a push or a pull. Forces can make things stay still, speed up, slow down or stay at a steady speed.

1) Stationary Object — All Forces in Balance

1) The weight of an object acts downwards on the surface.
2) This causes a REACTION FORCE from the surface pushing up on the object.
3) The forces are balanced — they're the same size but acting in opposite directions.
4) The balanced forces mean that the object won't accelerate in any direction.
5) Any HORIZONTAL forces must be equal and opposite otherwise the object will accelerate sideways.

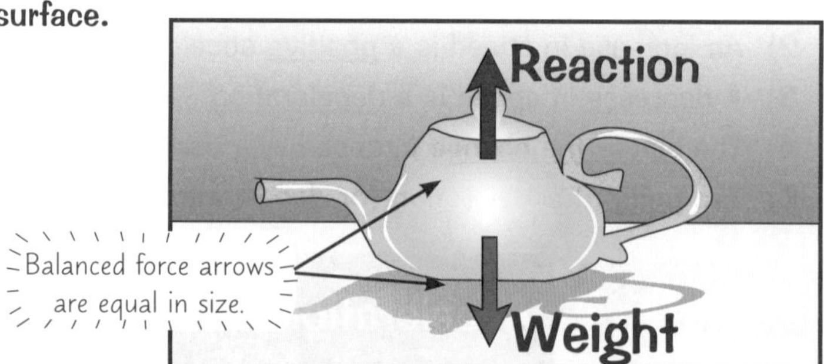

Reaction
Balanced force arrows are equal in size.
Weight

2) Steady Horizontal Speed — All Forces in Balance

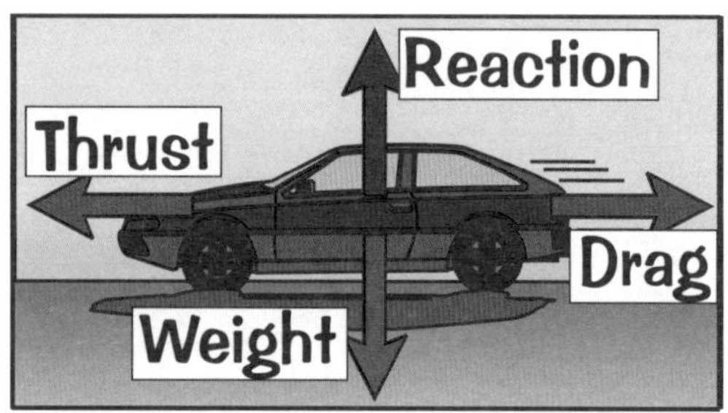

3) Steady Vertical Speed — All Forces in Balance

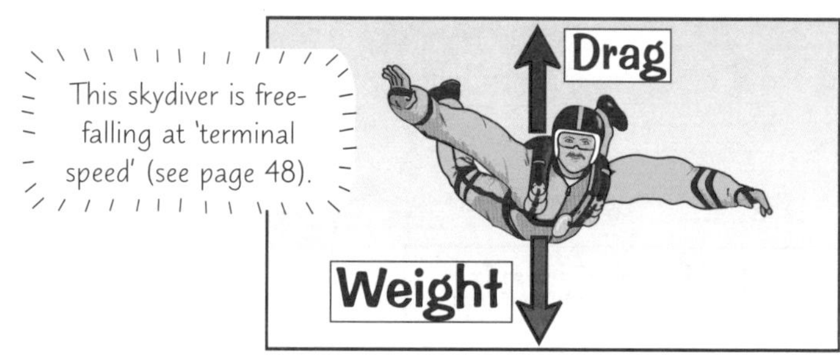

To move with a steady speed the forces must be in BALANCE.
If there is an unbalanced force then you get acceleration, not steady speed.

4) Horizontal Acceleration — Unbalanced Forces

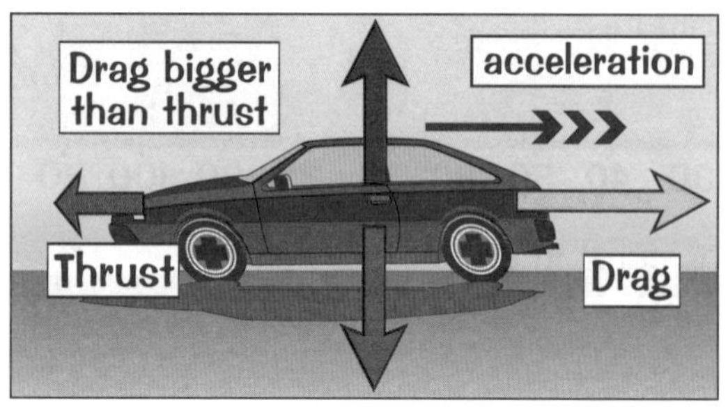

5) Vertical Acceleration — Unbalanced Forces

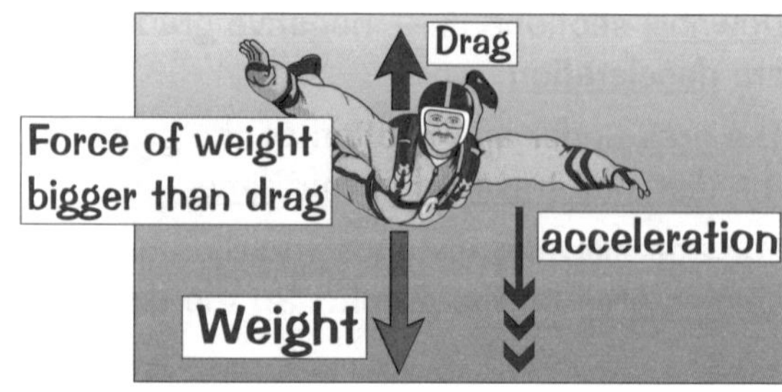

1) You only get acceleration or deceleration with unbalanced forces.
2) The bigger this unbalanced force, the greater the acceleration or deceleration.
3) On a force diagram the arrows will be unequal.

Accelerate your learning — force yourself to revise...

So, things only accelerate in a particular direction if there's an unbalanced force in that direction. Simple.

Friction

Ever wondered why it's so hard to run into the wind whilst wearing a sandwich board? Read on to find out...

Friction is Always There to Slow Things Down

1) Friction is a force that always acts in the opposite direction to movement.
2) You get friction when two surfaces rub together, or when an object passes through a fluid (but then it's called drag).
3) If an object has no force driving it along it will always slow down and stop because of friction and drag.
4) In space, where there is no atmosphere, there is nothing to rub against. This means there is no drag to slow down a moving object.
5) To travel at a steady speed, the driving force needs to balance the frictional forces.
6) To speed up, an object needs to have a bigger driving force than the frictional forces.
7) This means it has to put in more energy to move.
8) More of this energy is wasted overcoming friction.
9) So big frictional forces make things like cars less efficient.

Friction Occurs in Two Main Ways:

FRICTION BETWEEN SOLID SURFACES

1) Static friction acts between two surfaces that are gripping each other.
2) Friction between surfaces that are sliding past each other is sliding friction.
3) You can reduce both these types of friction by putting a lubricant like oil or grease between the surfaces.

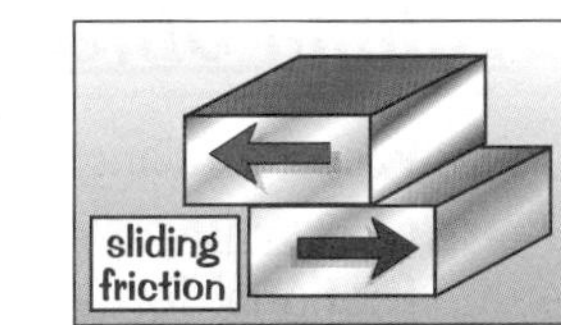

RESISTANCE OR DRAG FROM FLUIDS (air or liquid)

1) Most of the frictional forces on a moving object are caused by air resistance or drag.

2) The shape of an object affects the drag on it as it moves through a fluid.
3) Some things are designed to reduce drag by being aerodynamic (streamlined).
4) For example, sports cars and aeroplanes are aerodynamic.

5) Parachutes are designed to have a large amount of air resistance.
6) The faster an object moves, the more air resistance there is.

Learning about air resistance — it can be a real drag...

There are a couple of really important things on this page. 1) When you move, there's usually a frictional force to stop you. 2) The faster you move, the greater the frictional force that acts on you. Got that? Lovely.

Weight and Terminal Speed

Now for something a bit more attractive — the force of gravity. Enjoy...

Weight is due to Gravity

1) Gravity attracts (pulls) all masses towards each other.
2) Gravitational field strength (g) is a measure of how strongly the gravity of an object (such as a planet) pulls on other objects.
3) On Earth, the gravitational field strength is 10 m/s^2.
4) This means that any object falling to Earth will accelerate due to the force of gravity at 10 m/s^2.
5) An object's weight is the force of gravity acting on its mass:

weight =	mass ×	gravitational field strength
(N)	(kg)	(m/s^2)

EXAMPLE: What is the weight, in newtons (N), of a 5 kg chicken, both on Earth ($g = 10\ m/s^2$) and on the Moon ($g = 1.6\ m/s^2$)?

ANSWER: Weight = mass × gravitational field strength
On Earth: Weight = 5 × 10 = 50 N
On the Moon: Weight = 5 × 1.6 = 8 N

Falling Objects Reach a Terminal Speed

1) When a falling object first sets off, the force of gravity pulling it down is greater than the frictional force slowing it down.
2) This means the object accelerates (speeds up).
3) As the speed increases, the friction builds up.
4) This slowly reduces the acceleration.
5) Eventually the frictional force is equal to the force of gravity.
6) The overall force is zero.
7) This means the object can't accelerate any more (see next page).
8) It will have reached its terminal (maximum) speed and will fall at a steady speed.

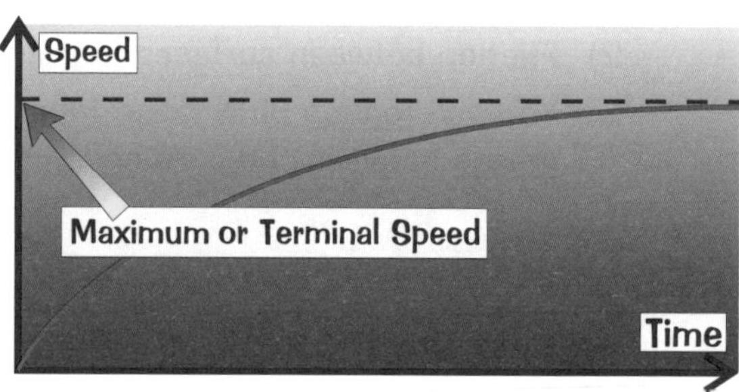

An open parachute has a lot of air resistance. This allows skydivers to reach terminal speed sooner than they would without it — and that terminal speed is a lot slower (and safer).

Oh terminal speed — I've really fallen for you...

On the Moon, the gravitational field strength is smaller than it is on Earth. So even though your mass stays the same, you'd weigh less on the Moon than you do on Earth. Beats dieting any day. Now, where's my space suit...

Forces and Acceleration

Things only accelerate if you give them a push. Makes sense.

A Balanced Force Means a Steady Speed

If the forces on an object are all BALANCED, then it'll keep moving at the SAME SPEED in the SAME DIRECTION (so if it starts off still, it'll stay still).

1) If an object is moving in a straight line at a steady speed then the forces on it must all be balanced.
2) Things definitely DON'T need a constant overall force to keep them moving — NO NO NO NO!
3) To keep going at a steady speed, there must be zero resultant (overall) force.

An Unbalanced Force Means Acceleration

If there is an UNBALANCED FORCE, the object will ACCELERATE in the direction of the force.

1) An unbalanced force will always produce an acceleration.
2) This 'acceleration' could be starting, stopping, speeding up or slowing down.
3) The arrows on a force diagram will be unequal: 

The Overall Unbalanced Force is called the Resultant Force

Any resultant force will produce acceleration. This is the formula for it:

Force = mass × acceleration
(N) (kg) (m/s^2)

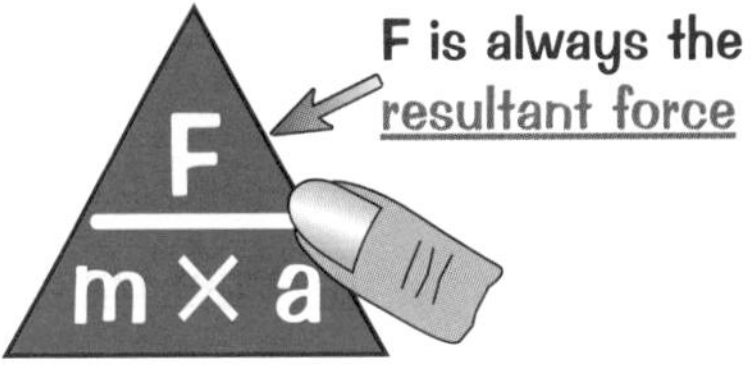

EXAMPLE: Calculate the acceleration of a 1000 kg car with a resultant force of 2000 N acting forwards.

ANSWER:
- Cover up the 'a' on the formula triangle and write down what's left showing: $a = F \div m$.
- Plug in the numbers from the question: $a = 2000 \div 1000 = 2\ m/s^2$

Everyday Example — Pushing a Trolley

1) The bigger the force you push with, the greater the acceleration.
2) The bigger the mass (as you put more things in), the smaller the acceleration.
3) To get a big mass to accelerate as fast as a small mass, it needs a bigger force.

Resultant force... I'm pretty sure that's a Steven Seagal film...

You need to remember these simple rules: balanced forces = steady speed, resultant force = acceleration.

Stopping Distances

The stopping distance of a car is the distance covered in the time between the driver first spotting a hazard and the car coming to a complete stop. Examiners are pretty keen on this stuff, so make sure you learn it.

Many Factors Affect Your Total Stopping Distance

The longer it takes to stop after spotting a hazard, the higher the risk of crashing into whatever's in front. The distance it takes to stop a car is divided into the THINKING DISTANCE and the BRAKING DISTANCE:

STOPPING DISTANCE = THINKING DISTANCE + BRAKING DISTANCE

Thinking Distance

"The distance the car travels in the time between the need for braking occurring and the brakes starting to act."

It's affected by FOUR MAIN FACTORS:

1) TIREDNESS
2) ALCOHOL or other drugs
3) DISTRACTIONS or lack of concentration

   These first three all increase 'reaction time' — the time between the hazard appearing and the driver hitting the brakes.

4) SPEED — whatever your reaction time, the faster you're going, the further you'll travel before you hit the brakes.

Braking Distance

"The distance taken to stop once the brakes have been applied."

It's affected by THREE MAIN FACTORS:

1) ROAD CONDITIONS
   a) If the road's slippy, it takes longer to stop and the braking distance increases.
   b) This could be due to a poor road surface — from loose material, diesel spills or wet leaves.
   c) Or weather conditions — wet or icy roads are always much more slippy than dry roads.

2) CAR CONDITIONS
   a) A heavier car — with the same brakes, the heavier the vehicle the longer it takes to stop. For example, a car won't stop as quickly when it's full of people or towing a caravan.
   b) Brakes — if your brakes are worn or faulty you won't be able to brake with as much force, so you won't slow down as quickly.
   c) Tyres — By law, tyres should have a minimum tread depth of 1.6 mm. This gets rid of the water in wet conditions. A tyre without tread will ride on a layer of water and skid very easily.

3) SPEED

   The faster you're going, the further it takes to stop (see next page).

Stop right there — and learn this page...

Makes you think, doesn't it. Learn the details and write yourself a mini-essay to see how much you really know.

More on Stopping Distances

So now you know what affects stopping distances, let's have a look at the facts and figures.

Stopping Distances are Huge at High Speed

1) The figures below for typical stopping distances are from the Highway Code.

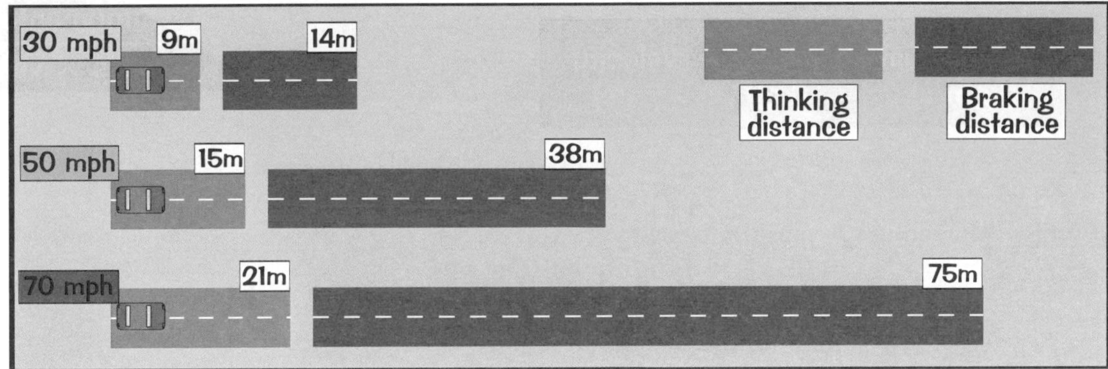

2) It's scary to see just how far it takes to stop when you're going at 70 miles per hour (mph).

EXAMPLE:
Use the chart above to find the total stopping distance for a car travelling at 70 mph.

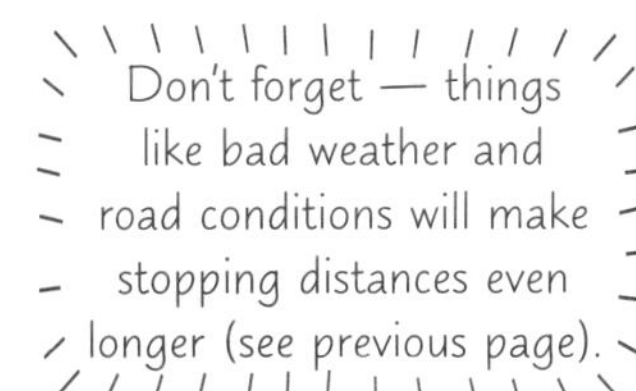

Don't forget — things like bad weather and road conditions will make stopping distances even longer (see previous page).

ANSWER:
The thinking distance is 21 m and the braking distance is 75 m.
Stopping distance = thinking distance + braking distance
= 21 + 75 = 96 m (That's the length of a football pitch.)

Leave Enough Space to Stop

1) To avoid an accident, drivers need to leave enough space between their car and the one in front.
2) This is so that if they had to stop suddenly they would have time to do it safely.
3) 'Enough space' means the stopping distance for whatever speed they're going at.
4) So even at 30 mph, you should drive no closer than 6 or 7 car lengths away from the car in front — just in case.
5) And if the road conditions are bad, leave even more space.
6) Speed limits are really important because speed affects the stopping distance so much.
7) Some residential areas are now 20 mph zones.

There's a little rhyme that goes: "Only a fool breaks the two second rule". It's a handy way of making sure you leave enough space when driving. When the car in front passes a street light or a tree, count the seconds until you pass the same thing. If it's less than two seconds you're too close.

If you live life in the fast lane — leave plenty of space in front...

If the road's icy, stopping distances can be 10 times as far as on a dry road — eek! If only there was a little rhyme like that to help you pass your exams... Learning this page should do the trick though, so get a move on.

Momentum

A large rugby player running very fast is going to be a lot harder to stop than a small one out for a Sunday afternoon stroll. That's momentum for you.

Momentum = Mass × Velocity

1) The greater the mass or velocity of an object, the more momentum it has.

Momentum (kg m/s)	=	Mass (kg)	×	Velocity (m/s)

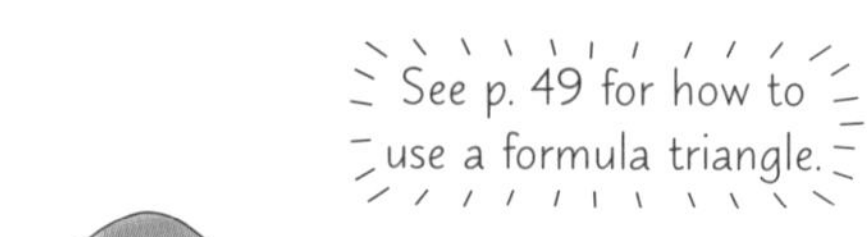

See p. 49 for how to use a formula triangle.

EXAMPLE: A 65 kg kangaroo is moving in a straight line at 10 m/s. Calculate its momentum.

ANSWER: Momentum = mass × velocity
= 65 kg × 10 m/s = 650 kg m/s

2) Momentum has size and direction — like velocity (but not speed).

Forces Cause Changes in Momentum

1) When a force acts on an object, it causes a change in momentum.

$$\text{Force acting (N)} = \frac{\text{Change in momentum (kg m/s)}}{\text{Time taken for change to happen (s)}}$$

EXAMPLE: A rock and a comet collide in space. The collision lasts for 0.7 s. The rock's momentum changes from 15 kg m/s to 1765 kg m/s during the collision. Calculate the force of the comet on the rock.

ANSWER: Change in momentum = 1765 – 15 = 1750 kg m/s
Force acting = change of momentum ÷ time
= 1750 kg m/s ÷ 0.7 s = 2500 N

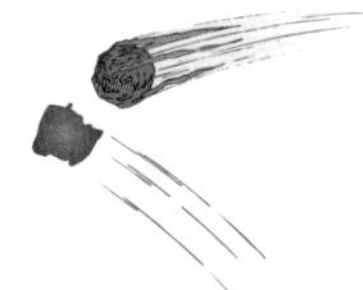

2) For the same change in momentum:
   - if the time taken is small, the force will be big,
   - if the time taken is big, the force will be small.
3) So if someone's momentum changes very quickly (like in a car crash), the forces on the body will be very large, and more likely to cause injury.
4) Car safety features slow people down over a longer time in a crash.
5) The longer it takes for a change in momentum, the smaller the force, which reduces the injuries.

- CRUMPLE ZONES crumple and change shape during a crash, increasing the time taken for the car to stop.
- SEAT BELTS stretch slightly, increasing the time taken for the wearer to stop. This reduces the forces acting on the chest.
- AIRBAGS also slow you down more gradually.

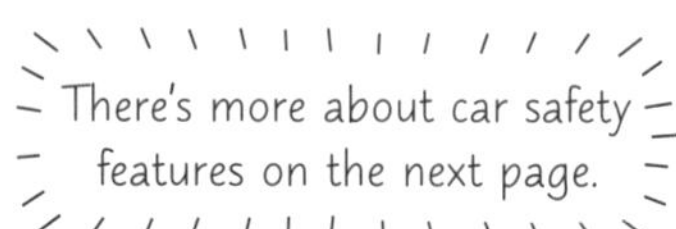

There's more about car safety
features on the next page.

Learn this stuff — it'll only take a moment... um...

Momentum's pretty important — so make sure you learn it properly. Momentum depends on mass and velocity. A force causes a change in momentum. Safety features on cars work by slowing down the change in momentum.

Car Safety

Cars have different types of safety features to help keep you as safe as possible inside the car.

Safety Features Help to Prevent Accidents and Reduce Injuries

There are two main types of car safety feature:

Features that PREVENT ACCIDENTS

ABS brakes and traction control: These prevent the car from skidding, making it easier for the driver to stay in control.

Electric windows and paddle-shift controls: Many cars have lots of their controls either on or near the steering wheel, to help the driver to stay safely in control.

Features that REDUCE INJURIES if you crash

Safety cage: This rigid cage surrounds the people in the car. It doesn't easily change shape, even in a bad crash, so it stops the passengers getting crushed.

Crumple zones, airbags, seat belts and collapsible steering columns: These all change shape during an impact to reduce the forces acting on the passengers (see previous page) and absorb energy (see below).

Some Safety Features Absorb Kinetic Energy

See page 55 for more on kinetic energy.

1) When a car stops suddenly, its kinetic energy has to be changed to other forms.
2) Many car safety features absorb energy to help reduce injuries in a crash.
3) The brakes absorb a lot of energy by heating up.
4) Seat belts, crumple zones and airbags absorb energy by changing shape during a crash.
5) For example, seat belts stretch slightly.
6) This is why seat belts need to be replaced after a crash. If they have stretched once, they might have been weakened, so they won't be as stretchy if you have a second accident.

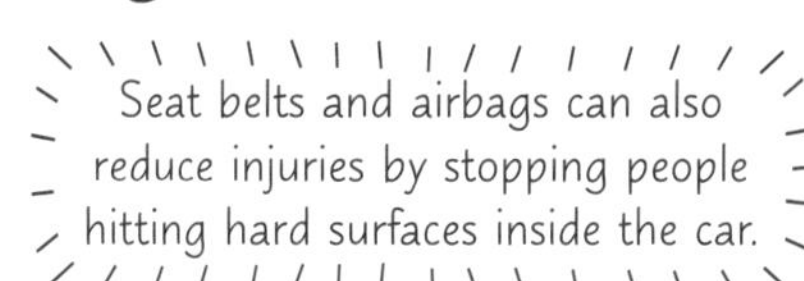

Seat belts and airbags can also reduce injuries by stopping people hitting hard surfaces inside the car.

Safety Features Save Lives

1) Safety features are tested to see how well they save lives or stop injuries in an accident.
2) Testing involves crashing cars both with and without the safety feature in place, and watching slow motion film footage to see the results.
3) The cars contain crash test dummies.
4) These have sensors at different places on their 'bodies' to show where a real person would be injured, and how bad the injury would be.
5) The tests are repeated using different cars, at different speeds, and using different sized dummies.
6) The results can then be compared with real data on deaths and severe injuries from actual road accidents.

Belt up and start revising...

Back seat passengers who don't wear a seat belt will hit the front seat with a force of between 30 to 60 times their body's weight in an accident at 30 mph. This is like the force you'd feel if you were sat on by an elephant.

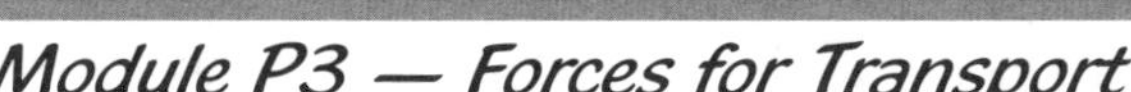

Work Done and Power

Time to get some work done on... er... work done. You'll need to use some energy for this.

Work is Done When a Force Moves an Object

1) Whenever something moves, there must be a force to move it.
2) For example, when you lift a weight, climb the stairs, pull a sledge or push a shopping trolley.
3) The thing providing the force needs a supply of energy (like fuel or food or electricity).
4) It then does 'work' by moving the object.
5) The energy it receives is transferred into other forms.
6) Whether the energy is transferred usefully or is wasted, work is done.
7) Just like Batman and Bruce Wayne, 'work done' and 'energy transferred' are 'one and the same'. (And they're both given in joules.)
8) The amount of work done on an object depends on the size of the force and the distance it has moved.

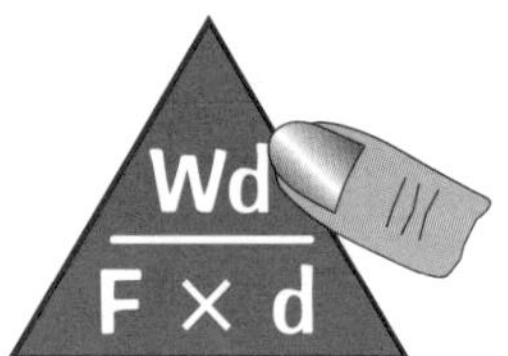

Work Done = Force × Distance
(J) (N) (m)

See p. 49 for how to use a formula triangle.

EXAMPLE: Some kids drag an old tractor tyre 5 m over rough ground. They pull with a total force of 340 N. Find the work done dragging the tyre.

ANSWER: Work done = Force × Distance = 340 N × 5 m = 1700 J

Power is the 'Rate of Doing Work'

1) Power is a measure of how quickly work is being done:
2) The proper unit of power is the watt (W).
3) 1 W = 1 J of energy transferred per second.

$$\text{Power (W)} = \frac{\text{Work done (J)}}{\text{Time taken (s)}}$$

EXAMPLE: A motor transfers 4800 J of useful energy in 120 seconds. Find its power output.

ANSWER: Power = Work done ÷ time
= 4800 J ÷ 120 s = 40 W

Revise work done — what else...

Remember "energy transferred" and "work done" are the same thing. If you need a force to make something start moving (p.49), all that means is that you need to give it a bit of energy. Makes sense.

Kinetic and Gravitational Potential Energy

Anything that's moving has kinetic energy. There's a slightly tricky formula for it, so you'll have to concentrate.

Kinetic Energy is Energy of Movement

1) The kinetic energy (K.E.) of something is the energy it has when moving.
2) The kinetic energy of something depends on both its mass and speed:

$$\text{Kinetic Energy (J)} = \tfrac{1}{2} \times \text{mass (kg)} \times \text{speed (m/s)}^2$$

$$\text{K.E.} = \tfrac{1}{2} \times m \times v^2$$

EXAMPLE: A car of mass 1450 kg is travelling at 28 m/s. Calculate its kinetic energy.

ANSWER: You just plug the numbers into the formula — but watch the 'v^2'!
K.E. = $\tfrac{1}{2} \times m \times v^2 = \tfrac{1}{2} \times 1450 \times 28^2$ = 568 400 J. (Joules because it's energy.)

3) If you double the mass, the K.E. doubles.
4) If you double the speed, though, the K.E. quadruples (it's 4 times as big).

Gravitational Potential Energy is Energy Due to Height

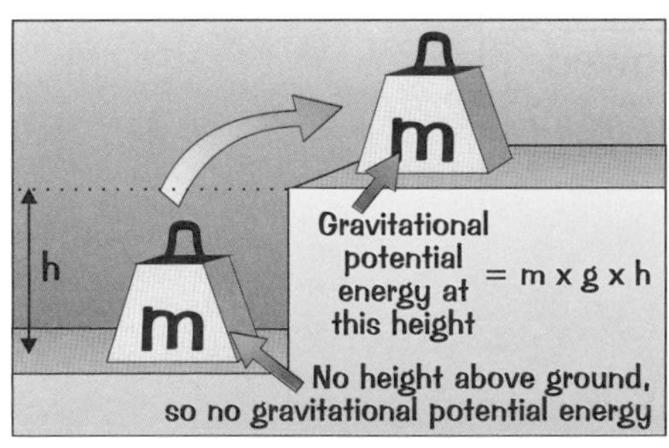

1) Gravitational potential energy (G.P.E.) is the energy that something has because of its mass and its height above the ground.
2) For example, a lift has a lot more G.P.E. on the top floor than it does at lower floors, because it is higher above the ground.
3) G.P.E. can be found using this formula:

$$\text{G.P.E. (J)} = \text{mass (kg)} \times g\ (\text{m/s}^2) \times \text{height (m)}$$

$$\text{G.P.E.} = m \times g \times h$$

4) The g in the formula is gravitational field strength (see p.48). On Earth, g is about 10 m/s^2 (or 10 N/kg).

EXAMPLE: A sheep of mass 47 kg is lifted by 6.3 m. Find its increase in gravitational potential energy.

ANSWER: Just plug the numbers into the formula:
G.P.E. = $m \times g \times h = 47 \times 10 \times 6.3$ = 2961 J.
(Joules because it's energy.)

!
What do you call a sheep with no eyes and no legs?
Dunno?
A Cloud!

Kinetic energy — just get a move on and learn it, OK...

So, kinetic energy is all to do with movement, and gravitational potential energy is all to do with height. Both of them depend on mass too. Think you've got the hang of it? Good. Now get practising those formulas...

Falling Objects and Roller Coasters

What goes up must come down — and change its gravitational potential energy to kinetic energy on the way.

Falling Objects Convert G.P.E. into K.E.

1) When something falls, its gravitational potential energy is transferred (changed) into kinetic energy.
2) So the further it falls, the faster it goes.

Kinetic Energy gained = Gravitational Potential Energy lost

In real life, some of the potential energy will be changed into heat due to air resistance — it won't all get changed to kinetic energy. But in exam questions they'll usually tell you to ignore air resistance, so you can say it all changes to kinetic energy.

Roller Coasters Transfer Energy

1) At the top of a roller coaster (position A) the car has lots of gravitational potential energy.

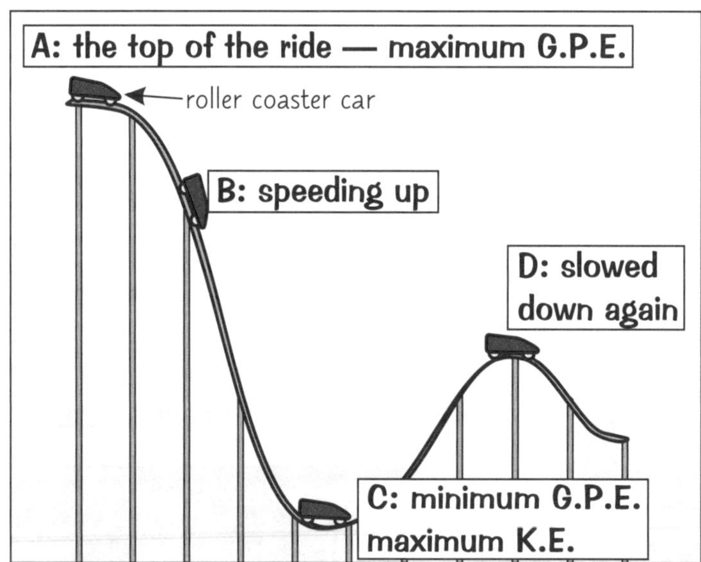

2) As the car drops towards position C, gravitational potential energy is transferred to kinetic energy. The car speeds up.
3) If you ignore any air resistance or friction, the car will have as much energy at C as it did at A.
4) That energy must have been transferred from gravitational potential energy to kinetic energy.
5) So at C the car has minimum gravitational potential energy and maximum kinetic energy.
6) In a real roller coaster (that does have friction to deal with), the car has to have enough kinetic energy at point C to carry it up the hill again to D.

Life is a roller coaster — just gotta ride it...

Now then, who said physics couldn't be fun? This has been a pretty exciting module so far — I hope you're enjoying the ride. Even if you're not, you still need to know all this stuff for the exam, so get learning.

Fuel Consumption and Emissions

Cars and lorries would be pretty useless if they didn't have any fuel to get them moving...

Cars Have Different Power Ratings

Typical Power Ratings

Sports car power = 100 kW

Small car power = 50 kW

1) A car's power rating depends on the size and design of the engine.
2) The larger or more powerful an engine, the more energy it transfers from its fuel every second.
3) This means it usually has a higher fuel consumption.

Fuel Consumption is All About the Amount of Fuel Used

1) The fuel consumption of a car is usually given as the amount of fuel used to go a certain distance.
2) Fuel consumption is often given in litres per 100 km (l/100 km).
3) For example, a car with a fuel consumption of 5 l/100 km will travel 100 km on 5 litres of fuel.
4) It can also be given in miles per gallon (mpg) — how many miles the car can travel on a gallon of fuel.
5) Cars that use a lot of fuel compared to other cars are more expensive to run, because fuel costs money.
6) They're also more damaging to the environment, because fossil fuels pollute (see below and next page).

Shape Can Affect Fuel Consumption

1) Energy from the fuel is needed to do work against air resistance (drag).
2) So, things that increase air resistance will increase a car's fuel consumption:
    a) Roof boxes spoil the streamlined shape of the car which increases air resistance.
    b) Driving with the windows open increases air resistance too.
3) Things that decrease air resistance will decrease fuel consumption:
    a) The wedge shape of sports cars makes them very streamlined which reduces air resistance.
    b) Deflectors on lorries and caravans are shaped bits of plastic that reduce air resistance.

The shape of a car affects the speed too. A shape that increases the air resistance will lower the top speed of the car.

When Cars Burn Fuel they Release Emissions

1) As fossil fuels are burnt they release emissions.
2) These are gases like CO_2, nitrogen dioxide (NO_2) and water vapour.
3) In general, the higher the fuel consumption, the more emissions a car gives out, and the worse it is for the environment.
4) Older cars often have worse fuel consumption and emission figures.
5) If you have to interpret data on emissions, read it carefully and check the units.
6) There are lots of different units that could be used, such as g/mile or g/km — these tell you how many grams of emissions are given out for every mile or km you travel.

I bet this page has fuelled your enthusiasm...

You might get asked how to reduce fuel consumption by reducing drag. Make sure you know how.

Fuels for Cars

We can't keep filling our fuel tanks with petrol and diesel forever.
Not only are they running out fast, but they're also bad for the environment. Eeep!

Most Cars Run on Fossil Fuels

1) Most cars and lorries use petrol or diesel as a fuel.
2) Petrol and diesel are fuels that are made from oil, which is a fossil fuel.
3) The pollution released when these fuels are burnt can cause environmental problems like acid rain and climate change.
4) Fossil fuels are also non-renewable, which means they'll run out one day.
5) This means that in the future we may have to rely on renewable energy sources such as biofuels or solar energy to power our vehicles (see below).

Some Cars Run On Biofuels

1) Biofuels are made from plants and organic waste.
2) They are renewable — they won't run out because we can keep growing more.
3) Growing and burning biofuels doesn't increase the total amount of carbon dioxide in the air.
4) Burning biofuels also produces less other pollution than burning fossil fuels.
5) So scientists are developing cars that run on biofuels instead.

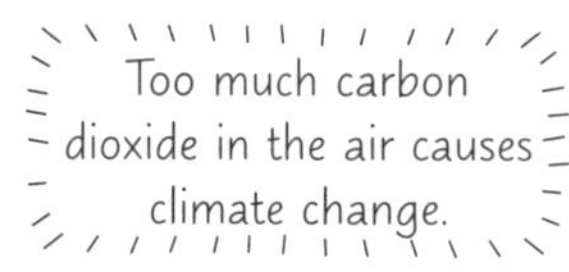

Too much carbon dioxide in the air causes climate change.

Electric Cars Need To Be Recharged

1) A few vehicles use large batteries to power electric motors.
2) These vehicles don't release any pollution as you drive along (at the 'point of use'), unlike fossil fuel cars.
3) But their batteries need to be recharged using electricity.
4) This electricity is likely to come from power stations.
5) Most power stations create pollution when they burn fossil fuels to produce electricity.
6) One way around this is to use solar power.
7) Solar-powered cars have solar panels that change energy from the sun into electricity to power the motor.
8) Solar power is renewable, and solar-powered vehicles produce no pollution after they're built.
9) But electric cars and solar panels are expensive to make and buy, so not everyone can afford them.
10) And pollution is created during their production too.

"I pity the fuel" — Mr T, campaigner for electric vehicles...

Almost done for another section — just one lovely little page of questions to go. Make sure you learn this page first though. You need to know about the ways we can power our cars without fossil fuels — biofuels, batteries and solar panels — and why we might have to. Of course, the humble bicycle is always an option too...

Revision Summary for Module P3

Well done, you've made it to the end of this section. There are loads of bits and bobs about forces, motion and fast cars which you definitely have to learn. And the best way to find out what you know is to get stuck in to these lovely revision questions, which you're going to really enjoy (honest)...

1)* A mouse starting from rest reaches a speed of 0.08 m/s in 35 seconds. How far does it travel in that time?

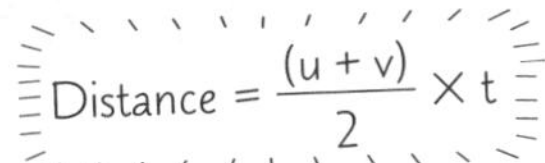

2) How do average speed cameras work?

3) Sketch a typical distance-time graph and point out all the important parts of it.

4)* What's the acceleration of a soggy pea flicked from rest to a speed of 14 m/s in 0.4 seconds?

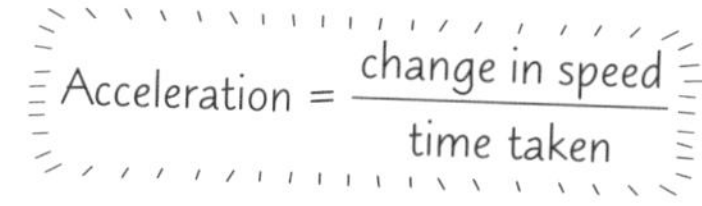

5) Explain how to find the distance travelled from a speed-time graph.

6) Draw and label a diagram to show the forces acting on a stationary owl sat on a (stationary) rock.

7) What could you do to reduce the friction between two surfaces?

8) What's the formula for weight?

9) What is "terminal speed"?

10) If an object has zero resultant force on it, can it be moving?

11)* What force is needed to accelerate a 4 kg mass at 7.5 m/s^2?

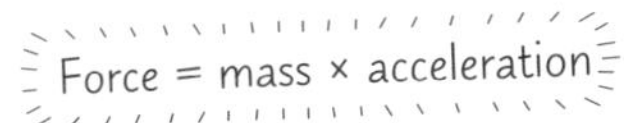

12) What are the two different parts of the overall stopping distance of a car?

13) List three factors that affect each of the two parts of the stopping distance.

14)* A 6 kg ferret has a momentum of 45 kg m/s. What is its velocity?

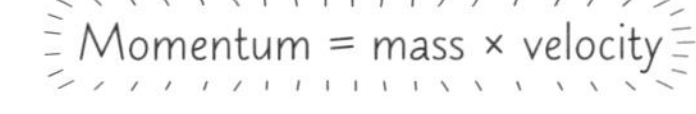

15) The same ferret is hit by a speeding vole, which changes its momentum. How will the time taken for the change in momentum affect the force acting on the ferret?

16) List four safety features of cars and describe how each one makes driving safer.

17) Bruce tries to lift a weight but can't move it. Explain why no work has been done on the weight.

18)* An electric motor does 540 000 J of work in 270 s. What is its power output?

19) What happens to your kinetic energy if you double your speed?

20)* Find the gravitational potential energy of a box of mass 12 kg at a height of 4.5 m. (g = 10 N/kg.)

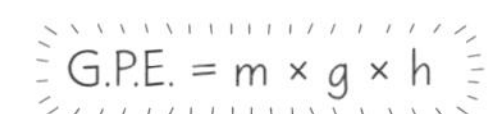

21)* At the top of a roller coaster ride a carriage has 150 kJ of gravitational potential energy. Ignoring friction, how much kinetic energy will the carriage have at the bottom (where G.P.E. = 0)?

22) Describe the relationship between the power rating of a car and its fuel consumption.

23) Give two ways to reduce the fuel consumption of a car or lorry by reducing drag.

24) What are the two main fuels used in cars?

25) Why might we have to rely on biofueled or solar-powered cars in the future?

26) Electric vehicles don't give out polluting gases when you drive them, but they still cause pollution. Explain why.

* Answers on page 116.

Collecting Methods

Welcome to Module B4 — it's the one you've all been waiting for. If you're hoping to collect lots of marks in your exam, you'll need to know how to collect organisms — which is what this page is all about.

Organisms form Populations and Communities

You need to know the difference between a population and a community.

1) A POPULATION is all the organisms of one species living in an area.
2) Populations of different species in an area make up a COMMUNITY.

...looks like a member of the local bear population has been through here in the last few days...

You Need to Know How to Use These Collecting Methods

In order to study the organisms in a population or community, you've got to catch them first. Here's how:

COLLECTING METHOD		DESCRIPTION
Nets		• Nets are used for catching flying insects and organisms that live in water. • To catch the organisms, the net is trailed along in the air or water.
Pitfall Traps	jar; cover propped up with stones; food	• Pitfall traps are used to catch insects that walk across the ground. • The insects fall into the trap and can't get out again.
Pooters	Mouthpiece; Mesh filter; Collection tube	• Pooters are used to suck up individual insects. • The user sucks on the mouthpiece and the insect is sucked in through the collection tube.

Counting methods — avoid the pit-falls...

This stuff sounds fun — running around waving nets and setting traps for some poor insect to fall into. All in the name of science too. Remember — some animals prefer certain environments. E.g. there'll be loads more woodlice hanging out underneath rocks than there are running about in an open field.

Counting and Identifying Organisms

Sometimes, you need to count organisms rather than catch them. That's where quadrats come in...

Use a Quadrat to Help you Count Organisms

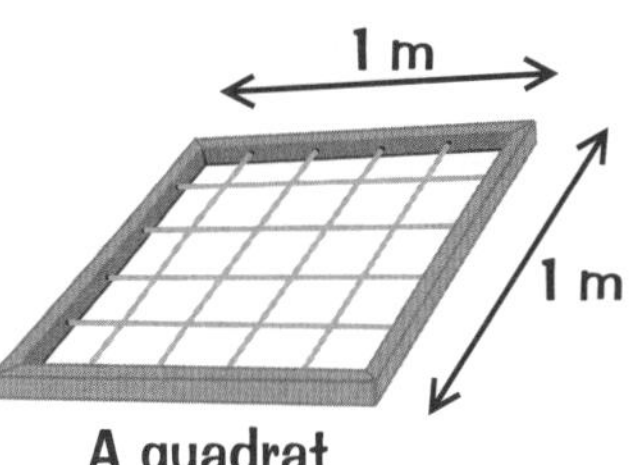

A quadrat

1) A quadrat is a square frame enclosing a known area e.g. 1 m^2.
2) You just place it on the ground and count the organisms inside it.
3) If you put the quadrat down somewhere like a field, or a forest floor, you'll be able to see a variety of plant and animal species inside it.
4) If it's difficult to count every single organism in the quadrat, you can estimate what percentage of the quadrat's area is covered by the organisms.

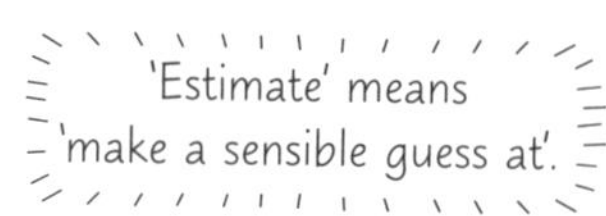

Keys are Used to Identify Plants and Animals

1) A key is a list of questions that you can use to work out what an unknown organism is.
2) You start at question 1. You can work out the answer by looking at your mystery organism.
3) As you answer more questions you narrow down your options until you're just left with one possible species your organism could be.

Example: A student saw the following living things in a pond. Using the key provided, work out what each organism is.

1) Has the organism got leaves?	......................YES, then it's a ..waterlily.. ....NO — go to question 2

2) Does the organism have a backbone?	......................YES — go to question 3 ....NO, then it's a ..dragonfly..

3) Does the organism have gills?	......................YES, then it's a ..fish... ....NO, then it's a ..frog...

4) You might get a 'key diagram' in the exam. It works using basically the same idea as the key above — just follow the lines that lead you to the next question or answer.

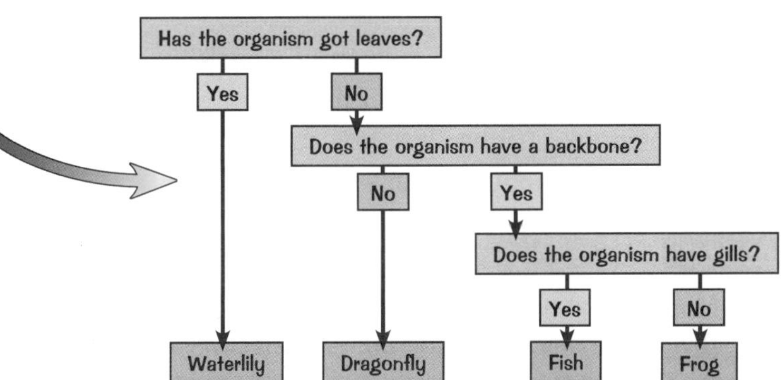

Drat, drat and double drat — that's the only quadrat I know...

It's worth getting to know the simple quadrat. It crops up again on the next couple of pages for a start, but you'll probably use them if you do any ecology experiments. They might not look particularly fun to use, but it beats sitting in the classroom on a Friday afternoon, right?

Estimating Population Sizes

Remember: a population is all the organisms of one species living in an area.

Estimate Population Sizes by Scaling Up from a Small Sample Area

To estimate the population size of organisms in a large area,
you can study the small area within a quadrat and scale up your findings:

1) Count all the organisms in a 1 m^2 quadrat.
2) Multiply the number of organisms in the quadrat by the total area (in m^2) of the habitat.

Example:
- A 1 m^2 quadrat contains 90 grass plants, 30 buttercups and 25 daisies.
- Estimate the total populations of the different species in a 120 m^2 field.

Answer: Multiply the figures for the 1 m^2 quadrat by 120 to estimate the populations in the whole field.

Grass	Buttercups	Daisies
$90 \times 120 = 10\,800$	$30 \times 120 = 3600$	$25 \times 120 = 3000$

So the field will contain about 10 800 grass plants, 3600 buttercups and 3000 daisies.

Estimate Population Sizes Using Capture-Recapture

'Capture' just means 'catch'.

To estimate population size using the capture-recapture method:

1) Capture a sample of the population and mark the animals in a harmless way.
2) Release them back into the environment.
3) Recapture another sample of the population.
4) Count how many of this sample are marked.
5) Estimate population size using this equation:

$$\text{Population Size} = \frac{\text{number in first sample} \times \text{number in second sample}}{\text{number in second sample previously marked}}$$

Example:
- A pitfall trap, set up in an area of woodland, caught 30 beetles in an hour.
- The beetles were marked on their shell, before being released back into the environment.
- The next day, 35 beetles were caught in an hour, only 5 of which were marked.
- Estimate the population size.

Answer:
1) Multiply the number of beetles in the first sample by the number in the second sample: $30 \times 35 = 1050$
2) Divide the answer by the number that were marked in the second sample: $1050 \div 5 = 210$
3) So the area of woodland will contain about $(30 \times 35) \div 5 = 210$ beetles.

I don't know about you, but this page has really captured my imagination...

The best way to learn how to estimate a population size is to practise doing the sums. So go over the example questions again — but this time cover up the answers and try to work them out for yourself.

Ecosystems and Distribution of Organisms

If you like getting down on your hands and knees and poking around at plants, you're in for a treat...

Ecosystems are NOT the Same as Habitats

1) An ECOSYSTEM is all the organisms living in a particular area, as well as all the non-living, physical conditions, e.g. light, temperature (see next page).
2) An ecosystem isn't the same as a HABITAT — a habitat is just the place where an organism lives.

Transects are used to Study the Distribution of Organisms

1) Distribution is where organisms are found.
2) You can study distribution using lines called transects.
3) To do a transect, you mark out a line using a tape measure and place quadrats next to each other all the way along the line.
4) You then count and write down the organisms you find in the quadrats.
5) You can draw the results of a transect on a kite diagram (see below). This allows you to map the distribution of organisms in an area.

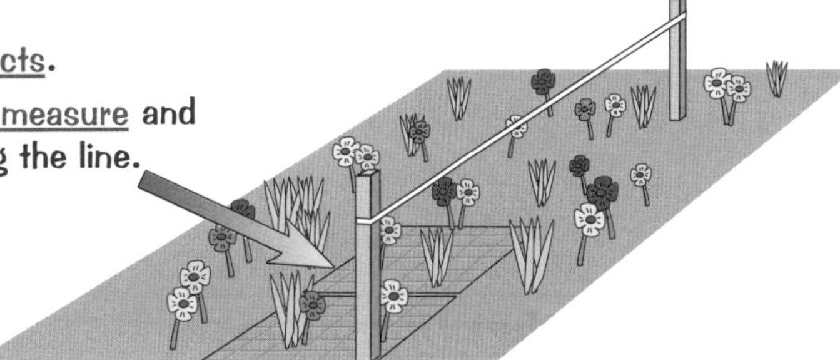

Kite Diagrams Show the Distribution of Organisms

The kite diagram below shows the distribution of organisms along a transect in a field:

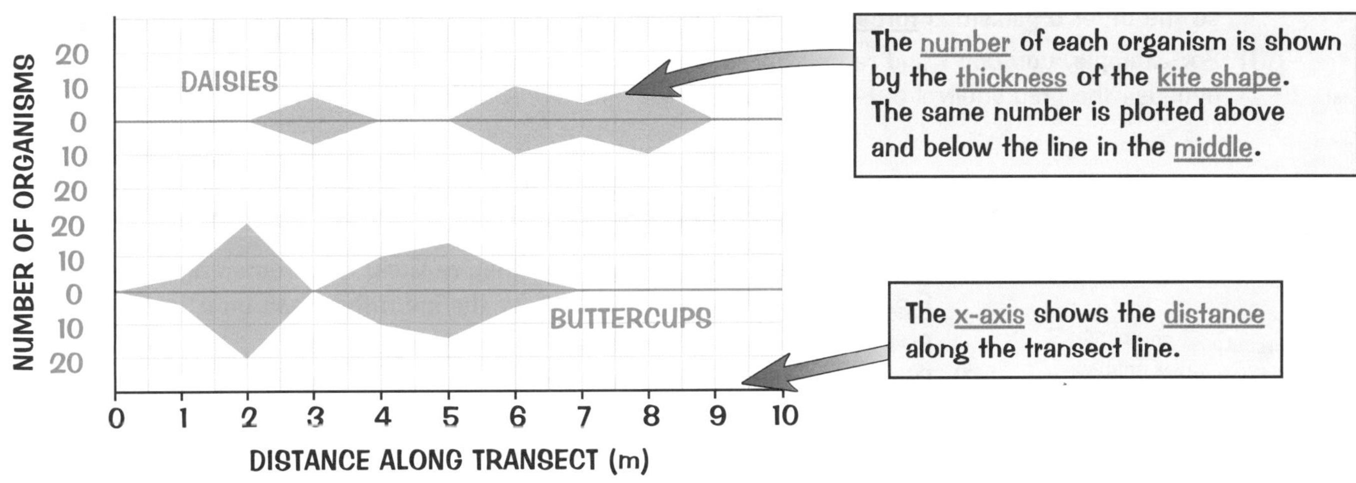

1) From the kite diagram you can see that buttercups were found between 0 and 7 m along the transect.
2) Daisies were found between 2 and 9 m along the transect.
3) At 2 m along the transect there were 20 buttercups. At 6 m there were 5 buttercups and 10 daisies.

Kite diagrams — to show your parents exactly how it got stuck in the tree...

Granted — this isn't the most exciting page in the world — but you still need to know it. Making sure you know the basics from this page and the previous one will make the rest of this section seem a lot easier. Trust me.

Distribution of Organisms

You might never have thought about it before, but organisms aren't just spread out randomly. They live where they do some very good reasons and this page will tell you what they are.

The Distribution of Organisms is Affected by Physical Factors...

1) The physical factors in an environment are non-living things like light, temperature, water, oxygen, and soil quality.
2) The distribution of organisms is affected by physical factors because:
   - Organisms are adapted to live in certain physical conditions.
   - This means they're more likely to survive and reproduce in areas with these conditions.

E.g. woodland ferns are adapted to living in shade, so you don't often find them growing in sunny areas.

...and by Other Organisms

The distribution of organisms can also be affected by other organisms — for example, through competition or predator-prey relationships:

Competition

1) Competition happens when different organisms in the same area need the same resource (e.g. food, water).
2) One type of organism is often better at getting the resource, so the other organism is forced out of the area.
3) For example, you don't find red and grey squirrels in the same place because the grey squirrel out-competes the red for food and shelter.

Predator-Prey Relationships

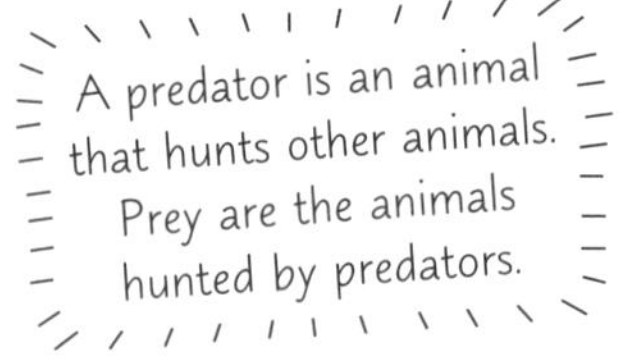

A predator is an animal that hunts other animals. Prey are the animals hunted by predators.

1) Prey will often avoid areas where they're likely to be eaten by a predator. E.g. seals spend a lot of time under the ice rather than on it to avoid predators like polar bears.
2) Predators are found in areas where there's plenty of prey for them to eat. E.g. there might be loads of ladybirds in your mum's rosebushes — because that's where you find their prey (aphids).

Believe it or not — there's a reason that giraffes don't live in the sea...

...and penguins don't live in the Sahara desert. It sounds pretty straightforward, but make sure you can explain everything on this page — even the tricky stuff, like the competition bit.

Biodiversity

Biological + diversity = Biodiversity. Simple. There's a bit more to it than that actually, but if you learn the definition in the red box, you'll be sorted — enjoy.

You Need to Know What Biodiversity is...

BIODIVERSITY is the VARIETY of different SPECIES living in a habitat.

Natural Ecosystems have a Higher Biodiversity than Artificial Ones

1) Natural ecosystems look after themselves without any help from humans. E.g. native (natural) woodlands and natural lakes.
2) Artificial ecosystems are created and looked after by humans. E.g.
    - Forestry plantations — areas of forest, where just one type of tree is grown for wood.
    - Fish farms — fenced-off areas of water, where one type of fish is kept for food (see page 80 for more).

Native Woodlands have a Higher Biodiversity than Forestry Plantations...

A forestry plantation.

Native Woodlands	Forestry Plantations
Lots of different tree species.	One species of tree.
Lots of different plant species, e.g. flowers, moss.	Few plant species.
Lots of different animal species, e.g. birds, insects.	Few animal species.

...and Lakes have a Higher Biodiversity than Fish Farms

Lakes	Fish Farms
Lots of different fish species.	One fish species.
Lots of different plant and animal species.	Very few plant and animal species.

Biodiversity — sounds like a washing powder...

Getting your head around exactly what biodiversity actually is is really important. That definition's one that you definitely need to know — so make sure you learn it. Sorted.

Plants and Photosynthesis

Well, here's where the plant stuff really begins (groan). You might think that they're boring, but don't forget — we rely on plants to live.

Photosynthesis Produces Glucose from Sunlight

1) Photosynthesis uses energy from the Sun to change carbon dioxide and water into glucose and oxygen.
2) Photosynthesis takes place in the chloroplasts of plant cells.
3) Chloroplasts contain pigments (coloured chemicals) like chlorophyll to absorb the light energy.
4) Some plant cells don't have chloroplasts — these are cells in parts of the plant that don't photosynthesise, e.g. the roots.
5) Learn these equations for photosynthesis:

$$\text{carbon dioxide} + \text{water} \xrightarrow[\text{chlorophyll}]{\text{LIGHT ENERGY}} \text{glucose} + \text{oxygen}$$

$$6CO_2 + 6H_2O \xrightarrow[\text{chlorophyll}]{\text{LIGHT ENERGY}} C_6H_{12}O_6 + 6O_2$$

6) The glucose produced by photosynthesis has lots of different uses (see next page).
7) Oxygen is a waste product of photosynthesis.

The Rate of Photosynthesis can be Increased in Several Ways

1) Plants need light and carbon dioxide to photosynthesise.
   This means you can make plants photosynthesise faster by giving them...

   ...more LIGHT... ...more CARBON DIOXIDE...

2) Photosynthesis is carried out by enzymes (see page 12 for more on enzymes).
3) Enzymes work better when it's warm so you can also make plants photosynthesise faster by giving them...

   ...a higher TEMPERATURE.

   Increasing the temperature only works up to a certain point.

4) The faster plants photosynthesise, the faster they are able to grow.
5) Plants photosynthesise and grow faster in the summer because it's warmer and there's more light.

Aaaaarrrggh — there's chemistry on the page...

Photosynthesis can seem pretty tricky at first (there's that nasty-looking chemical equation after all), but it's all must-learn stuff. Remembering the three ways of increasing the rate of photosynthesis is easy-peasy, but don't forget you might need to be able to link them to plant growth too.

More on Photosynthesis

Right, that wasn't too bad. Basically photosynthesis makes loads of glucose. Here's what happens next...

Glucose is Converted into Other Substances

1) GLUCOSE is transported around the plant as soluble sugars.
2) Soluble sugars can dissolve in water, which makes it easy to transport them to other places in the plant.
3) Here's how plants use the glucose they make:

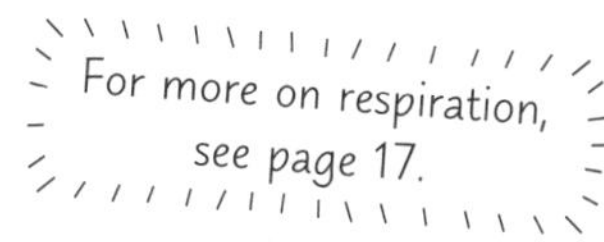
For more on respiration, see page 17.

1 For Respiration

1) Plants use some of the GLUCOSE for RESPIRATION.
2) This releases energy so the rest of the glucose can be converted into other useful substances.

2 Making Cell Walls

GLUCOSE is converted into CELLULOSE for making cell walls.

3 Stored in Seeds

GLUCOSE is turned into FATS and OILS for storing in seeds.

4 Stored as Starch

1) Some GLUCOSE is turned into STARCH and stored.
2) Starch is insoluble — it doesn't dissolve in water.
3) Starch is converted back into glucose when supplies of the sugar are low.

17
Hi Mr Starch, it's Tony from next door. May I borrow some sugar?

5 Making Proteins

1) GLUCOSE is combined with other things to make PROTEINS.
2) Proteins are used for growth and repair.

Cell walls made of cellulose — that'll keep the criminals in...

Sorry, I couldn't help myself — those plant cell/prison cell jokes get me every time. You might not think they're funny, but they could just help you remember my words of wisdom when you're sat in the exam.

Understanding Photosynthesis

We now know that plants get their food from photosynthesis — but it's taken us a while to work it out.

There Have Been Different Ideas About How Plants Gain Mass

1) When plants grow, they get heavier — they gain mass.
2) Ancient Greek scientists thought that plants gained mass from soil minerals.
3) But a scientist called van Helmont later discovered that plants also gain mass from other sources:

- He dried some soil, weighed it, and put it in a pot.
- He weighed a small willow tree and planted it in the soil.
- He added rainwater to the pot whenever it was dry.
- 5 years later, the tree had grown and was much heavier than at the start.
- The mass of the soil had hardly changed at all.

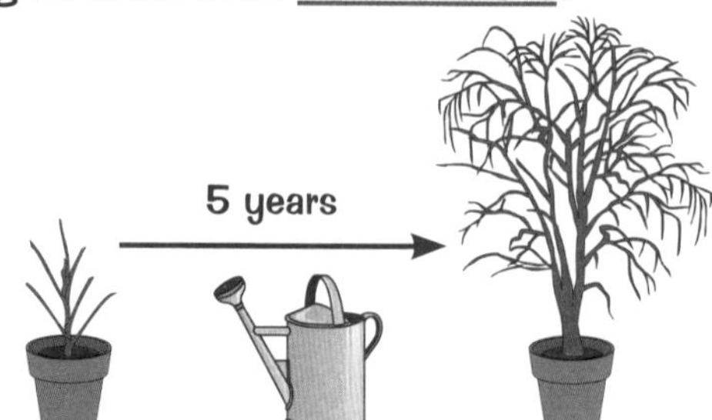

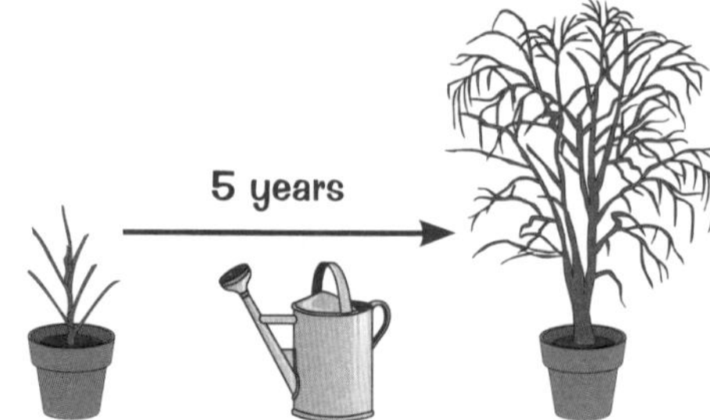

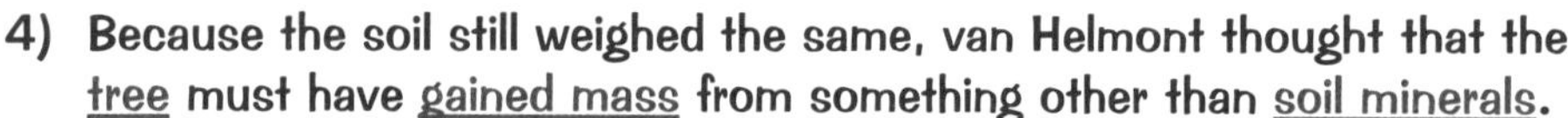

4) Because the soil still weighed the same, van Helmont thought that the tree must have gained mass from something other than soil minerals.
5) The only thing he'd added to the pot was rainwater — so he concluded the tree must have gained mass by taking in water.

Priestley's Experiments Showed that Plants Produce Oxygen

1) Many years after van Helmont, a scientist called Priestley did this experiment:

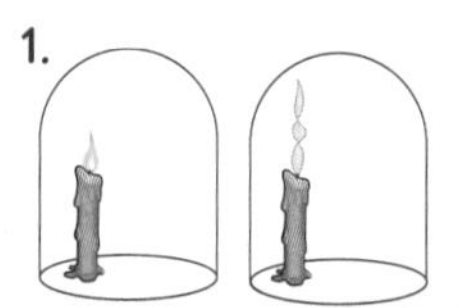

- He placed a burning candle in a sealed container.
- The flame went out and couldn't be re-lit.
- He then placed a living plant in the container.
- After a few weeks the candle could be re-lit.

2) He also did this experiment:

- He also put a mouse in a sealed container full of breathed-out air. The mouse died after a few seconds.
- He filled another container with breathed-out air.
- He put a living plant in the container and waited for a few days.
- He then put a mouse in the container — this time it survived for a few minutes (lucky thing).

3) He thought that the candle flame went out and that the mouse died because burning and breathing had taken something out of the air.
4) From these experiments, Priestley decided that plants somehow return this substance to the air.
5) Today we know that this substance is oxygen — a product of photosynthesis.

I don't understand 'Understanding Photosynthesis'...

Putting a mouse in a jar of carbon dioxide and noticing that it dies doesn't sound like a particularly cutting-edge investigation. But the experiments on this page were all important in helping us to understand photosynthesis.

Diffusion

There's a reason why you can always smell Jonny's gym bag from the other side of the changing room. That reason is diffusion, and you need to know all about it for your exams.

Don't be Put Off by the Fancy Word

1) Diffusion is just the movement of particles from places where there are lots of them to places where there are fewer of them.
2) It's just stuff spreading out.
3) Unfortunately you also have to learn the fancy way of saying the same thing, which is this:

DIFFUSION is the NET MOVEMENT OF PARTICLES from an area of HIGHER CONCENTRATION to an area of LOWER CONCENTRATION

4) Diffusion happens in both liquids and gases — that's because the individual particles in these substances are free to move about randomly.
5) For example, the smell of a perfume diffuses through the air in a room:

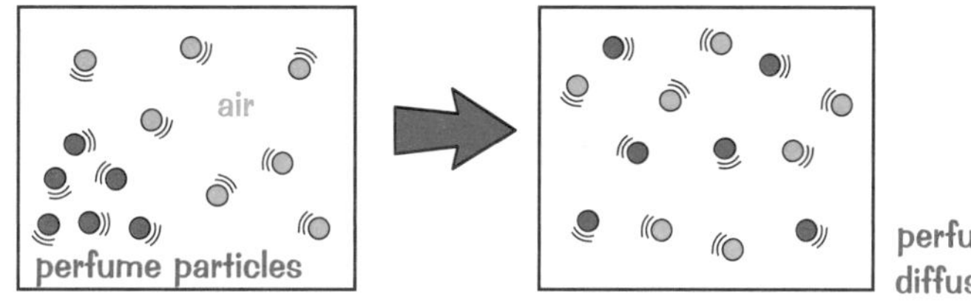

Cell Membranes are Kind of Clever...

1) A cell is surrounded by a cell membrane.
2) It holds the cell together BUT it lets stuff in and out as well.
3) Only very small molecules can diffuse through cell membranes — things like glucose and amino acids.
4) Big molecules like starch and proteins can't pass through the membrane.

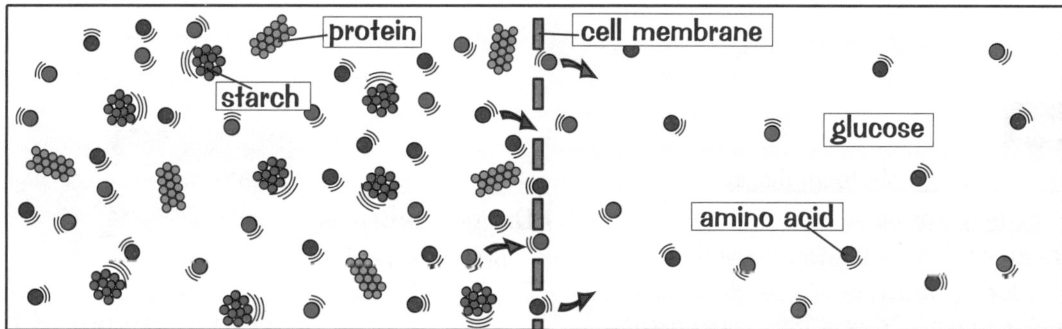

5) Just like with diffusion in air, particles flow through the cell membrane from where there's a higher concentration (a lot of them) to where there's a lower concentration (fewer of them).

Whoever smelt it dealt it... Whoever said the rhyme did the crime...

Because, of course, it's not just perfume that diffuses through a room. Anyway. All living cells have membranes, and their structure allows small molecules to drift in and out as needed. Don't forget, the membrane doesn't control diffusion, it happens all by itself — but the membrane does stop large molecules passing through.

Leaves and Diffusion

This page is all about leaves, what they get up to in the dark, and how they exchange gases.

Plants Carry Out Both Photosynthesis and Respiration

1) Photosynthesis and respiration are opposite reactions:

> Photosynthesis: carbon dioxide + water → glucose + oxygen (Uses energy)

> Respiration: glucose + oxygen → carbon dioxide + water (Energy released)

For more on respiration, see page 17.

2) Photosynthesis uses energy from light so it can only take place during the day.
3) Respiration releases energy for life processes — so it needs to take place all the time.

Plants Exchange Gases by Diffusion

1) Carbon dioxide and oxygen are gases.
2) They move in and out of leaves by diffusion.
3) Diffusion of gases in the leaves is important for both photosynthesis and respiration. Here's how it works:

PHOTOSYNTHESIS

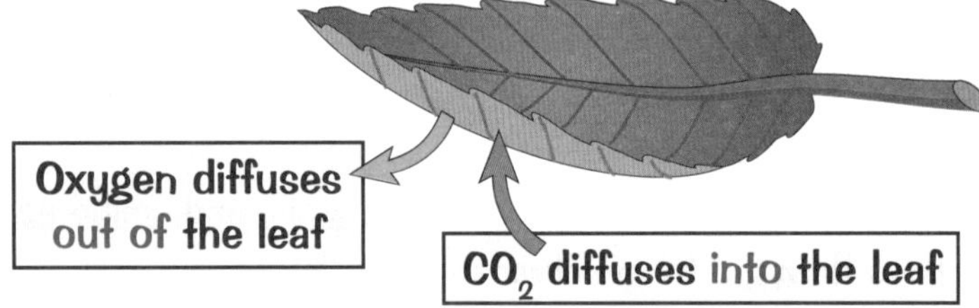

1) During photosynthesis the plant uses up lots of carbon dioxide.
2) This causes more carbon dioxide to move into the leaf by diffusion.
3) At the same time the plant makes lots of oxygen.
4) Some is used in respiration, and the rest diffuses out of the leaf.

RESPIRATION

1) At night, there's no photosynthesis.
2) Lots of carbon dioxide is made by respiration and lots of oxygen is used up.
3) There's a lot of carbon dioxide in the leaf — but not much oxygen. So now it's mainly carbon dioxide diffusing out and oxygen diffusing in.

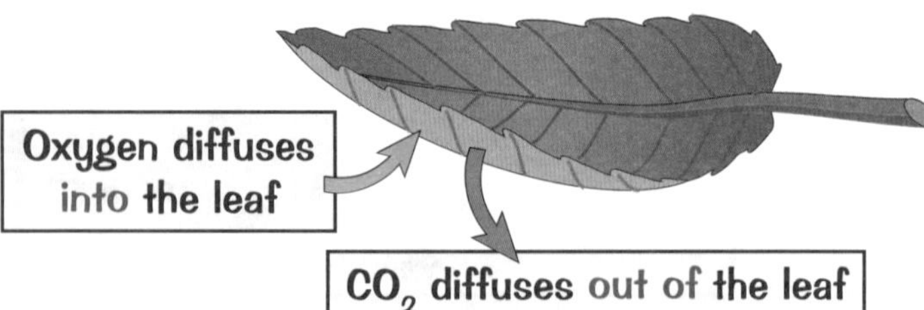

I tried really hard to leaf the dodgy jokes out of this page...

... and I got so close. Oh well — sorry about that. Remember: photosynthesis can only take place during the day (when there is light shining on the leaves), but respiration happens all the time — even when it's dark.

Leaves and Photosynthesis

Leaves are pretty important — that's why there's another page on them. Get this stuff learnt.

You Need to Learn The Structure of A Leaf

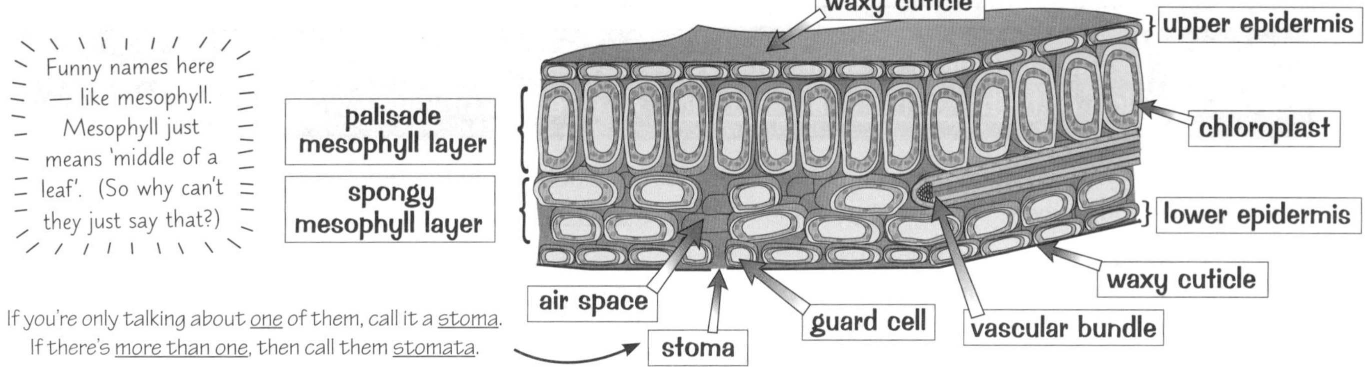

Leaves are Adapted for Efficient Photosynthesis

Leaves have adaptations to help them get the carbon dioxide, water and light they need for photosynthesis.

Leaves are Adapted for Diffusion

broad

thin

stoma

1) Leaves are BROAD (wide). This gives them a LARGE SURFACE AREA for carbon dioxide and oxygen to diffuse.
2) They're also THIN, which means the gases only have to diffuse a short distance.
3) The lower surface is full of little holes called STOMATA.
   - Stomata let gases like carbon dioxide into the leaf and oxygen out of the leaf.
   - They also allow water to escape — which is known as transpiration (see page 74).

4) Leaves have GUARD CELLS around each stoma (see above) to control when the stoma opens and closes.

Leaves are Adapted to Absorb Light

1) The leaves being broad also means there's a large surface area to absorb light energy.
2) Leaf cells contain lots of CHLOROPLASTS.
3) Chloroplasts contain CHLOROPHYLL and other PIGMENTS (coloured chemicals). The pigments absorb light energy from different parts of the spectrum (i.e. different wavelengths of light).

Leaves Have a Network of Vascular Bundles

1) Vascular bundles are the transport vessels, xylem and phloem (see page 73).
2) They transport water and other nutrients to every part of the leaf.
3) The vascular bundles help to support the leaf structure.

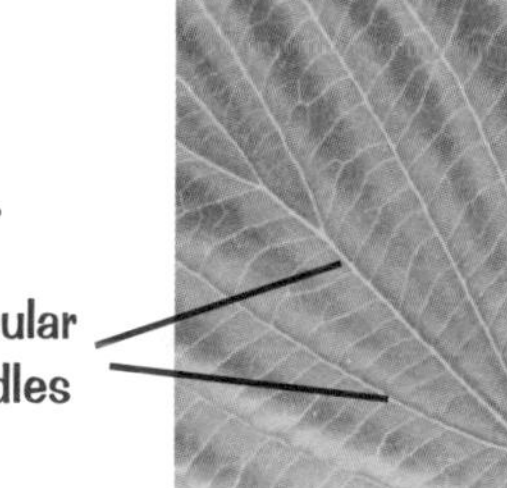

If you don't do much revision, it's time to turn over a new leaf...

So how do they know all this stuff? Well, scientists know how leaves are adapted for photosynthesis because they've used microscopes to see the structure of leaves and the cells inside them.

Osmosis

'Osmosis' is one of those scary science words that frightens a lot of people off, but don't worry — it's a lot easier than it sounds.

Osmosis is a Special Case of Diffusion, That's All

Osmosis is the movement of water molecules across a partially permeable membrane from a region of higher water concentration to a region of lower water concentration.

1) A partially permeable membrane is just one with very small holes in it. Only tiny molecules (like water) can pass through the holes — bigger molecules (e.g. sucrose) can't.
2) During osmosis water molecules move across the membrane from the side with lots of water molecules, to the side with fewer water molecules.
3) Osmosis is a type of diffusion.
4) Water moves in and out of plant and animal cells by osmosis across the cell membrane.

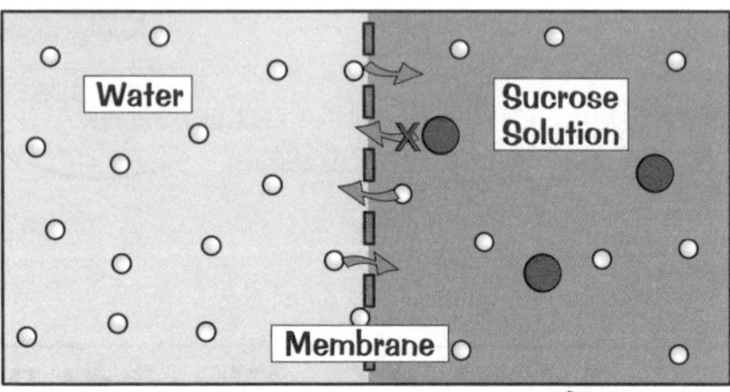

Turgor Pressure Supports Plant Tissues

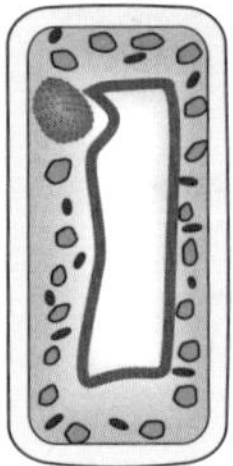
Normal Cell

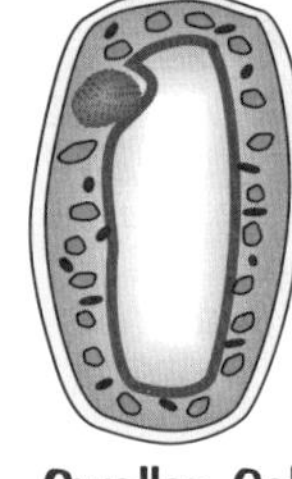
Swollen Cell

1) A plant cell wall is inelastic (stiff). It supports the cell.
2) When a plant is well watered, all its cells will draw water in by osmosis. This makes them plump and swollen.
3) The contents of the cell push against the inelastic cell wall — this is called turgor pressure.
4) Turgor pressure helps support the plant tissues.
5) If there's no water in the soil, a plant starts to wilt (droop). This is because the cells start to lose water and so lose their turgor pressure.

Animal Cells Don't Have an Inelastic Cell Wall

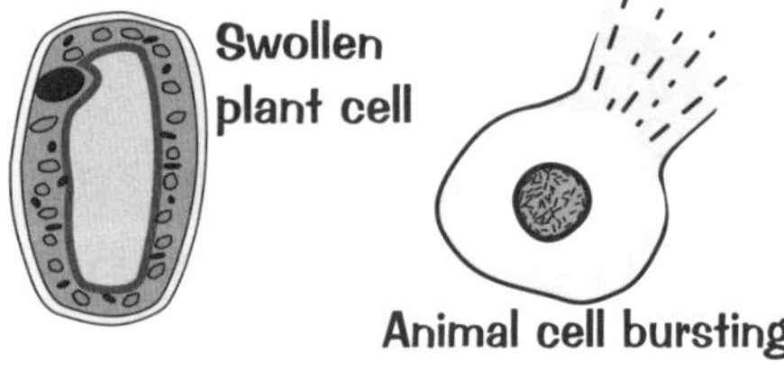

Animal cells don't have a cell wall. This means that:

- If an animal cell takes in too much water, it bursts.
- If it loses too much water it shrivels up.

Revision by osmosis — you wish...

Wouldn't that be great — if all the ideas in this book would just gradually drift across into your mind, from an area of higher concentration (in the book) to an area of lower concentration (in your mind — no offence). Actually, that probably will happen if you read it again. Why don't you give it a go...

Transport Systems in Plants

Plants have two separate types of vessel for transporting stuff around. These are the xylem and phloem. Both types of vessel go to every part of the plant in a continuous system, but they're totally separate.

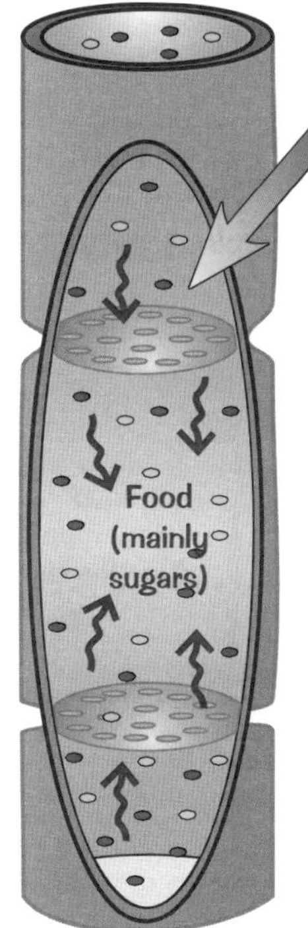

Phloem Tubes Transport Food:

1) Phloem transport food substances (mainly sugars) both up and down the stem to growing and storage tissues.
2) This movement of food substances around the plant is called translocation.

Xylem Vessels Take Water UP:

1) Xylem carry water and minerals from the roots up the shoot to the leaves.
2) This movement of water up the plant is caused by transpiration (see next page).

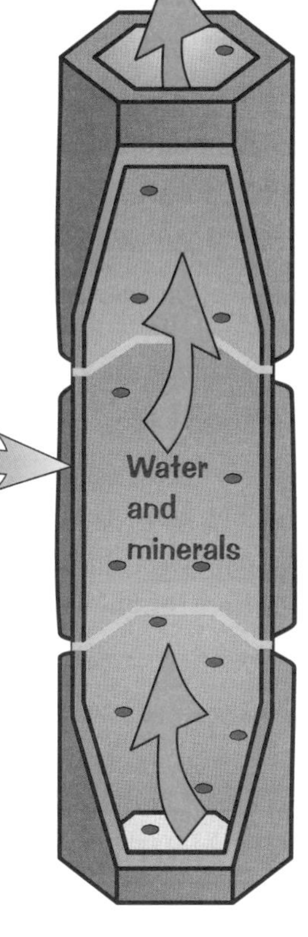

You can Recognise Xylem and Phloem by Where They Are

1) They usually run alongside each other in vascular bundles (like veins).
2) They're found in different places in different parts of the plant.

You need to learn these three examples:

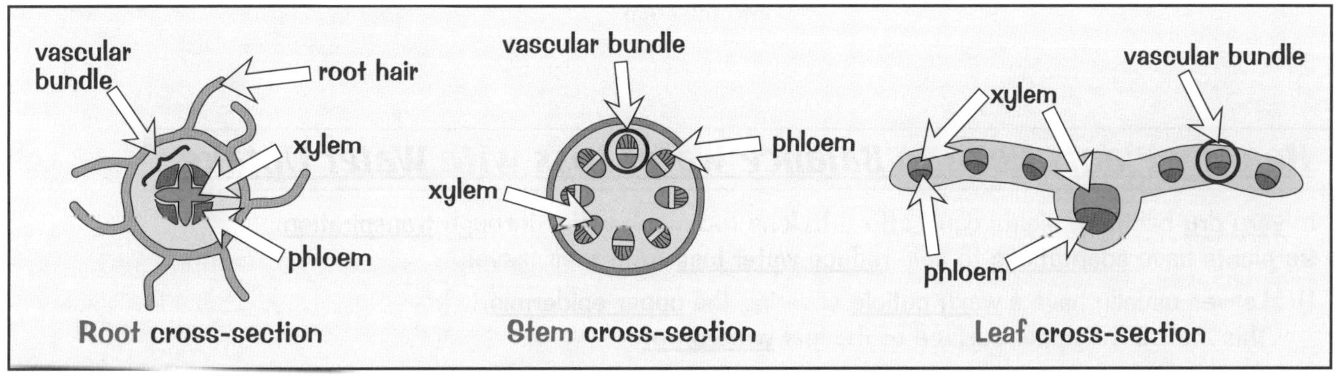

Don't let revision stress you out — just go with the phloem...

Phloem and xylem are both weird-looking words. You might have heard your teacher talking about them and not known what they were on about — 'phloem' is pronounced 'flow-em' and 'xylem' sounds like 'zy-lem'. Er right.

Water Flow Through Plants

If you don't water a house plant for a few days it starts to go all droopy. Then it dies, and the people from the Society for the Protection of Plants come round and have you arrested. Plants need water.

Transpiration is the Loss of Water from the Plant

1) Water from the soil is absorbed through the root hairs.
2) It's transported up the stem to the leaves, where some of it is lost through transpiration.
3) Transpiration caused by is the evaporation and diffusion of water vapour from inside the leaves.
4) This creates a shortage of water in the leaf. More water is drawn up from the rest of the plant through the xylem vessels (see previous page) in the stem to replace the lost water.

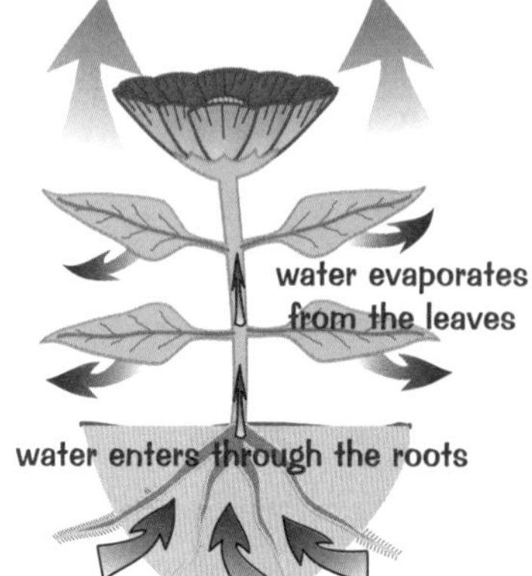

Transpiration has some benefits for the plants:

1) It helps to keep the plant cool.
2) It provides the plant with a constant supply of water for photosynthesis.
3) The water allows the plant cells to become rigid, which helps support the plant (see page 72).
4) Minerals needed by the plant (see page 76) can be brought in from the soil along with the water.

Root Hairs Take in Water by Osmosis

Root hairs are specially adapted for absorbing the water that plants need for photosynthesis.

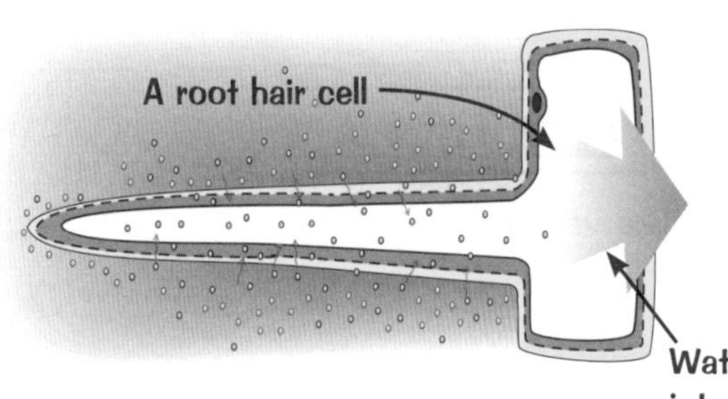

1) The cells on plant roots grow into long 'hairs' which stick out into the soil.
2) Each branch of a root will be covered in millions of these tiny hairs.
3) This gives the plant a big surface area for absorbing water from the soil.

Healthy Plants Need to Balance Water Loss with Water Uptake

In very dry habitats, plants can't afford to lose too much water through transpiration. So plants have adaptations to help reduce water loss from their leaves.

1) Leaves usually have a waxy cuticle covering the upper epidermis. This makes the upper surface of the leaf waterproof.
2) Most stomata are found on the lower surface of a leaf, where it's darker and cooler. This helps slow down transpiration (see next page).

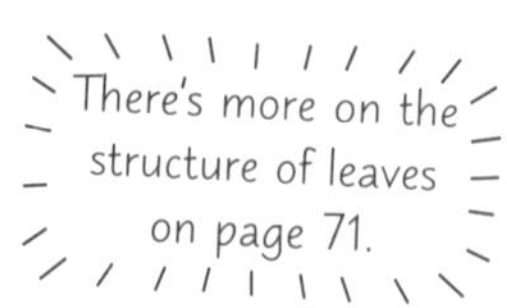

There's more on the structure of leaves on page 71.

Transpiration — the plant version of perspiration...

Here's an interesting fact — a biggish tree loses about a thousand litres of water from its leaves every single day. That's as much water as the average person drinks in a whole year.

Water Flow Through Plants

Plants don't always lose water quickly — it depends on their environment.

You Can Carry Out Experiments to Measure Transpiration Rate

You can do a nice little experiment to show transpiration happening in a plant.

1) All you need is a beaker with some brightly coloured water in it — just add some blue or red food colouring.
2) Then add a plant with a fairly see-through stem, e.g. celery (daffodils and white carnations will also work well).
3) Wait for a few hours and you'll see the coloured water slowly move up the stem, through their xylem (see page 73).

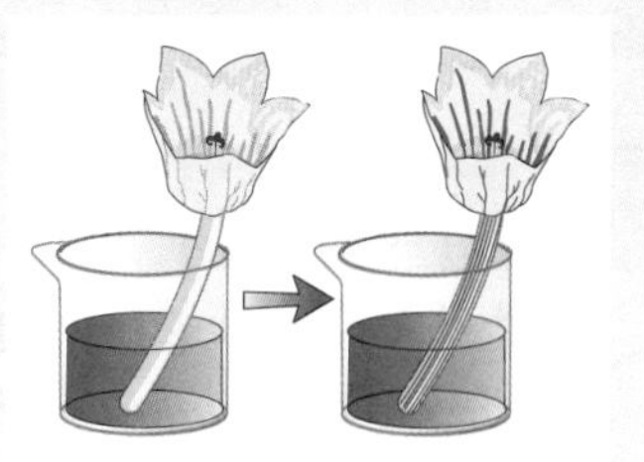
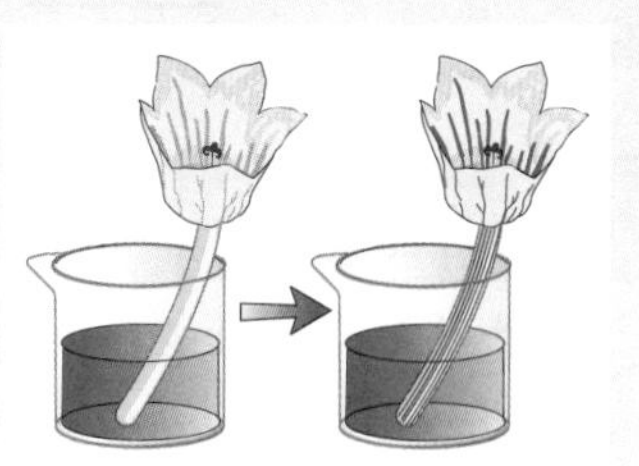

During transpiration, plants lose mass as water. You can use this and adapt the experiment above to measure the rate of transpiration.

1) Put the plant into a beaker of water. Weigh the plant and the beaker.
2) Leave the plant for a set amount of time.
3) Weigh the plant and the beaker again.
4) Work out how much mass is lost in a certain amount of time, e.g. milligrams per hour. This is the transpiration rate.

The greater the rate of transpiration, the more water the plant will lose.

The rate of transpiration varies depending on:

Light Intensity

- The brighter the light, the greater the transpiration rate.
- To investigate this, you could place one plant in a dark cupboard and one on a windowsill during the day.

Temperature

- The warmer it is, the faster transpiration happens.
- To see what effect the temperature has on rate, you could put one plant in a fridge and one into a similar dark cupboard that's warmer.

Air Movement

- If there's lots of air movement (wind) around a leaf, transpiration happens faster.
- In the lab you could place a cool fan beside a plant to sweep the water vapour away.

Air Humidity

- If the air around the leaf is very dry, transpiration happens more quickly.
- If you place a polythene bag around a plant, it creates a very humid environment.

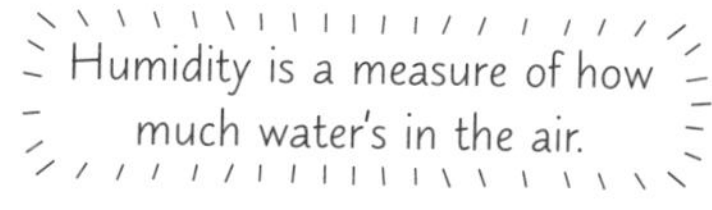

Humidity is a measure of how much water's in the air.

Plants — they're pretty much upside-down water slides...

You'll be pleased to hear that there's an easy way to remember the four factors that increase transpiration rate — they're the same as perfect kite-flying conditions: sunny, warm, windy and dry.

Minerals Needed for Healthy Growth

Plants are important in food chains and nutrient cycles because they can take minerals from the soil and energy from the Sun and turn it into food. And then, after all that hard work, we eat them.

Plants Need Three Main Minerals

'Deficiency' means that there's not enough of something.

Plants need certain minerals to live. They get these minerals from the soil.
If there aren't enough of these minerals in the soil, the plants will suffer symptoms of mineral deficiency.

1) Nitrates

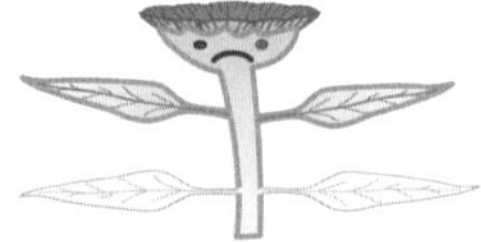

Needed for making proteins, which are needed for cell growth. If a plant can't get enough nitrates, its growth will be poor and it'll have yellow leaves.

2) Phosphates

Needed for respiration and growth. Plants without enough phosphate have poor root growth and discoloured leaves.

3) Potassium

Needed for photosynthesis and respiration. If there's not enough potassium in the soil, plants have poor flower and fruit growth and discoloured leaves.

Magnesium is Also Needed in Small Amounts

1) Small amounts of the mineral magnesium are needed for photosynthesis.
2) Plants without enough magnesium have yellow leaves.

Root Hairs Take in Minerals From the Soil

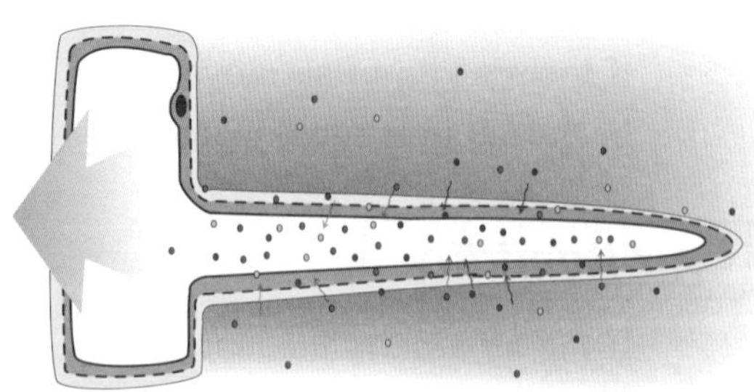

1) Root hairs (see page 74) absorb minerals from the soil dissolved in solution (i.e dissolved in water).
2) The concentration of minerals in the soil is usually pretty low.

Roses are red, violets are blue... *(but their leaves will be yellow if they don't get enough nitrates)*

Believe it or not, soil's not just dirt — it's full of really important minerals, that plants would be completely snookered without. Make sure you know what all four of the ones on this page do, as well as what plants will look like if they're missing out on them. Once you can do that, you'll have definitely earned a break and a biscuit.

More on Minerals

If plants have a mineral deficiency, it means that they're not getting enough of a particular mineral. This is bad for their growth.

You Can Do Experiments to Show the Effects of Mineral Deficiencies

1) A soil-less culture is where plants are grown in a solution of nutrients, rather than soil.
2) You can grow plants in soil-less cultures and control what minerals are available to them.
3) By missing out one mineral from the culture, you can see the effects that a deficiency in this mineral has on plant growth.
4) In the experiment on the right, one culture has all four minerals.
5) Each of the other cultures contains all the minerals except one.
6) After being left to grow in the solutions for a bit, some of the plants will start to shown the signs of mineral deficiencies.

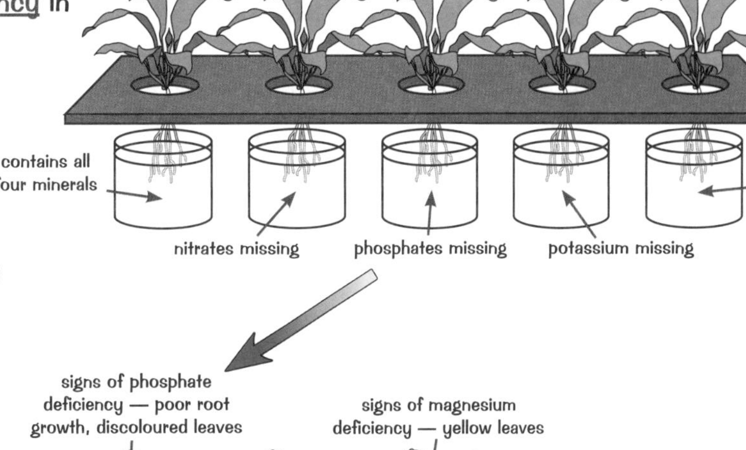

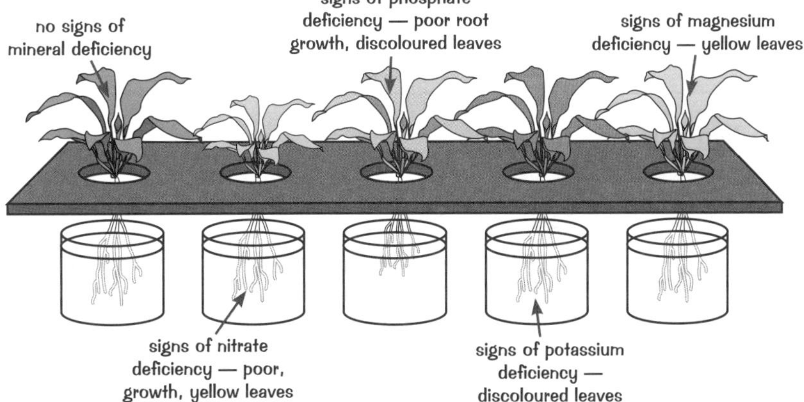

Fertilisers Contain the Main Nutrients

Gardeners and farmers often add fertilisers to the soil to make their plants and crops grow better.

1) Fertilisers contain a mixture of the minerals that plants need to grow — e.g. nitrates, phosphates, potassium and magnesium.
2) Chemical fertilisers are given an NPK value. This shows the percentage of nitrates (N), phosphates (P) and potassium (K) in the mixture — so you can pick the right one for your plants and soil.
3) For example, if your plants weren't growing well and had yellow leaves, it might be because they can't get enough nitrates from the soil. You could use a fertiliser with a high N value to improve their growth.
4) A fertiliser with an NPK value of 24-20-6 would have 24% nitrates, 20% phosphates and 6% potassium. A fertiliser with an NPK value of 30-15-12 would have 30% nitrates, 15% phosphates and 12% potassium.

FERTILISER
NPK value:
24-20-6

NPK — easy as one, two, three...

When you're looking at NPK values, you need to be careful not to get the P and the K muddled up. Remember — the P stands for phospates, and the K stands for potassium (like in the periodic table).

Decay

Microorganisms break down dead plant and animal remains. This includes plant and animal remains in our food.

Things Decay Because of Microorganisms...

1) Decomposers are microorganisms like soil bacteria and fungi.
2) When living things die they're broken down by decomposers. This is known as decay.
3) Decomposers also decay plant waste (e.g. in compost heaps) and human waste (e.g. in sewage works).
4) Plants rely on decay — it releases the minerals they need to grow.
5) The rate of decay depends on four main things:
   a) Presence of microorganisms — decomposers need to be present for decay to happen.
   b) Temperature — a warm temperature makes things decay faster.
   c) Moisture — things decay faster when they're moist.
   d) Oxygen (air) — decay is faster when there's oxygen available.

...You Can Do An Experiment to Show This

You can do an experiment to show that bacteria and fungi (acting as the decomposers) carry out decay:

1) Heat some broth in two flasks — this kills off any bacteria or fungi that are in the broth.
2) One of the flasks should have an S-shaped neck — this allows fresh air to get in, but not any decomposers. These collect in the curved neck, so they can't get to the broth.
3) Leave the flasks for a few days.
4) The broth in the flask with the S-shaped neck stays fresh.
5) The broth in the other flask will go cloudy and 'off' — this shows that it's the bacteria and fungi in air that cause things to decay.

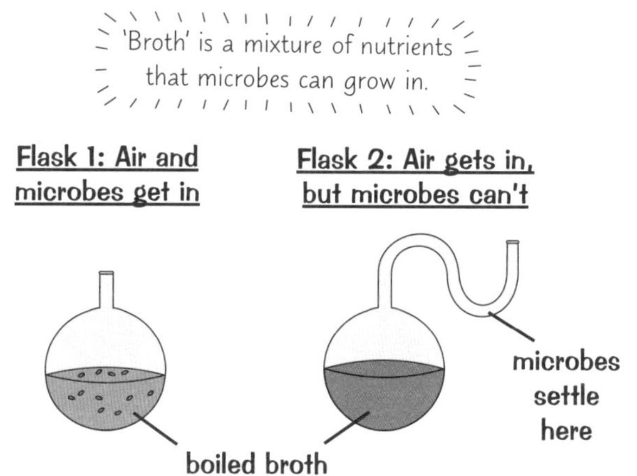
'Broth' is a mixture of nutrients that microbes can grow in.
Flask 1: Air and microbes get in
Flask 2: Air gets in, but microbes can't
microbes settle here
boiled broth

Detritivores Feed on Decaying Material

1) Detritivores are important organisms in decay.
2) They feed on dead and decaying material (called detritus).
3) Detritivores are things like earthworms, maggots and woodlice.
4) As these detritivores feed on the decaying material, they break it up into smaller bits.
5) This gives a bigger surface area for other decomposers to work on, which increases the rate of decay.

Decomposers — they're just misunderstood...

OK, so it's annoying when you go to the cupboard and find that everything has turned a funny green colour. But imagine the alternative — when a plant or animal died, it would just stay there, hanging around. Ugh.

Preventing Decay

We may not be able to stop our food going off, but there's certain things we can do to slow it down.

Food Preservation Methods Reduce the Rate of Decay

Decomposers are good for returning nutrients to the soil, but they're not so good when they start decomposing your lunch. So people have come up with ways to stop them:

1. **Canning**

   Basically, this involves putting food in a sealed can. This keeps the decomposers out.

2. **Cooling**

   The easiest way to keep food cool is to put it in a fridge. Cooling slows down decay because it slows down the decomposers' reproduction.

3. **Freezing**

   Food lasts longer in the freezer than in the fridge because the decomposers can't reproduce at all at such low temperatures.

4. **Drying**

   Dried food lasts longer because decomposers need water. Lots of fruits are preserved by drying them out, and sometimes meat is too.

5. **Adding Salt/Sugar**

   If there's a high concentration of salt or sugar around decomposers, they'll lose water by osmosis. This damages them and means they can't work properly. Things like tuna and olives are often stored in brine (salt water).

6. **Adding Vinegar**

   Mmm, pickled onions. Vinegar is acidic, and it kills the decomposers.

So should I brush my teeth with vinegar every day...

Uggghh... or salt. I can't decide what would be worse. Even with these methods of preventing decay, things do still go off, and it's not always easy to tell. If only I had a penny for every time some cheese or bread has gone mouldy in my fridge, I'd be extremely rich by now. But as it is, I'm not.

Intensive Farming

Make sure you're sitting down, because this page is pretty intense.

Intensive Farming is Used to Produce More Food

1) Intensive farming means trying to produce as much food as possible from your land, animals and plants.
2) Farms that can do this are said to have high productivity. Here are some examples of how they do it:
   - Fish farming — fish can be reared in tanks or fenced-off natural areas of water. Here they are fed lots of food and protected from any predators.
   - Glasshouses (greenhouses) — by growing plants in glasshouses, the conditions (like temperature) can be controlled. This increases the rate of photosynthesis.

   - Hydroponics — this is where food such as tomatoes are grown in nutrient solutions (water and fertilisers) instead of in soil. Hydroponics is also used in areas with barren (poor) soil.
   - Battery farming — where animals are kept close together indoors in small pens. This stops them wasting energy on moving around and keeping warm.

Intensive Farming Uses Pesticides

1) Pests are any organisms that damage crops.
2) Pesticides are chemicals that kill pests.
3) Using pesticides reduces damage to crops. The crops grow better, which allows farmers to grow more food.

Pesticides include:
- Insecticides — which kill insects.
- Fungicides — which kill fungi.
- Herbicides — which kill weeds.

Intensive Farming Can Harm the Environment

1) Intensive farming methods are efficient — this means it only takes a little effort to produce lots of food.
2) But they also raise ethical dilemmas (moral problems) because they can damage the environment. The main problems are:
   - Removing hedges to make larger fields can destroy habitats.
   - Careless use of fertilisers pollutes rivers and lakes.
   - Pesticides disturb food chains — see below.
   - Many people think that intensive farming of animals such as battery hens is cruel.

Pesticides Disturb Food Chains

Food chains show what eats what in an ecosystem.

1) Pesticides kill pests, but they can also kill organisms that aren't pests, like bees.
2) This can cause a shortage of food for animals further up the food chain.
3) Some pesticides are persistent — this means they stick around in ecosystems and are hard to get rid of.
4) There's a danger that pesticides will accumulate (build up) in the food chain, killing the animals further up.
5) Pesticides could cause health risks if they build up in food chains and are eaten by humans.

Plants without soil? It's not like when I was a lad...

One of the saddest things about intensive farming is that it reduces the wildlife in the countryside.
If there are no plants (except crops) and few insects, there's not much around for other animals to eat.

More on Farming

Biological control is growing more popular, as people get fed up with all the problems caused by pesticides.

You Can Use Biological Control Instead of Pesticides

1) Biological control means using living things instead of chemicals to control a pest.
2) Predators can be used to kill pests. E.g. ladybirds are used to kill aphids that eat vegetables.

You need to be able to explain the advantages and disadvantages of biological control:

ADVANTAGES:

- No chemicals are used, so there's less disruption of food chains and risk to people eating the food that's been sprayed.
- There's no need to keep repeating the treatment — like you would with chemical pesticides.

DISADVANTAGES:

- The predator that you introduce might not eat the pest — making it useless.
- The predator could eat useful species, e.g. insects that carry pollen between flowers.
- The predator's population might increase and get out of control.
- The predator might not stay in the area where it's needed.

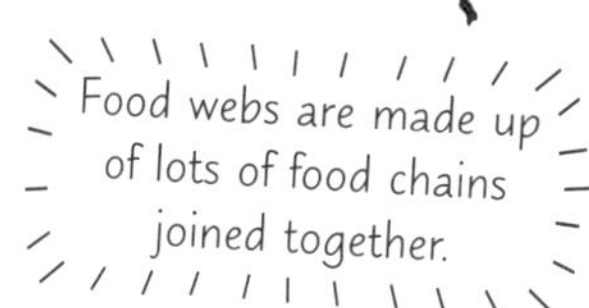

3) Removing a pest from a food web can affect all the other organisms too. E.g. if you remove a pest insect, you're removing a source of food from all the organisms that normally eat it. This might cause them to die out.

Food webs are made up of lots of food chains joined together.

Organic Farming Doesn't Use Artificial Fertilisers or Pesticides

You need to know about these organic farming techniques:

1) Using ANIMAL MANURE and COMPOST — these add nutrients to the soil.
2) CROP ROTATION — growing a cycle of different crops in a field each year. This stops the pests and diseases of one crop building up, and stops nutrients running out.
3) Planting NITROGEN-FIXING CROPS (e.g. peas and beans) — these help put nitrates (see page 76) back in the soil. Nitrogen-fixing crops are often included in crop rotations.
4) WEEDING — this means pulling out the weeds, rather than just spraying them with a herbicide.
5) VARYING SEED PLANTING TIMES — sowing seeds at different times of year helps avoid major pests.

Organic Farming Methods Have Their Advantages and Disadvantages

Advantages

1) Using fewer chemicals lowers the risk of toxic chemicals remaining on food.
2) It's better for the environment. There's less chance of polluting rivers with fertiliser. Organic farmers also avoid using chemical pesticides, so are less harmful to wildlife.
3) There's no battery farming on organic farms — which is better for the animals.

Disadvantages

1) Organic farming takes up more space than intensive farming.
2) It's also a lot more work. This makes the food more expensive.
3) You can't grow as much food using organic farming techniques.

Don't just skip ahead to your favourite page — you need biological control...

Ah, good old organic farming methods — there's nothing quite like good, honest, hard work (except for revision).

Revision Summary for Module B4

What a nice leafy section that was. Things started to get a bit mouldy at one point, but that's life I suppose. Now, just to make sure you've taken it all in, here's a little revision summary so you can check what you've learned. You know what to do by now — whizz through the questions and make a note of any you can't answer. Then go back and find the answer in the section. It's actually kind of fun, like a treasure hunt... well, okay, it's not — but it works.

1) Explain the words 'community' and 'population'.
2) Name three different methods that are used to collect insects.
3) What is a quadrat? Describe how you would use it.
4)* Estimate the total ant population in a 4000 m^2 car park if a 1 m^2 area contained 80 ants.
5)* You catch 23 woodlice one day and mark their shells. The next day you catch 28 woodlice and find that four of them are marked. Estimate the population size.
6) Explain the meaning of the word 'ecosystem'. How is an ecosystem different to a habitat?
7) Describe how you'd carry out a transect to investigate the distribution of plant species in a field.
8) Name three physical factors that could affect the distribution of an organism.
9) What is competition? How can it affect the distribution of organisms?
10) What is biodiversity?
11) Describe how the biodiversity is different in a native woodland compared to a forestry plantation.
12) Write down the balanced symbol equation for photosynthesis.
13) Give two ways to increase the rate of photosynthesis.
14) Name five things that a plant can use glucose for.
15) How did ancient Greek scientists think that plants gained mass?
16) What were the conclusions of Priestley's experiments with mice and plants?
17) Write a definition of the word 'diffusion'.
18) Why can't molecules like starch and proteins pass through cell membranes?
19) Why does more oxygen move into leaves during the night?
20) Describe how leaves are adapted for efficient diffusion.
21) Describe how leaves are adapted to absorb light energy.
22) Explain what osmosis is.
23) What is turgor pressure?
24) What do xylem vessels transport?
25) Draw a diagram to show where the xylem and phloem are found in a root.
26) What is transpiration?
27) Give three ways in which transpiration benefits a plant.
28) What is the advantage to a plant of having root hairs?
29) Name four factors that affect the rate of transpiration.
30) Name the three main minerals plants need for healthy growth.
31) What is magnesium needed for in a plant?
32) What does an NPK value tell you about a fertiliser?
33) Give an example of a detritivore.
34) Why does pickling food in vinegar help it to last for longer without decaying?
35) Name three other ways of preventing decay.
36) Give four different intensive farming techniques.
37) Give three problems associated with intensive farming.
38) Give one disadvantage of chemical pesticides.
39) Write down one advantage and one disadvantage of biological pest control.
40) Give two organic farming methods.

*Answers on page 116.

The History of the Atom

If you kept cutting something into millions and millions of tiny pieces — just how small could you get them and what would the stuff you end up with look like... Scientists have been trying to work it out for years...

The Theory of Atomic Structure Has Changed Throughout History

1) Atoms are the tiny particles which make up everything in the universe.
2) At the start of the 19th century a scientist called Dalton described atoms as solid balls.
3) He said that different balls made up the different elements (see page 85).
4) Later on another scientist, J J Thomson, discovered that atoms contained electrons.
5) Electrons are very small, negative (–) particles.
6) The discovery of the electron meant that Dalton's model had to be wrong.
7) So ideas about what the atom was like changed.

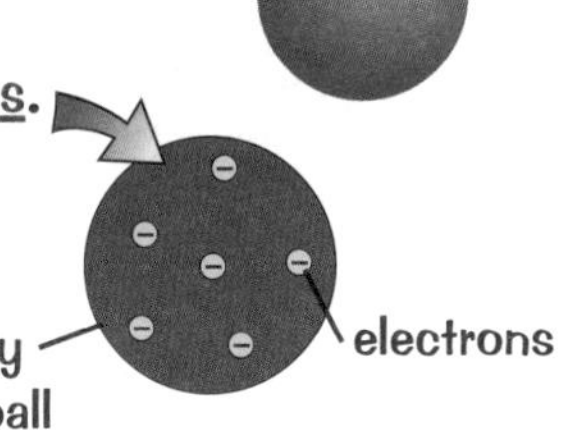

Rutherford Showed that Thomson's Model Was Wrong

1) A few years later, Rutherford found evidence that most of an atom is just empty space.
2) This meant that Thomson's model couldn't be right.
3) Rutherford came up with the theory of the nuclear atom:
   - There's a tiny, positively charged nucleus at the centre.
   - Negative electrons are scattered around the nucleus.
   - Most of the atom is empty space.

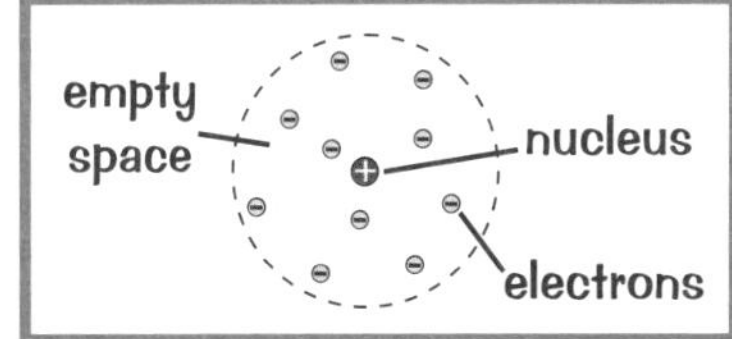

The Bohr Model Explains a Lot...

1) Scientists realised that the atoms in Rutherford's model wouldn't be stable (they would collapse).

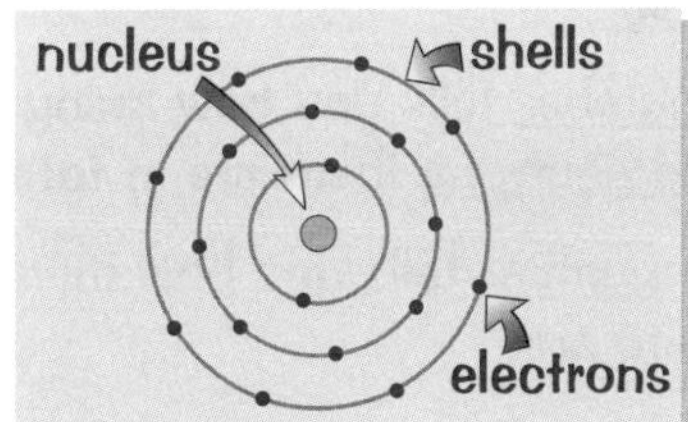

2) Bohr suggested that electrons can only exist in orbits, or shells around the nucleus.
3) Bohr's theory of atomic structure was supported by many experiments.
4) It was pretty close to our current version of the atom (have a look at the next page to see what we now think atoms look like).

Scientific Theories Have to be Backed Up by Evidence

1) What we think the atom looks like now is completely different to what people used to think.
2) As new evidence was found our theory of the structure of the atom changed to fit it.
3) This is how science works... New evidence forces people to come up with new ideas.
4) These new ideas can be tested by using them to predict what might happen in an experiment — if they can then the idea could be right.

I love a good model — Kate Moss is my favourite...

Scientists love a good theory but what they love more is trying to disprove their mate's one. That's how science works.

Atoms

You can use this model of the atom to explain pretty much the whole of chemistry... which is nice.

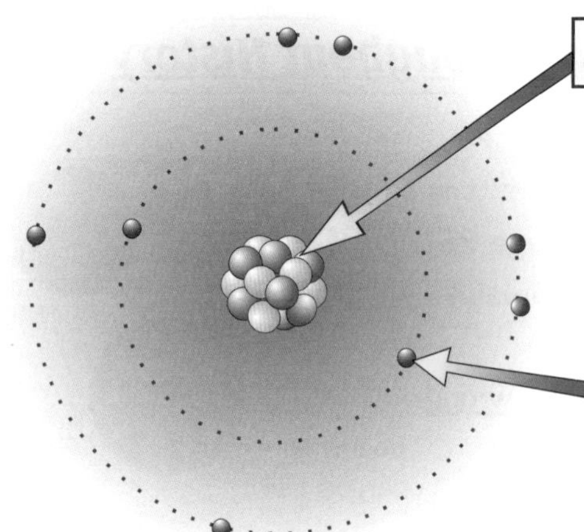

The Nucleus

1) The nucleus is in the middle of the atom.
2) It contains protons and neutrons.
3) It has a positive charge (because of the protons — see below).

The Electrons

1) Electrons move around the nucleus in electron shells.
2) They're negatively charged.

Atoms are Neutral

1) Atoms are very small and have a very small mass.
2) You need to know the relative masses and charges of protons, neutrons and electrons:

PARTICLE	MASS	CHARGE
Proton	1	+1
Neutron	1	0
Electron	0.0005	–1

(Electron mass is often rounded down to zero.)

3) An atom is neutral overall — it doesn't have a charge.
4) This is because it has the same number of protons as electrons.

Atomic Number and Mass Number Describe an Atom

1) These two numbers tell you how many of each kind of particle an atom has.

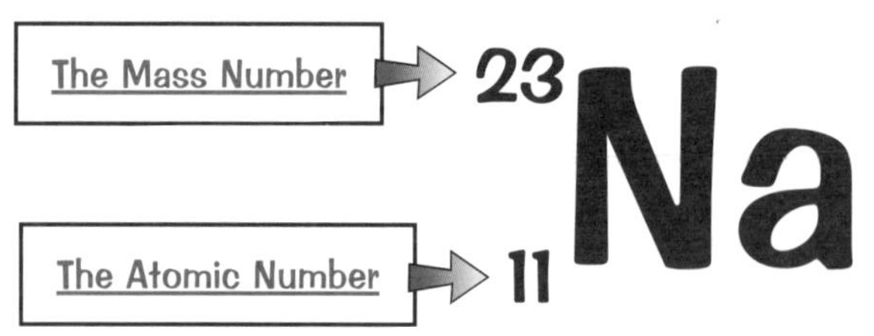

2) The mass number tells you how many protons and neutrons there are in total.
3) The atomic number tells you how many protons there are.
4) So the number of neutrons is just the mass number minus the atomic number.
5) Isotopes are elements that have the same atomic number but different mass numbers.
6) For example carbon-12 and carbon-14 are isotopes of carbon:

Carbon-12

$^{12}_{6}C$

6 PROTONS
6 ELECTRONS
6 NEUTRONS

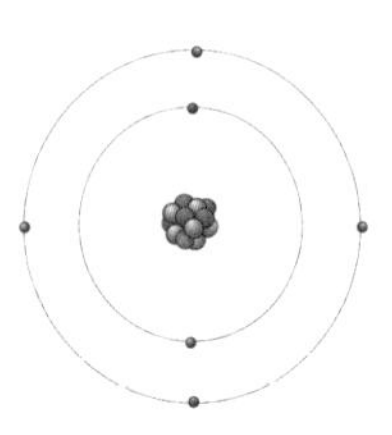

Carbon-14

$^{14}_{6}C$

6 PROTONS
6 ELECTRONS
8 NEUTRONS

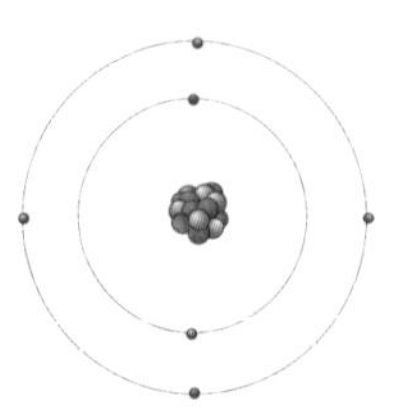

The atomic number is sometimes called the proton number.

Neutron walks into a bar and asks the bartender 'how much is a pint?'...

Bartender says 'for you — no charge'. Sorry. Couldn't help myself. Anyway... This stuff might seem a bit useless at first, but you need to make sure you know it like it's stamped on your forehead. Learn it now :)

Elements and the Periodic Table

Elements are those friendly fellows you find in the periodic table. They're made up of only one type of atom.

The Periodic Table is a Table of All Known Elements

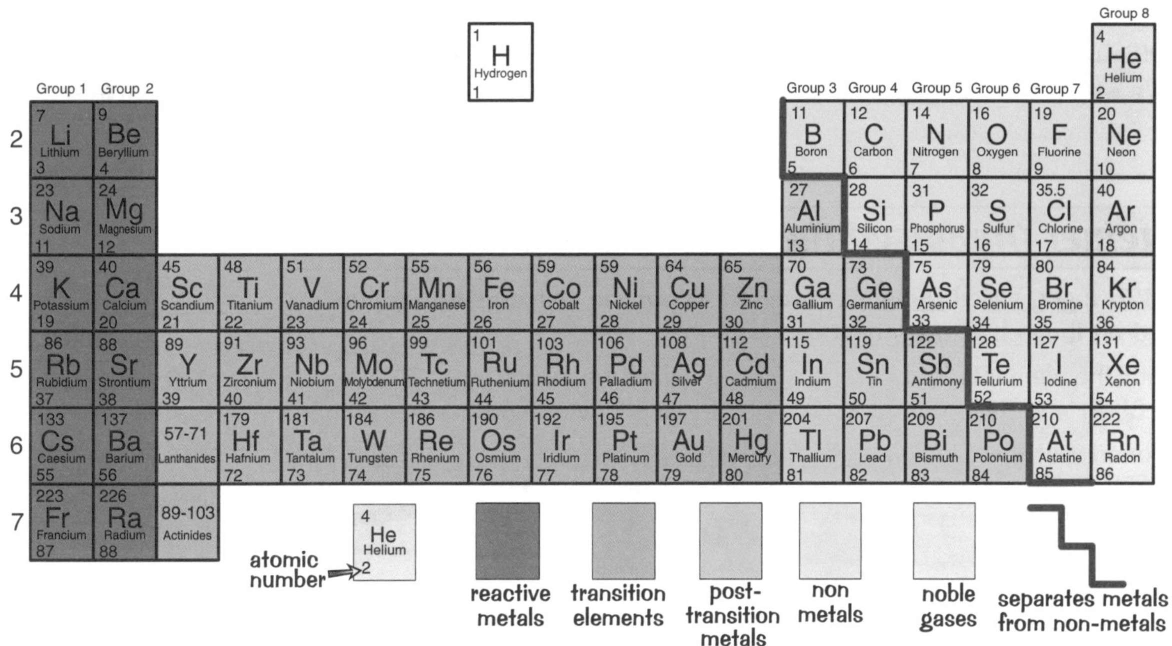

1) Elements are substances made up of only one type of atom.
2) The periodic table shows the elements in order of atomic number.
3) The periodic table is laid out so that elements with similar properties form columns.
4) These vertical columns are called groups.
5) Group 1 elements have 1 electron in their outer shell, Group 2 elements have 2 electrons in their outer shell, Group 3 elements have 3 and so on...
6) The rows of the table are called periods.
7) Elements in the 1st period only have electrons in the first shell. Elements in the 2nd period have electrons in the first two shells. Elements in the 3rd period have electrons in the first three shells, and so on.

You can use the periodic table to find the atomic number of each element.

Compounds Are Made Up of More Than One Element

1) On a periodic table, the elements are shown using symbols (like Ca and Fe).
2) You can tell from a formula (the chemical written in symbols) if it's an element or a compound.
3) Compounds have more than one symbol in their formula (see page 28).
4) For example NaCl is a compound because it has two element symbols, Na and Cl.

What do you do with a dead chemist? — Barium...

Well, there it is. The periodic table in all its glory. Isn't it smashing. But it's not just to stare at, it can also be used to work out lots of interesting things, like the different elements in a compound. Isn't that just grand.

History of the Periodic Table

We haven't always known as much about Chemistry as we do now. No sirree. Take the periodic table...

Scientists Organised Elements Based on Evidence

1) Scientists in the 1800s didn't know as much about elements as we do now.
2) To organise the elements they could only use evidence that was around at the time.
3) That's why it took so long, and so many scientists, to work out the periodic table we have today.

Döbereiner Organised the Elements into Groups of Three

1) In 1828 a guy called Döbereiner started to put the elements into groups based on their chemical properties.
2) He put the elements into groups of three, which he called triads. E.g. Cl, Br and I were one triad, and Li, Na and K were another.
3) He found that the middle element of each triad had a relative atomic mass that was the average of the other two.

Element	Relative atomic mass
Lithium	7
Sodium	23
Potassium	39

$(7 + 39) \div 2 = 23$

Newlands' Law of Octaves Was the First Good Effort

1) Later on a chap called Newlands listed the elements in order of relative atomic mass.
2) He noticed that every 8th element had similar properties.
3) He listed some of the known elements in rows of seven.
4) This meant that elements had similar properties to the ones directly above or below them. E.g. Li, Na and K all have similar properties.
5) These sets of eight were called Newlands' Octaves. Unfortunately the pattern broke down on the third row.
6) But he was getting pretty close, as you can see.

H	Li	Be	B	C	N	O
F	Na	Mg	Al	Si	P	S
Cl	K	Ca	Cr	Ti	Mn	Fe

Dmitri Mendeleev Left Gaps and Predicted New Elements

1) In 1869, Mendeleev arranged all the known elements into a Table of Elements.
2) Mendeleev put the elements in order of atomic mass (like Newlands did).
3) But Mendeleev left some gaps in the table.
4) This kept elements with similar properties in the same vertical groups.
5) The gaps meant that the pattern didn't break down like in Newland's Octaves.

Mendeleev's Table of the Elements

H																	
Li	Be												B	C	N	O	F
Na	Mg												Al	Si	P	S	Cl
K	Ca	*	Ti	V	Cr	Mn	Fe	Co	Ni	Cu	Zn	*	*	As	Se	Br	
Rb	Sr	Y	Zr	Nb	Mo	*	Ru	Rh	Pd	Ag	Cd	In	Sn	Sb	Te	I	
Cs	Ba	*	*	Ta	W	*	Os	Ir	Pt	Au	Hg	Tl	Pb	Bi			

Julie Andrews' octaves — do-re-mi-fa-so-la-ti-do...

This is a good example of how science often changes. A scientist has a good idea. Other scientists laugh and mock. So the idea is changed a bit to fit the new evidence, and then bam — into the textbooks it goes.

Electron Shells

Remember those atoms on page 84. Well they're back and they've brought their electrons along for the ride.

Electron Shell Rules:

1) Electrons are found in shells.
2) The inner shells are always filled first.
3) Only a certain number of electrons are allowed in each shell:

1st shell	2nd shell	3rd shell
2 electrons	8 electrons	8 electrons

Electron shells are sometimes called 'energy levels'.

The number of electrons in an atom can be given as an electronic structure.
For example, silicon has the electronic structure 2,8,4.

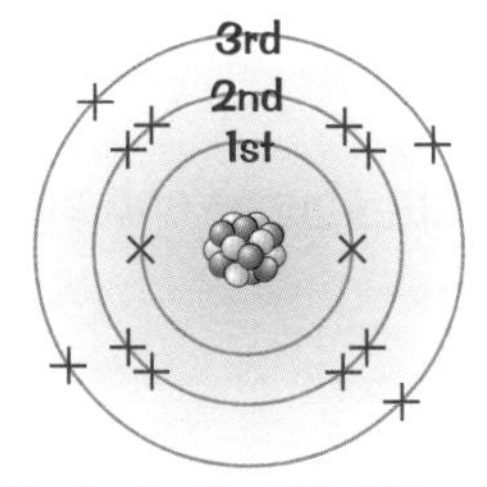

3rd shell still filling

There are 2 electrons in the first shell.

There are 8 electrons in the second shell.

2 , 8 , 4

There are 4 electrons in the third shell.

Electronic Structures Can Be Used to Identify Elements

1) You can use the electronic structure to work out the atomic number of an element and then what the element is.
2) It's pretty simple really. All you have to do is add up the number of electrons.

Example: Element X has the electronic structure 2,8,2. Name element X.
Answer: Just add up the electrons... 2 + 8 + 2 = 12. So, the atomic number of element X is 12.
Then you just have to look it up in the periodic table.
Magnesium has the atomic number 12, so element X must be magnesium.

Electronic Structures Can Be Used to Find the Group and Period

1) The period of the element is the same as the number of shells that contain electrons.
2) The group number of an element is the same as the number of electrons in its outer shell.
3) For example:

Find the group and period of the element with electronic structure 2,3.
Answer: There are two shells filled so the element must be in period 2.
There are three electrons in its outer shell so the element must be in group 3.

One little duck and two fat ladies — 2, 8, 8...

Yeah, I know all this electron shell stuff is a bit strange — just roll with it. Make sure you know how the electrons are arranged in an atom (2 in the first shell, 8 in the second and 8 in the third). You also need to be able to work out the group and period numbers from the electronic structure of an element. Get practising.

Ionic Bonding

Atoms are lovely but they're a bit dull by themselves. What they need to do is join up to make more useful molecules and compounds. This is called bonding. Ionic bonding is the first type you have to learn.

Atoms That Lose or Gain Electrons are Called Ions

1) Ions are charged atoms.
2) Ions can be single atoms (e.g. Cl^-) or groups of atoms (e.g. NO_3^-).
3) Metals form ions by losing electrons. This makes them positive ions.
4) Non-metals form ions by gaining electrons. This makes them negative ions.

Ionic Bonding — Transferring Electrons

1) When a metal and a non-metal combine, they form an ionic bond.
2) An ionic bond is an attraction between a positive and a negative ion.
3) Ions are very reactive and will leap at the first passing ion with an opposite charge and stick to it like glue.
4) The reaction of sodium and chlorine is an example:

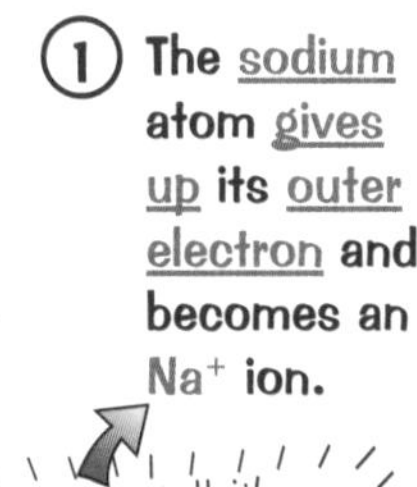

① The sodium atom gives up its outer electron and becomes an Na^+ ion.

You can tell it's an ion because it's got a charge next to it.

② The chlorine atom picks up the spare electron and becomes a Cl^- ion.

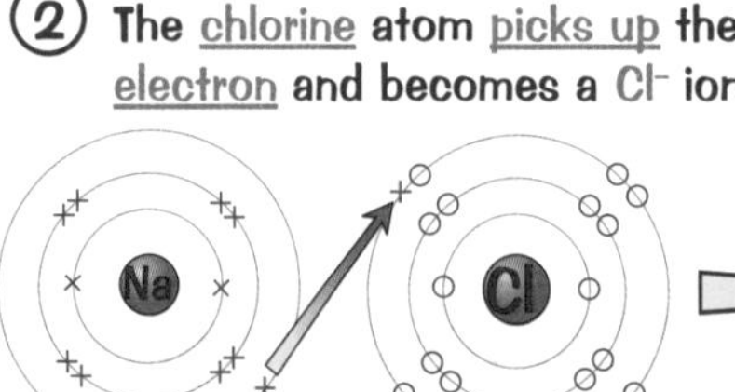

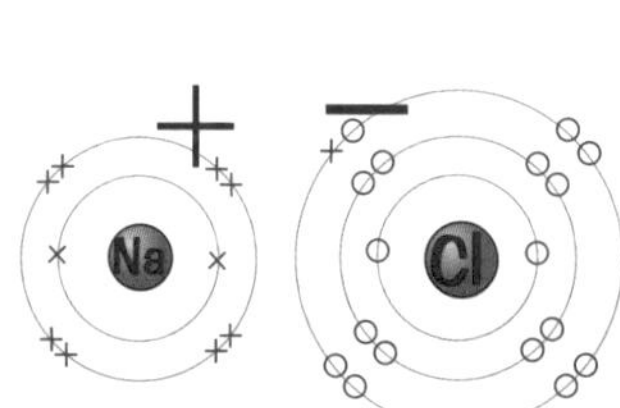

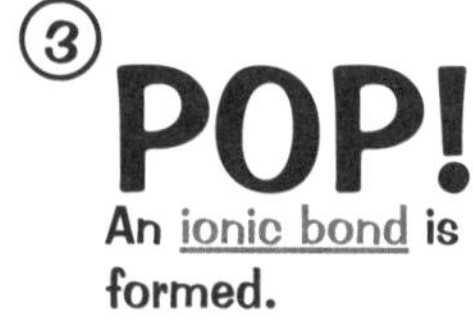

③ An ionic bond is formed.

MgO and NaCl are Both Giant Ionic Lattices

1) Magnesium oxide (MgO) and sodium chloride (NaCl) form giant ionic lattices.
2) Their ions form a regular lattice (an ordered group) where the positive ions are strongly attracted to the negative ions.
3) In the exam they could ask you to compare the properties of sodium chloride and magnesium oxide so make sure you learn them well:

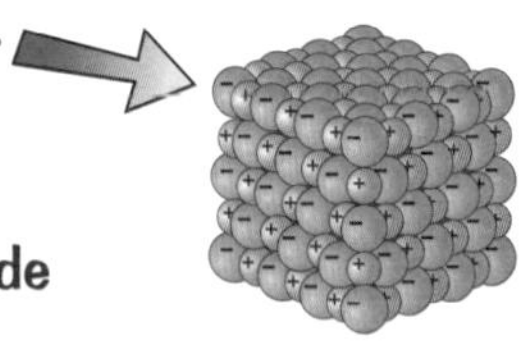

- Magnesium oxide and sodium chloride both have high melting points.
- MgO has much higher melting and boiling points than NaCl.
- They don't conduct electricity when they're solid.
- When they are molten, they will conduct electricity.
- NaCl dissolves in water to form a solution that will conduct electricity.

When something is 'molten' it just means that it's been heated until it melts.

The name's Bond, Ionic Bond — Taken not Shared...

Ionic bonding is the first type of bonding you're gonna have to learn for the exam — there's another type coming up in the next few pages. You've just got to remember that atoms lose or gain electrons to become ions and oppositely charged ions attract each other and form ionic bonds. There's one more page on ions up next...

Ions and Ionic Compounds

Ions crop up all over the place in chemistry. You're going to have to be able to work out the formulas of different compounds from their ions. It's not as tricky as it sounds but you've got to learn it properly.

All Ions Want is a Full Shell of Electrons

1) Atoms are always trying to get a full outer shell of eight electrons.
2) This will give them a "stable electronic structure".
3) To get a full outer shell some atoms need to lose or gain electrons.

- Metals such as sodium, magnesium etc., only have a few electrons in their outer shell.
- The easiest way for them to get a full outer shell is to lose these electrons.
- That's why they form positive ions.

- Non-metal elements, such as oxygen and chlorine, have almost full outer shells.
- The easiest way for them to get a full outer shell is to gain a few electrons.
- That's why they form negative ions.

4) The electrons lost from a metal can be transferred to a non-metal.
5) This means the metal and non-metal will both have full outer shells of electrons. Hooray.

You Can Use Ions to Find the Formula of a Compound

1) To work out the formula of an ionic compound, you have to balance the +ve and the –ve charges.
2) This just means that the charges have to add up to 0.
3) For example:

Potassium chloride is made up potassium and chloride ions.
A potassium ion has a 1^+ charge, K^+. A chloride ion has a 1^- charge, Cl^-.
The 1^+ charge on the potassium ion balances the 1^- charge on the chloride ion.
So, the formula for potassium chloride is just KCl.

Potassium oxide is made up of potassium and oxide ions.
A potassium ion has a 1^+ charge, K^+. An oxide ion has a 2^- charge, O^{2-}.
This time the charges don't balance. You need two potassium ions to create a 2^+ charge.
This will balance the 2^- charge from the oxide ion. So, the formula for potassium oxide is K_2O.

Full Shells — it's the name of the game...

You're gonna have to make sure you're dead good at working out the formulas for compounds for the exam. Remember to balance them, or you'll lose marks. Some elements like to gain electrons, some like to lose electrons, but they all want to have a full outer shell. Poor little electron shells, all they want in life is to be full...

Covalent Bonding

Ionic bonding isn't the only way atoms can join together. Atoms can also share electrons to make covalent bonds. Ah... ain't that nice.

Covalent Bonds — Sharing Electrons

1) Non-metal atoms join together using covalent bonds.
2) A covalent bond is made when atoms share pairs of electrons.
3) This way both atoms feel that they have a full outer shell, and that makes them happy (see page 89).

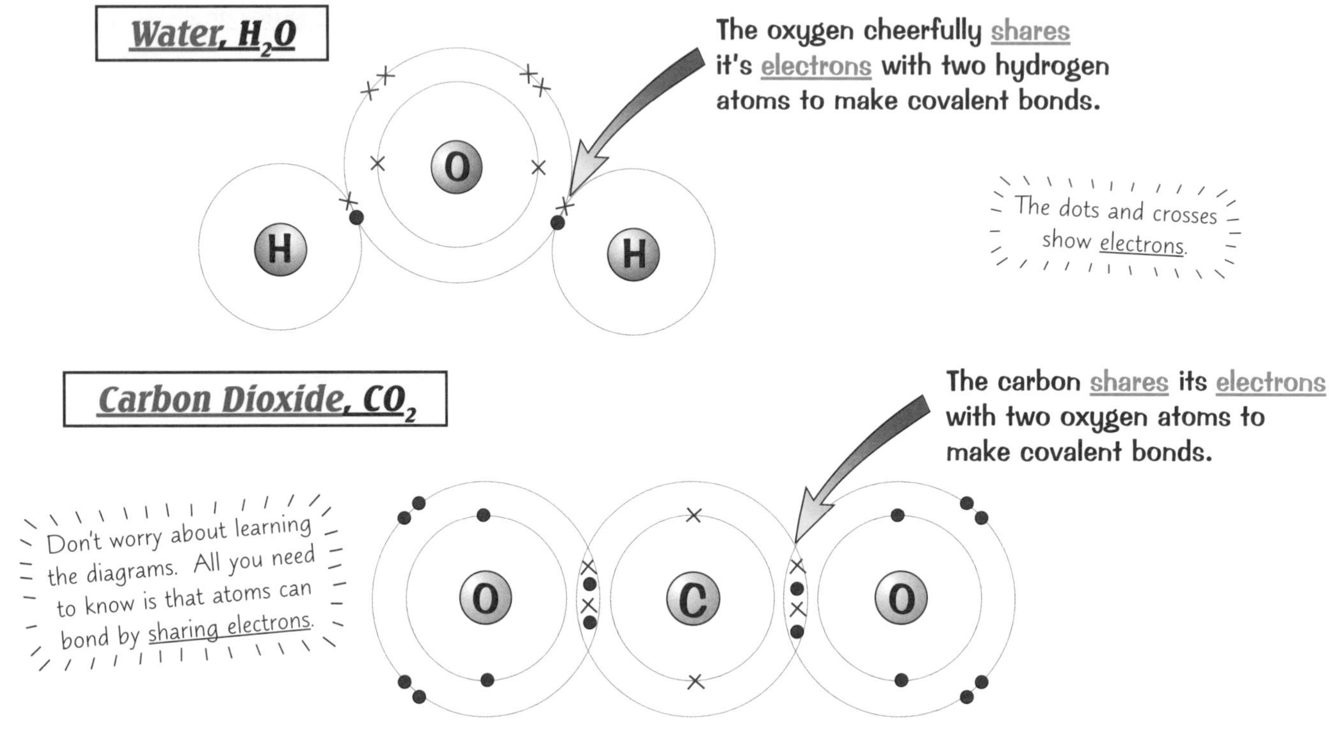

Water, H_2O
O
H
H
The oxygen cheerfully shares it's electrons with two hydrogen atoms to make covalent bonds.
The dots and crosses show electrons.
Carbon Dioxide, CO_2
The carbon shares its electrons with two oxygen atoms to make covalent bonds.
Don't worry about learning the diagrams. All you need to know is that atoms can bond by sharing electrons.
O
C
O

Simple Molecular Substances

1) Carbon dioxide and water are simple molecules.
2) This means that the atoms are joined together by strong covalent bonds, but the molecules are held together by weak forces.
3) The weak forces between molecules are called intermolecular forces.

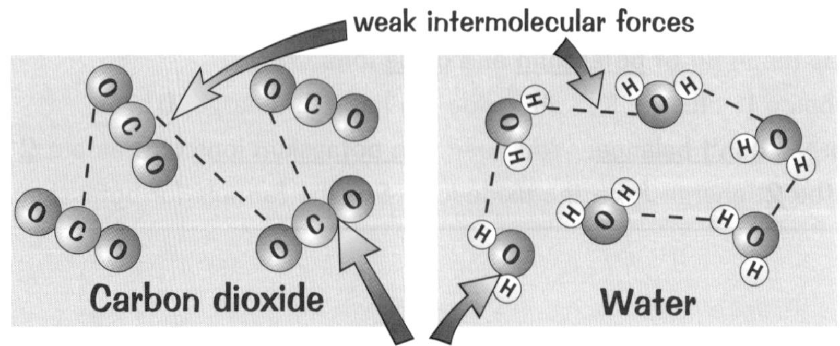

4) Carbon dioxide and water don't conduct electricity.

It's good to share — especially when it's somebody else's...

Make sure you know what covalent bonds are and the two examples of simple molecules. You never know when they'll come in handy... (hint: in your exam). Make sure you understand all about how covalent bonds form.

Group 1 — Alkali Metals

Welcome to the wonderful world of the alkali metals. May I introduce Li, Na, K, Rb, Cs and Fr...

Group 1 Metals are Known as the 'Alkali Metals'

1) Group 1 metals include lithium, sodium and potassium.
2) The alkali metals all have ONE outer electron — this gives them all similar properties.
3) The alkali metals are so reactive they have to be stored under oil to stop them reacting with moist air.

Reaction with Water Produces Hydrogen Gas

1) When lithium, sodium or potassium are put in water, they react very vigorously.
2) They move around the surface, they fizz and produce hydrogen.
3) An alkali forms which is the hydroxide of the metal. That's why they're called the 'alkali metals'.

$$2Li + 2H_2O \rightarrow 2LiOH + H_2$$
Lithium + Water → Lithium hydroxide + Hydrogen

$$2Na + 2H_2O \rightarrow 2NaOH + H_2$$
Sodium + Water → Sodium hydroxide + Hydrogen

$$2K + 2H_2O \rightarrow 2KOH + H_2$$
Potassium + Water → Potassium hydroxide + Hydrogen

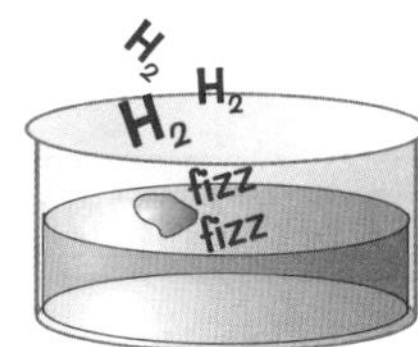

The Alkali Metals Get More Reactive as You go Down the Group

1) As you go DOWN Group 1, the alkali metals become more reactive.
2) This means the further down the group they are the more strongly they react with water.
3) The reaction between water and potassium gets hot enough to produce a lilac flame.
4) Rubidium and caesium are even more reactive than potassium. This means they react more violently with water. They even explode when they get wet.

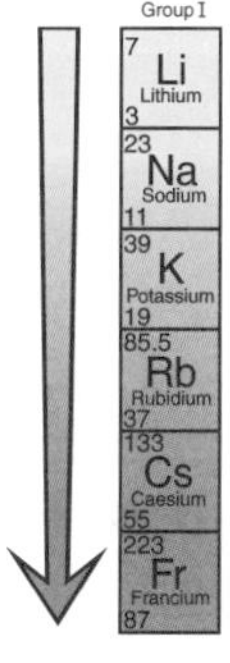

Alkali Metal Compounds Burn with Different Coloured Flames

You can use a flame test to help you find out if sodium, lithium or potassium are in a compound.

1) Dip a wire loop into some acid to make it moist.
2) Put the loop into a solid sample of the compound to be tested.
3) Place the end in a blue Bunsen flame.
4) Alkali metal ions will give pretty coloured flames — the colour of the flame tells you which alkali metal is present.

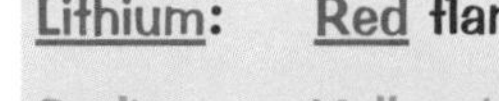

Lithium: Red flame

Sodium: Yellow/orange flame

Potassium: Lilac flame

Red and orange and pink and green — or something like that...

If you want to see some really awesome explosive chemistry check out the videos of alkali metals reacting with water online. Excellent. Learn the trends and characteristics of alkali metals before turning over.

Group 7 — The Halogens

Here's a page on another group in the periodic table — the halogens...

Group 7 Elements are Known as the 'Halogens'

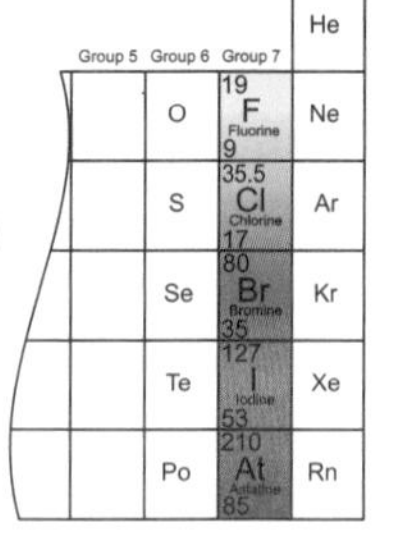

1) Group 7 includes fluorine, chlorine, bromine and iodine.
2) All Group 7 elements have got similar properties because they all have seven electrons in their outer shell.

As you go DOWN Group 7, the halogens become less reactive.

3) In the exam you might have to describe what the halogens look like at room temperature:
   - Chlorine (Cl_2) is a green gas.
   - Bromine (Br_2) is an orange liquid.
   - Iodine (I_2) is a grey solid.

4) Chlorine is used to sterilise water and to make plastics and pesticides. Iodine is used to sterilise wounds.

The Halogens React with Alkali Metals to Form Metal Halides

1) The halogens react vigorously with alkali metals (Group 1 elements, see page 91) to form 'metal halides'.
2) You can work out what compound will be formed by taking the name of the alkali metal and the name of the halogen with 'ine' taken off and 'ide' stuck on the end.
3) For example:

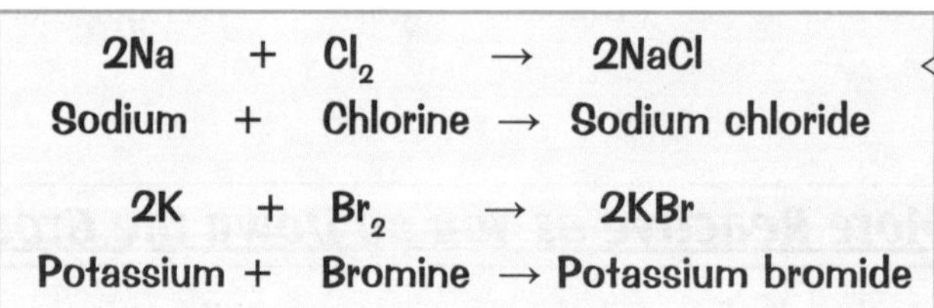

$2Na + Cl_2 \rightarrow 2NaCl$
Sodium + Chlorine → Sodium chloride

$2K + Br_2 \rightarrow 2KBr$
Potassium + Bromine → Potassium bromide

Make sure you can write equations for the reactions between all the Group 1 and Group 7 elements.

More Reactive Halogens Will Displace Less Reactive Ones

1) When a halogen reacts with a metal halide, the less reactive halogen gets displaced from the metal halide.
2) This means it'll be booted out and replaced by the more reactive halogen.
3) If the more reactive halogen is already in the metal halide it will stay where it is.
4) These reactions are called displacement reactions.
5) For example, chlorine can displace bromine and iodine because it's more reactive.
6) Bromine will displace iodine.

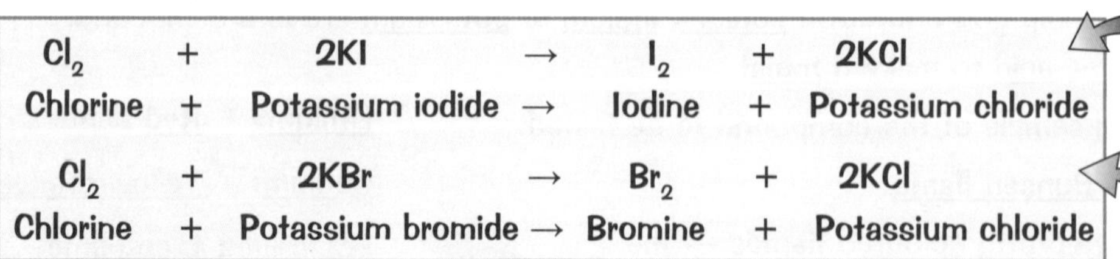

$Cl_2 + 2KI \rightarrow I_2 + 2KCl$
Chlorine + Potassium iodide → Iodine + Potassium chloride

$Cl_2 + 2KBr \rightarrow Br_2 + 2KCl$
Chlorine + Potassium bromide → Bromine + Potassium chloride

In this reaction the chlorine is more reactive than the iodine — it boots iodine out of the metal halide.

In this reaction the chlorine is more reactive than the bromine — so it boots bromine out of the metal halide.

7) In the exam you could be asked to predict the results of displacement reactions using other halogens.

What's a bakers favourite halogen — Fluor-ine...

The halogens are another group from the periodic table, and just like the alkali metals (p.91), you've got to learn their trends and the equations on this page. Learn them, cover up the page, scribble, check.

Metals

Loads of elements are metals and they all have really useful properties. Make sure you learn 'em well.

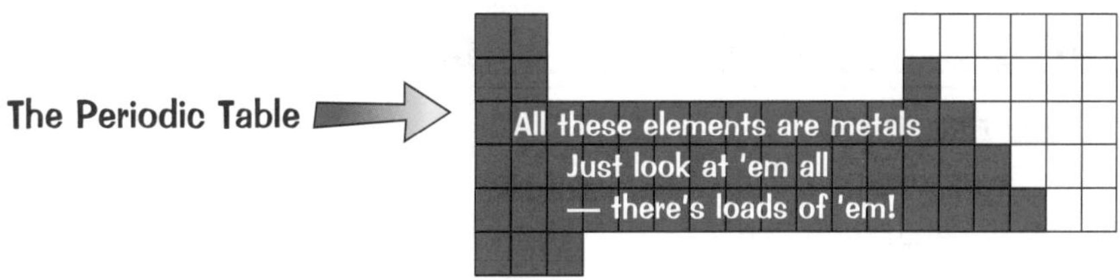
The Periodic Table
All these elements are metals
Just look at 'em all
— there's loads of 'em!

Metals Have Metallic Bonds

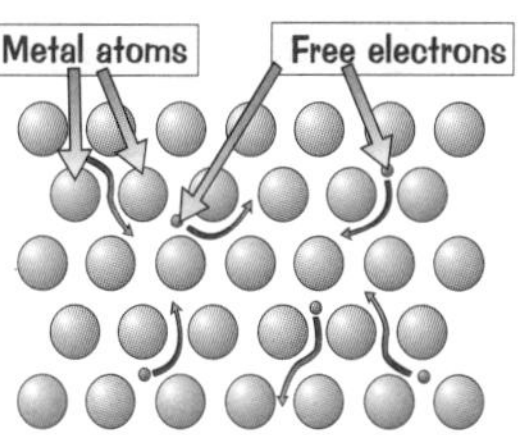
Metal atoms
Free electrons

1) The particles in metals are held together with strong metallic bonds.
2) These special bonds allow the outer electron(s) of each atom to move freely.
3) This creates a 'sea' of free electrons in the metal.
4) Metals conduct electricity really well.
5) This is due to the free electrons which can move through the metal, carrying the electrical current.

Metals Have Loads of Awesome Properties

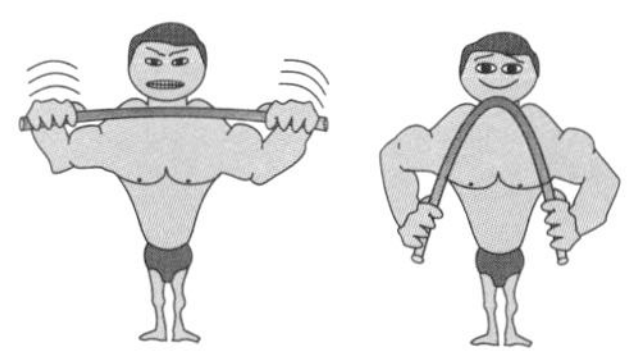

1) Metals are very hard, dense and lustrous (shiny).
2) They have a high tensile strength. In other words they're strong and hard to break.
3) Metals are also great conductors of heat.
4) Metals have high melting and boiling points. This is because of the strong metallic bonds between atoms.

You've Got to be Able to Match the Metal to the Use

Use	Properties Needed	Metal Used
Saucepans	Good conductor of heat, doesn't rust easily	Stainless Steel
Electrical Wiring	Good conductor of electricity, easily bent	Copper
Aeroplanes	Low density (light), strong, doesn't corrode	Aluminium
Bridges and Cars	Strong	Iron

In the exam you might have to suggest properties needed by a metal for a particular use.

Daniel Craig — he's definitely a strong Bond...

It's not just the main structure of an aeroplane that's made of aluminium — parts of the engines, the seat supports and even the cabin crew's trolleys are all made of aluminium. All this aluminium means the plane's light enough to fly.

Superconductors and Transition Metals

Oooooo, some interesting stuff...

At Very Low Temperatures, Some Metals are Superconductors

1) Normally, all metals have electrical resistance.
2) This means that when electricity flows through them they heat up, and some of the electrical energy is wasted as heat.
3) If you make some metals cold enough, their resistance disappears and the metal becomes a superconductor.
4) This means no electrical energy is wasted. Result.

So What's the Catch...

1) Using superconductors you can make:
   a) Power cables that don't lose any power (loss-free power transmission).
   b) Really strong electromagnets.
   c) Electronic circuits that work really fast.
2) But here's the catch — when I said cold, I meant REALLY COLD. Metals only start superconducting at less than –265 °C! Getting things that cold is very hard, and very expensive.

Metals in the Middle of the Periodic Table are Transition Metals

1) You'll have heard of a few of the transition metals (e.g. copper, iron) — but there are loads of others.
2) They are all found in the middle of the periodic table — the ones shown in yellow here:
3) Transition metals have typical 'metallic' properties (see page 93).

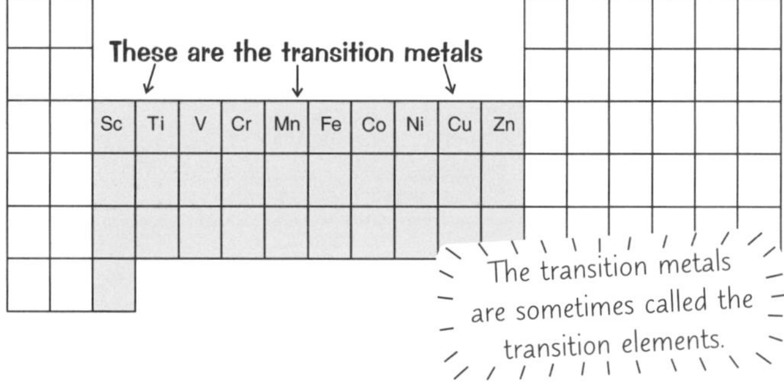

Transition Metals and Their Compounds Make Good Catalysts

1) Iron is the catalyst used in the Haber process for making ammonia.
2) Nickel is used as a catalyst in the manufacture of margarine.

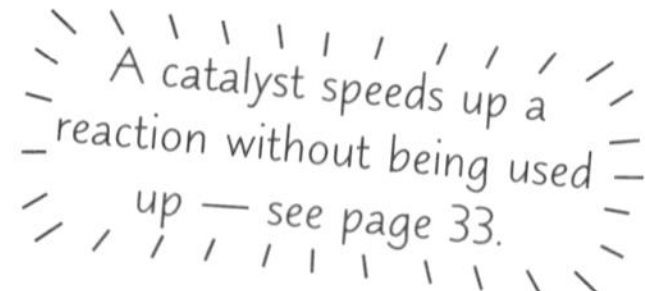

A catalyst speeds up a reaction without being used up — see page 33.

The Compounds are Very Colourful

1) A transition metal compound is just a compound that has a transition metal in it, for example $FeCO_3$
2) The compounds of transition elements are often colourful:

- Iron(II) compounds are usually light green.
- Iron(III) compounds are orange/brown.
- Copper compounds are often blue.

Why do superconductors always lose fights? — they put up no resistance...

Superconducting magnets are used in magnetic resonance image (MRI) scanners in hospitals. That way, the huge magnetic fields they need can be generated without using up a load of electricity. Great stuff...

Thermal Decomposition and Precipitation

Oooooh... More lovely long chemistry words to get your teeth into. Smashing.

Thermal Decomposition — Breaking Down with Heat

Thermal decomposition is when a substance breaks down into at least two other substances when it's heated.

1) Transition metal carbonates break down when they're heated.
2) Transition metal carbonates are things like copper(II) carbonate ($CuCO_3$), iron(II) carbonate ($FeCO_3$), zinc carbonate ($ZnCO_3$) and manganese carbonate ($MnCO_3$). In other words they've all got a CO_3 in them.
3) They break down into a metal oxide and carbon dioxide. For example:

copper(II) carbonate	⟶	copper oxide	+	carbon dioxide
iron(II) carbonate	⟶	iron oxide	+	carbon dioxide
magnesium carbonate	⟶	magnesium oxide	+	carbon dioxide
zinc carbonate	⟶	zinc oxide	+	carbon dioxide

4) These reactions usually show a colour change.
5) You can check that the gas is carbon dioxide by bubbling it through limewater. If it's carbon dioxide the limewater will turn milky.

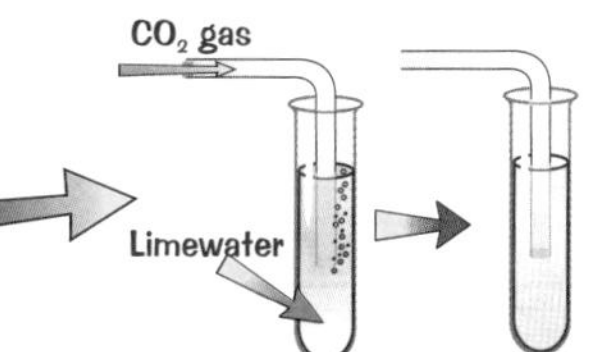

Precipitation — A Solid Forms in Solution

1) A precipitation reaction is where two solutions react and an insoluble solid forms.
2) The solid is called a precipitate.

Insoluble just means that something won't dissolve in water.

Use Precipitation to Test for Transition Metal Ions

1) You can use sodium hydroxide (NaOH) to see whether transition metal ions are in a solution.
2) All you have to do is add the sodium hydroxide to the solution and look at the colour of the precipitate...

If Cu^{2+} is in the solution you'll see a blue solid.
If Fe^{2+} is in the solution you'll see a grey/green solid.
If Fe^{3+} is in the solution you'll see an orange/brown solid.

Example: Sodium hydroxide is added to an unknown solution, and an orange/brown precipitate forms. What transition metal ions are in the solution?
Answer: An orange/brown solid means that there are Fe^{3+} ions in the solution.

My duffel coat's worn out — thermal decomposition...

Wow. This page is packed full of chemistry. I'm afraid you're gonna have to learn all the equations for thermal decomposition and the colours of the precipitates of transition metal ions if you want to impress the examiner.

Water Purity

Water, water, everywhere... well, there is if you live in Cumbria.

There are Limited Water Resources in the UK

1) Water is really important in industry.
2) It is used as a cheap raw material, to cool reactions and to dissolve reactants.
3) Between half and two thirds of all the fresh water used in the UK goes into industry.

In the UK, we get our water from:
1) Lakes, rivers and reservoirs (artificial lakes).
2) Aquifers (rocks that trap water underground).

4) All these resources are limited (they could run out).
5) When they will run out depends on the amount of rain we get and how much water people use.
6) Unless we try to save more water, experts think that by 2025 we might not have enough water to supply everybody's needs.
7) This is why it's important to conserve (save) water.

Water is Purified by Filtration, Sedimentation and Chlorination

1) Before it's purified (made cleaner) water may contain chemicals or solids that we don't want.
2) For example, dissolved salts and minerals, microbes, pollutants and insoluble materials may all be present.
3) The purification process includes:

1) Filtration — this is where any solid bits are taken out.
2) Sedimentation — chemicals are added to the water, which makes small particles clump together and settle at the bottom.
3) Chlorination — chlorine gas is bubbled through to kill harmful bacteria and other microbes.

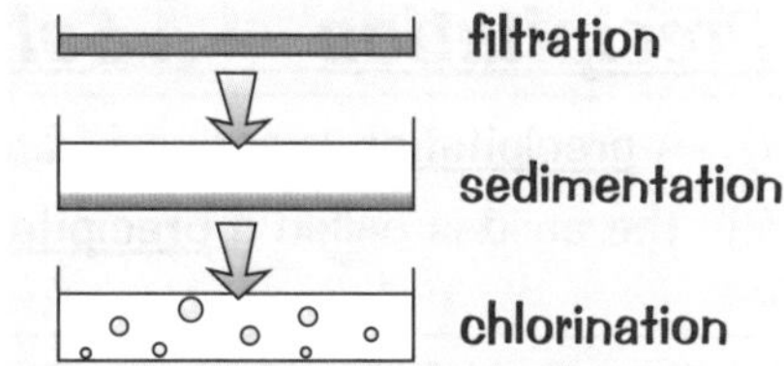

Tap Water Can Still Contain Pollutants

1) Low levels of pollutants are still found in water even after it's purified.
2) These pollutants come from a number of sources:

- Nitrate residues from excess fertiliser seeping into rivers and lakes.
- Lead compounds from old lead pipes.
- Pesticide residues from spraying pesticides too near to rivers and lakes.

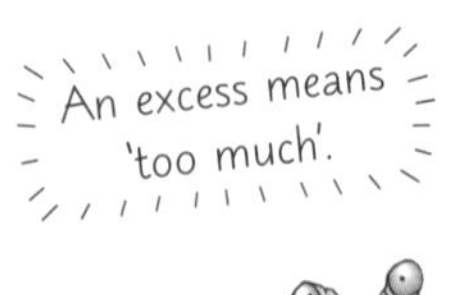

Who'd have thought there'd be so much to learn about water...

In the UK we're very lucky to have clean water available at the turn of a tap — but it's not a never-ending supply. Learn how water is purified in the UK, and what pollutants get through the cleaning process. Cover. Scribble.

Testing Water Purity

Here's another page on water and an interesting fact to keep you going... Taking a five-minute shower uses more water than a typical person in a slum in a developing country uses in a whole day. Crazy stuff.

You Can Test Water for Dissolved Ions

1) It's important that water companies test their water regularly for pollutants.
2) You can test for some dissolved ions using precipitation reactions.
3) A precipitation reaction is where two solutions react to make an insoluble solid (see page 95).

Test for Sulfate Ions Using Barium Chloride

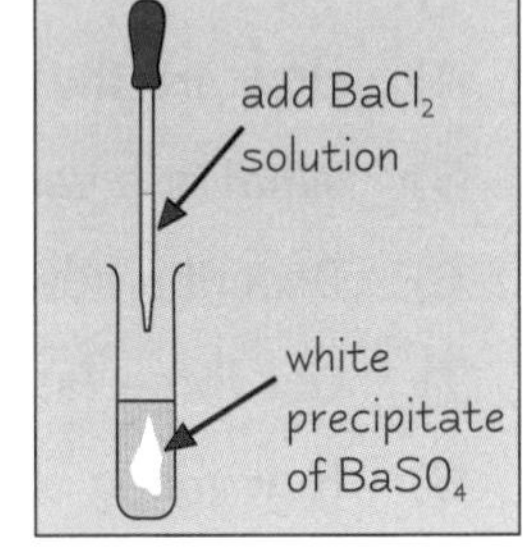

1) Add barium chloride solution to the test sample.
2) If you see a white precipitate, there are sulfate ions in the sample.
3) Here's an example where potassium sulfate is present in the sample:

barium chloride + potassium sulfate → barium sulfate + potassium chloride

Barium sulfate is the white precipitate.

4) Here's another example:

barium chloride + zinc sulfate → barium sulfate + zinc chloride

To work out what the products are just swap around the chloride and sulfate parts of the name. Simples.

Test for Halide Ions Using Silver Nitrate

1) Add silver nitrate solution to the test sample.
2) If halide ions are present a precipitate will form.

- Chloride ions give a white precipitate.
- Bromide ions give a cream precipitate.
- Iodide ions give a pale yellow precipitate.

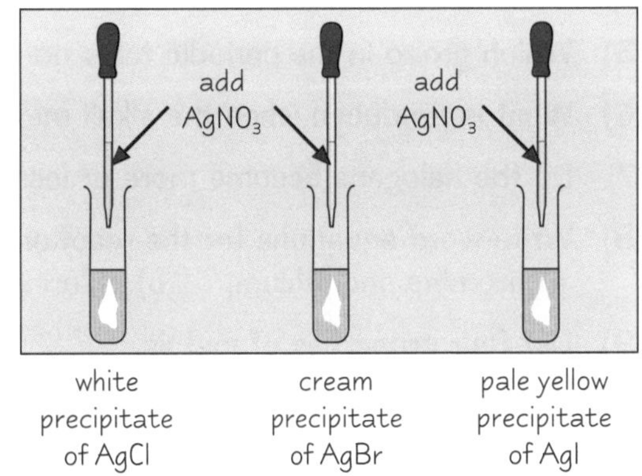

white precipitate of AgCl | cream precipitate of AgBr | pale yellow precipitate of AgI

3) These are the reactions you'll need to know for the exam:

silver nitrate + sodium chloride → silver chloride + sodium nitrate

silver nitrate + sodium bromide → silver bromide + sodium nitrate

silver nitrate + sodium iodide → silver iodide + sodium nitrate

For these reactions to work an acid has to be added to the test sample first. But don't worry, you won't be asked about that in the exam.

Two parts hydrogen, one part oxygen — hold the pollutants...

Water is amazingly important for us humans, but it's only safe to use if it's been tested properly for pollutants. One in eight people in the world don't have daily access to clean water and over two million people a year die from water related diseases. That's why it's so important for water companies to test their water regularly. Now, to brighten up your day, here comes a lovely revision summary. I know, I shouldn't have...

Revision Summary for Module C4

These certainly aren't the easiest questions you're going to come across. That's because they test what you know without giving you any clues. At first you might think they're impossibly difficult. Eventually you'll realise that they simply test whether you've learnt the stuff or not. If you're struggling to answer these then you need to do some serious learning.

1) Who discovered that atoms contain electrons?
2) What are the three types of particle found in an atom?
3) Explain what an isotope is.
4) How are the atoms ordered in the modern periodic table?
5) What is a vertical column of the periodic table called?
6) Describe how Newlands arranged the elements.
7) List three facts (or 'rules') about electron shells.
8) How many electrons are allowed in the second electron shell?
9) What is ionic bonding?
10) When does sodium chloride conduct electricity?
11) Do non-metals form positive ions or negative ions?
12)* A magnesium ion has a 2^+ charge and an oxide ion has a 2^- charge.
What is the formula of magnesium oxide?
13) What is covalent bonding?
14) What are the weak forces between water molecules called?
15) Which group in the periodic table contains the alkali metals?
16) What is produced when the alkali metals react with water?
17) Do the halogens become more or less reactive as you go down the group?
18)* Write word equations for the reactions between:
a) bromine and lithium, b) chlorine and potassium, c) iodine and sodium.
19) List four properties of metals.
20) Why is copper used for electrical wiring?
21) Give two uses of superconductors.
22) Name two transition metals that can work as catalysts.
23) What is thermal decomposition?
24) Two solutions react together and an insoluble solid forms. What type of reaction is this?
25) Describe three processes used to purify water.
26) A student adds dilute hydrochloric acid and barium chloride to a water sample and a white precipitate is produced. What ions are present in the water?

* Answers on page 116

Static Electricity

Static electricity is all about charges which are NOT free to move. This means they build up in one place and can make a spark or a shock when they do finally move.

The Build-up of Static is Caused by Rubbing

1) When two insulating materials are rubbed together, electrons will be transferred (moved) from one to the other.
2) Electrons have a negative (-) charge. The material with the extra electrons is left with a negative (-) charge.
3) The other material is left with a positive (+) charge because it has lost some electrons.
4) For example, when a polythene rod is rubbed with a cloth duster, electrons are scraped off the duster and dumped on the rod.
5) Some dusting cloths and brushes use static electricity. They become charged as they rub the surface, and this charge attracts the dust to them.

An insulating material is one where charges can't flow easily.

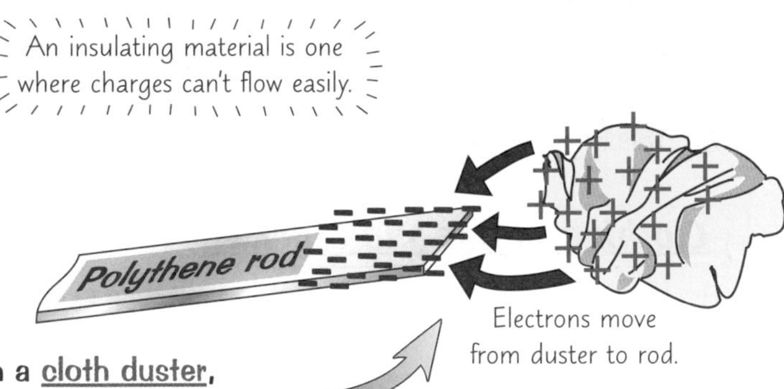

Electrons move from duster to rod.

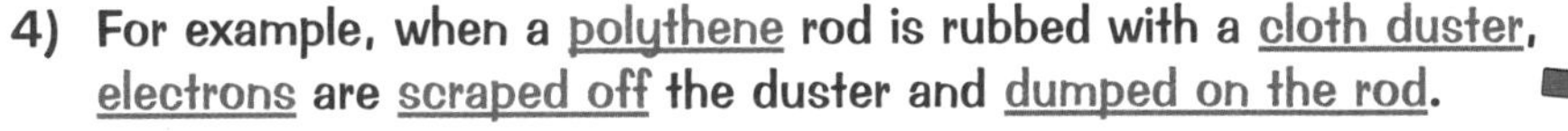

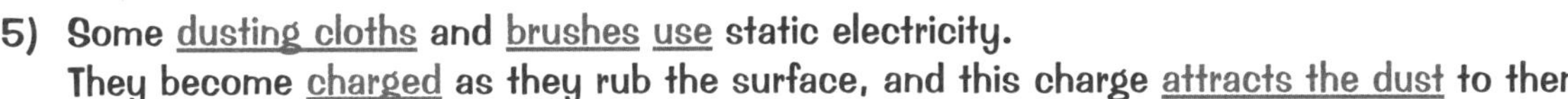

Only Electrons Move — Never the Positive Charges

1) Both positive and negative charges are only produced by the movement of negative electrons.
2) The positive charges definitely do not move.
3) A positive charge is always caused by electrons moving away elsewhere, as shown above. Don't forget!
4) If enough charge builds up, it can suddenly move.
5) This movement of charge can cause sparks or shocks that can be dangerous (see next page).

Like Charges Repel, Opposite Charges Attract

1) Two things with opposite charges will be attracted to each other.
2) Two things with the same charge ('like' charges) will repel each other. This means they push each other away.

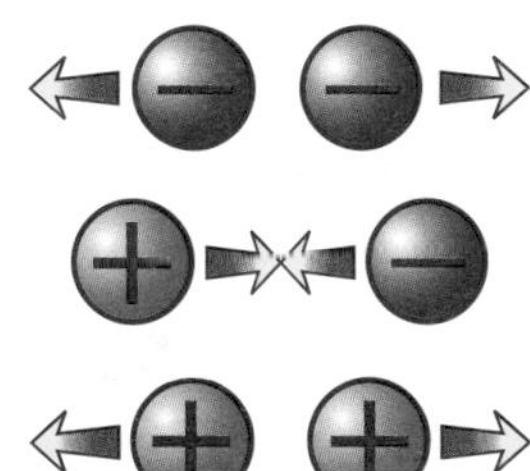

Come on, be positive — this stuff isn't so bad...

Static electricity's great fun. You must have tried rubbing a balloon against your clothes and trying to get it to stick to the wall. It really works... well, sometimes. And it's all due to the build-up of static. Bad hair days are also caused by static. It builds up on your hair, so your strands of hair repel each other.

More on Static Electricity

They could ask you to give quite detailed examples in exams. Make sure you learn all these details.

Static Electricity Can Be a Nuisance

Attracting Dust

1) Dirt and dust particles are charged and will be attracted to anything with the opposite charge.
2) Many objects around the house are made out of insulators — such as plastic containers and TV screens.
3) These get easily charged and attract the dust particles — making cleaning a nightmare.

Clothing Clings and Crackles

Synthetic things are made from man-made materials.

1) When synthetic clothes are dragged over each other, like in a tumble drier or over your head, electrons get scraped off.
2) This leaves static charges on both parts which makes them stick together or cling to you.
3) You can also get little sparks or shocks as the charges on the clothes rearrange themselves.

Shocks From Door Handles or Water Pipes

1) If you walk on a synthetic carpet, charge can build up on your body.
2) If you then touch a metal door handle or water pipe you become earthed.
3) This means the charge flows to the earth through the metal and you get a little shock.

Static Electricity Can be Dangerous

Lightning

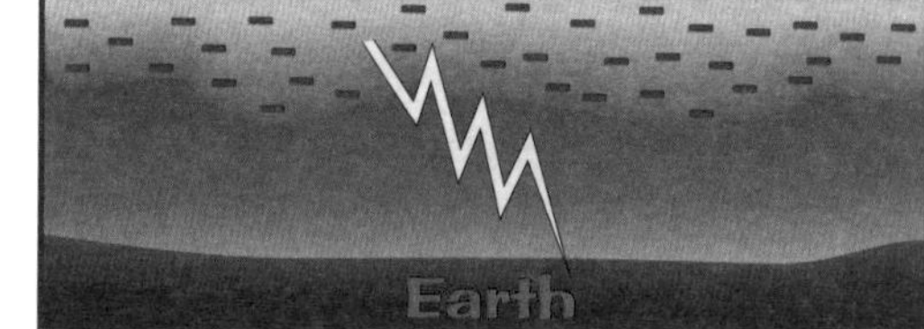

1) Rain drops and ice bump together inside storm clouds, knocking off electrons.
2) The electrons move around, and leave the top of the cloud positively charged and the bottom of the cloud negatively charged.
3) This creates a huge voltage and a big spark — lightning.

Grain Chutes, Paper Rollers and the Fuel Filling Nightmare

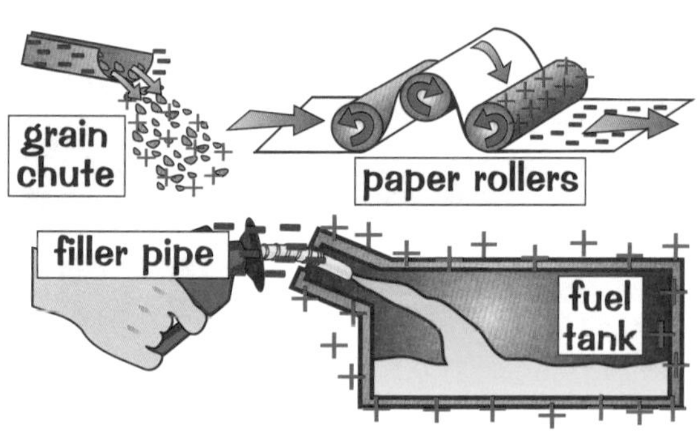

1) As fuel flows out of a filler pipe, charge can build up.
2) This can also happen when paper drags over rollers or grain shoots out of pipes (chutes).
3) The build up of static can easily lead to a spark.
4) This might cause an explosion in dusty or fumey places — like when filling up a car with fuel at a petrol station.
5) A spark could also cause an explosion in places where there are high concentrations of oxygen (like in a hospital operating theatre).

Static electricity — it's really shocking stuff...

Lightning always chooses the easiest path between the sky and the ground — that's the nearest, tallest thing. That's why it's never a good idea to fly a kite in a thunderstorm — you become part of the easiest path.

Uses of Static Electricity

Static electricity isn't always a nuisance. It's got loads of uses in medicine and industry. And now's your chance to learn all about them, you lucky thing...

Paint Sprayers — Getting an Even Coat

1) Bikes and cars are painted using electrostatic paint sprayers.
2) The spray gun is charged, which charges up the small drops of paint.

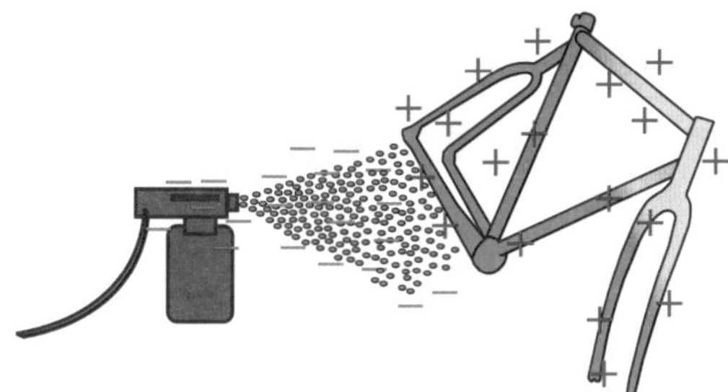

3) Each paint drop repels all the others, since they've all got the same charge, so you get a very fine spray.
4) The object to be painted is given an opposite charge to the paint.
5) This attracts the fine spray of paint.
6) This method gives an even coat and hardly any paint is wasted.
7) Parts of the object pointing away from the spray gun still attract paint so there are no paint shadows.
8) You can also spray crops this way.

Dust Precipitators — Cleaning Up Emissions

Chimney

Positively charged plates

Negatively charged grid or rods

1) Factories and power stations produce loads of smoke, which is made up of tiny particles of dust and soot.
2) The particles can be removed from a chimney with a precipitator.
3) At the bottom of the chimney, the particles pass through a charged metal grid or charged rods.
4) The particles become charged.
5) The particles are attracted to plates that are either earthed or have the opposite charge.
6) The plates are hit with a hammer to knock off the particles.
7) The dust falls to a collector at the bottom of the chimney and can be removed.
8) So the gases coming out of the chimney have very few smoke particles in them.

Defibrillators — Restarting a Heart

1) An electric shock to a stopped heart can make it start beating again.
2) Hospitals and ambulances have machines called defibrillators to do this.
3) The defibrillator has two paddles connected to a power supply.
4) The paddles of the defibrillator are placed firmly on the patient's chest to get a good electrical contact and then the paddles are charged up.
5) The charge passes through the paddles to the patient to make the heart contract (pump).
6) The person using the defibrillator needs to take care not to get an electric shock themselves.

If this doesn't get your heart going — nothing will...

You can get your very own special defibrillator now. One to carry around in your handbag, just in case. No, really, you can (okay, maybe it wouldn't fit in your handbag unless you're Mary Poppins, but it's still handy).

Charge and Resistance

If you've got a complete loop of conducting stuff connected to an electric power source, electricity flows round it. Isn't that great.

Charge Flows Around a Circuit

Voltage is sometimes called potential difference or p.d.

1) CURRENT is the flow of electrical charge around a circuit (loop). Current only flows in a circuit if there's a complete loop for it to flow around. It's measured in amps, A.
2) VOLTAGE is the driving force that pushes the current round. Voltage is measured in volts, V.
3) RESISTANCE is anything in the circuit which slows the flow down and reduces the current. Resistance is measured in ohms, Ω.
4) THERE'S A BALANCE: the voltage is trying to push the current round the circuit, and the resistance is trying to stop it.

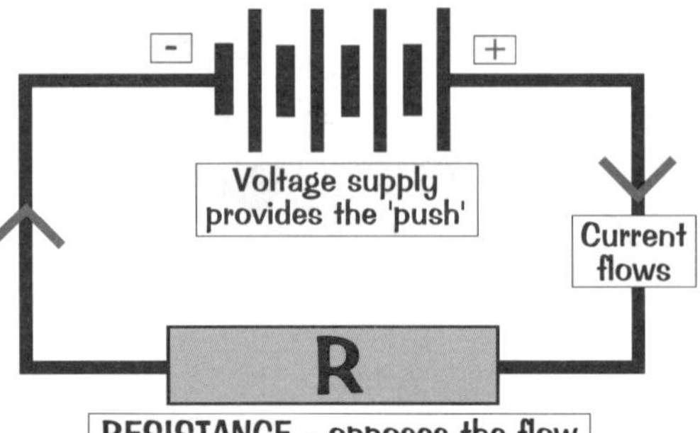

-
+
Voltage supply provides the 'push'
Current flows
R
RESISTANCE - opposes the flow

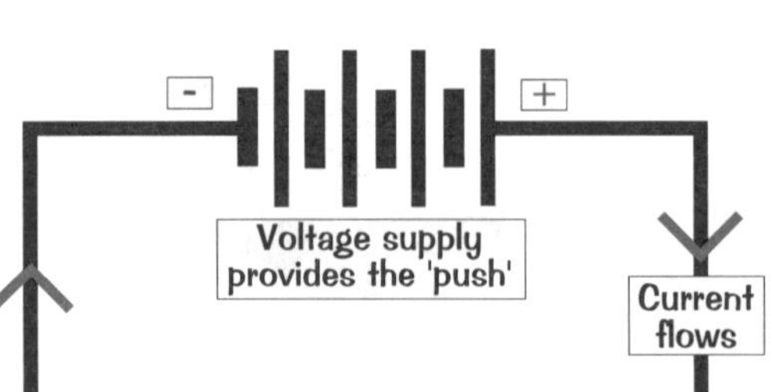

If you increase the VOLTAGE — then MORE CURRENT will flow.
If you increase the RESISTANCE — then LESS CURRENT will flow
(or MORE VOLTAGE will be needed to keep the SAME CURRENT flowing).

Variable Resistors

1) A resistor is something that reduces the current flowing in a circuit.
2) A variable resistor (or rheostat) is a resistor whose resistance can be changed.
3) This changes the amount of current flowing through the circuit.
4) Turn the resistance up and the current drops.
5) Turn the resistance down and the current goes up.
6) The old-fashioned ones are huge coils of wire with a slider on them.
7) As you move the slider, the length of wire that has current flowing through it changes.
8) Longer wires have more resistance, so have less current flowing through them.
9) The thickness of a wire also matters. Thinner wires have more resistance and so less current can flow.

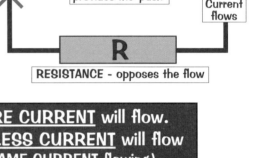

Calculating Resistance: R = V/I

A fixed resistor is one that has the same resistance all the time.

1) If you increase the voltage across a fixed resistor, the current increases as well.
2) For a fixed voltage, current increases as resistance decreases.
3) You can calculate resistance using this formula:

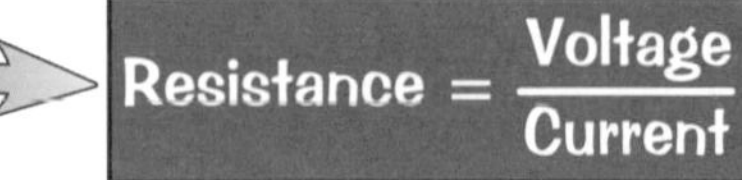

$$\text{Resistance} = \frac{\text{Voltage}}{\text{Current}}$$

EXAMPLE: A resistor is supplied with a voltage of 6 V and allows a current of 4 A to flow. What is its resistance?

ANSWER: Resistance = Voltage ÷ Current = 6 V ÷ 4 A = 1.5 Ω

You have to learn this — don't try to resist...

Sometimes you can get dimmer switches which fade the light in and out. Some of them work by resistance, and are perfect for getting that nice romantic atmosphere you want for your dinner for two. Handy.

Plugs, Fuses and Power

Now then, did you know... electricity is dangerous. It can kill you. Well just watch out for it, that's all.

All the Wires in a Plug are Colour Coded

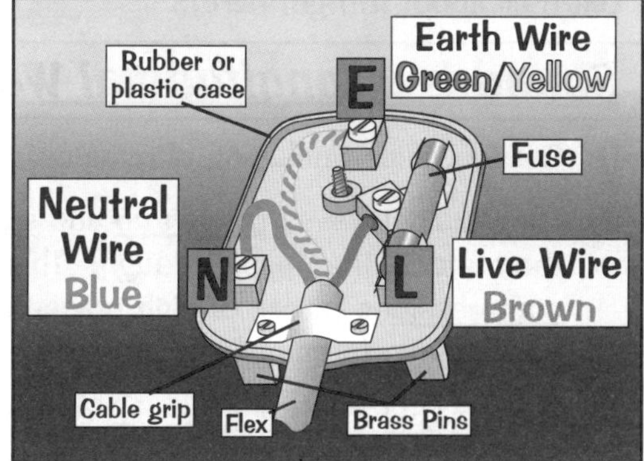

1) In plugs, the correct coloured wire is connected to each pin, and firmly screwed in place so no bare wires show.
2) The brown LIVE WIRE carries the high voltage.
3) The blue NEUTRAL WIRE completes the circuit — electricity normally flows in through the live wire and out through the neutral wire.
4) The yellow and green EARTH WIRE is a safety wire to stop the appliance becoming live.
5) Appliances with metal cases are "earthed" to reduce the danger of electric shock.
6) "Earthed" just means the case is attached to an earth wire.
7) An earthed conductor can never become live.
8) Appliances with cases made from non-conductors (such as plastic) are called double insulated appliances.
9) A double insulated appliance doesn't need an earth wire as it can't become live.

Fuses Prevent Fires

1) Sometimes a fault develops where the live wire touches the metal case of an appliance.
2) A current flows in through the live wire to the metal case.
3) Because the case is earthed, the current can flow through the case and out down the earth wire.
4) This large flow of current 'blows' the fuse and causes the wire inside it to melt.
5) With the fuse melted, the current stops flowing because it breaks the circuit.
6) This stops the flex overheating, which could cause a fire.
7) It also prevents further damage to the appliance.
8) Fuses break when they 'blow' and have to be replaced.
9) A circuit breaker works like a fuse but can be reset and used again.

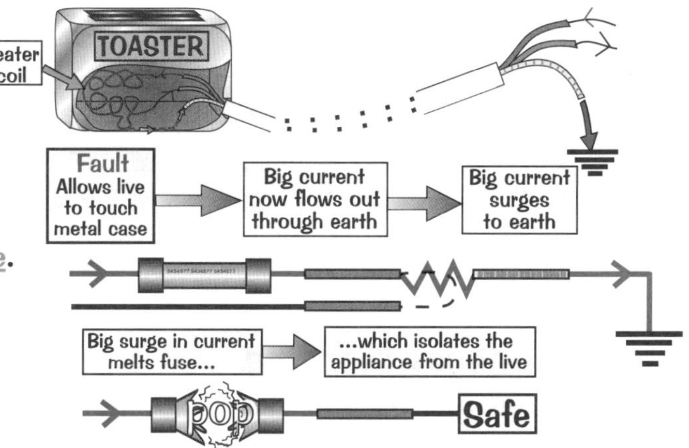

Electrical Power

The formula for electrical power is: **POWER (W) = VOLTAGE (V) × CURRENT (A)**

EXAMPLE: A toaster works off a supply voltage of 230 V and a current of 6 A. Find its power rating.

ANSWER: Power = Voltage × Current = 230 V × 6 A = 1380 W

CGP books are ACE — well, I had to get a plug in somewhere...

Have you ever noticed how if anything doesn't work in the house, it's always due to the fuse? It's annoying having to replace them when they blow, but they do make everything a whole load safer.

Ultrasound Treatments and Scans

Ultrasound is used for more than looking at babies, you know.
Learn all about it, right here...

Sound is a Longitudinal Wave

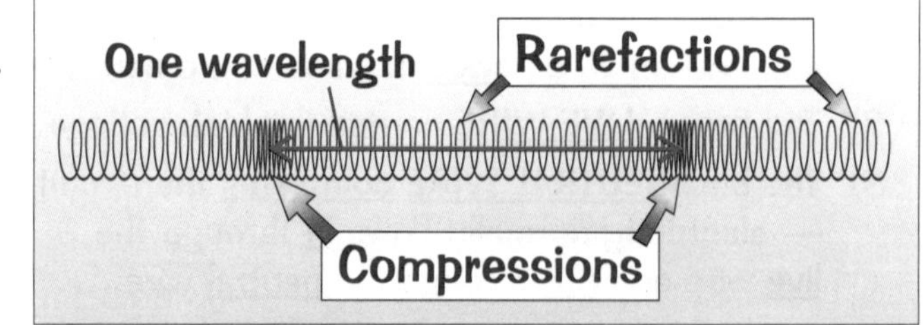

1) Sound waves (including ultrasound) are longitudinal.
2) Longitudinal waves squash up and stretch out the material they pass through. This makes compressions (areas of high pressure) and rarefactions (areas of low pressure) in the wave.
3) The WAVELENGTH is a full cycle of the wave. For example, from compression to compression.
4) FREQUENCY is how many complete waves there are per second passing a certain point.
5) Frequency is measured in hertz (Hz). 1 Hz is 1 complete wave per second.
6) For sound, high frequency = high pitch.

Ultrasound is Sound with a Higher Frequency Than We Can Hear

Sound with frequencies above the range of human hearing (20 000 Hz) is called ultrasound.
It has loads of uses in hospitals:

This means we can't hear it.

1) Breaking Down Kidney Stones

1) An ultrasound beam breaks down the kidney stone and turns it into sand-like particles.
2) These particles then pass out of the body in urine.
3) It's a good method because the patient doesn't need surgery.

2) For Body Scanning

1) Ultrasound can be used to look inside the body, to diagnose problems or do a scan of an unborn baby.
2) When an ultrasound wave passes through the body, some of the wave is reflected back and detected.
3) The detected waves form a picture.

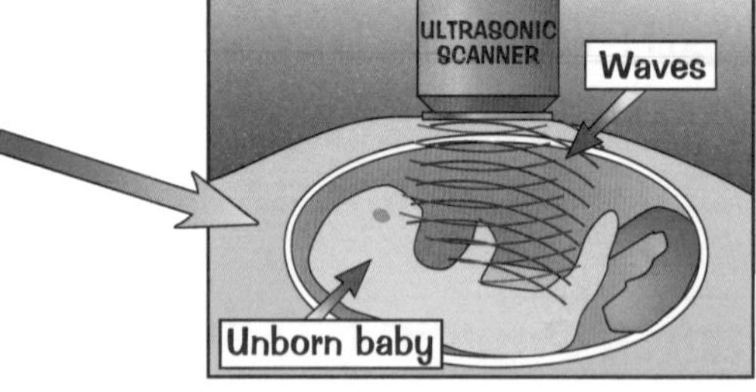

3) Measuring the Speed of Blood Flow

Ultrasound can also be used to measure how fast blood is flowing in the body.

Looking at things with sound — weird if you ask me...

Pity that you can't see into people's minds when they have headphones on... Well, you win some, you lose some.

Radioactive Decay and Background Radiation

Phew. Now all that electricity and sound stuff is out of the way we can get onto more exciting stuff. Ooooh.

Radioactivity Comes From an Unstable Nucleus

1) Radioactivity (or radiation) comes from the nucleus of an atom that is unstable.
2) An unstable nucleus can decay (break down) naturally at random.
3) As it decays, it can give out three forms of radiation — alpha (α), beta (β) and gamma (γ).
4) An alpha particle is a helium nucleus.
5) It is made up of two protons and two neutrons.
6) A beta particle is a fast-moving electron.
7) A gamma ray is an electromagnetic wave.

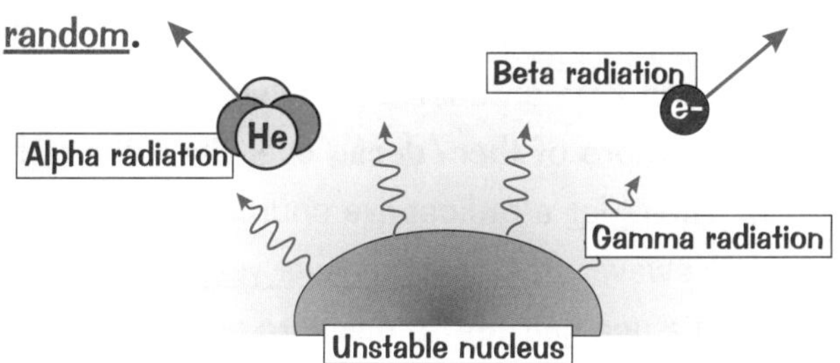

Background Radiation Comes from Many Sources

1) Anywhere you go there will be background radiation.
2) Background radiation comes from lots of different sources.
3) Natural radioactive substances are all around us — in the air, in food, in building materials and in the rocks under our feet. They have unstable atoms which decay.
4) Radiation from space, known as cosmic rays, comes mostly from the Sun.
5) Some background radiation comes from man-made sources like waste from industry and hospitals.

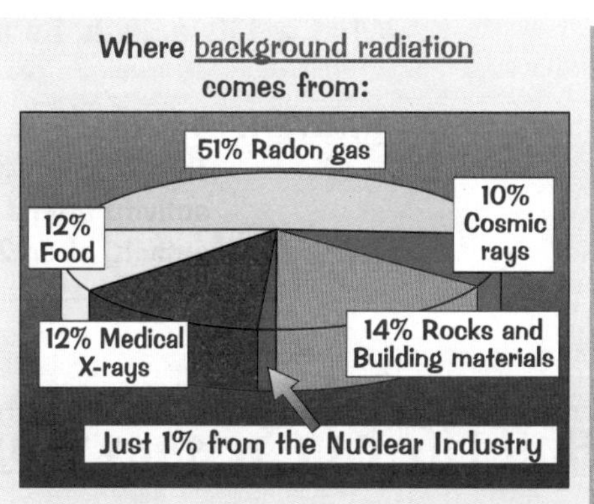

The Amount of Background Radiation Depends on Where You Are

1) The amount of background radiation can vary depending on where you are and your job.
2) For example, if your house is built on radioactive rocks, you may be exposed to more radiation.

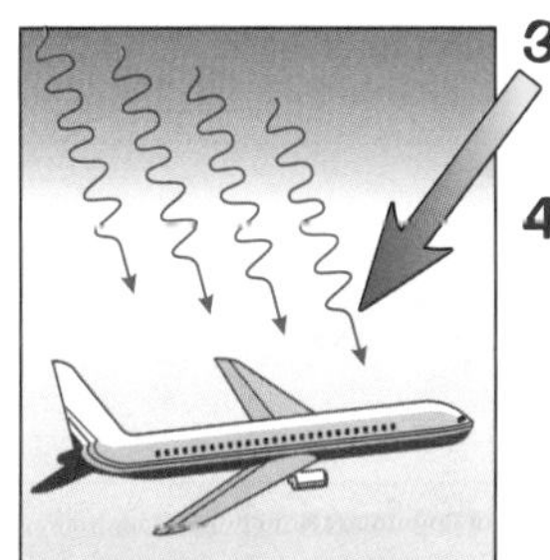

3) When you fly in an aeroplane you're exposed to more cosmic rays.
4) If you work in an industry that uses radiation, such as nuclear power or in a hospital, you will be exposed to more radiation.

If you are exposed to radiation it means that alpha, beta or gamma radiation comes into contact with your body.

I once beta particle — it cried for ages...

DON'T PANIC — background radiation won't harm you. So you can't use it as an excuse to get out of your exams...

Radioactivity and Half-Life

It's your lucky day... You get to do some maths on this page. Whoop.

Radioactivity Decreases Over Time

1) Radioactivity (or activity) is the number of decays per second.
2) It is measured in becquerels (Bq) or counts per minute (cpm). 1 Bq is 1 decay per second.
3) Each time an unstable nucleus decays, there is one less nucleus to decay later.
4) As more of them decay over time, the radioactivity of the source as a whole decreases.
5) The older a radioactive source is, the less radiation it gives out.
6) However, the activity never reaches zero.
7) We use half-life to measure how quickly the activity decreases:

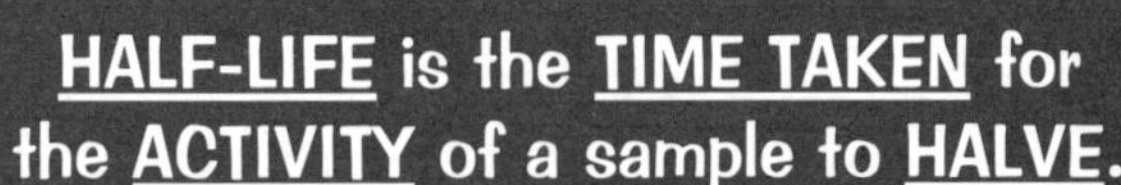

HALF-LIFE is the TIME TAKEN for the ACTIVITY of a sample to HALVE.

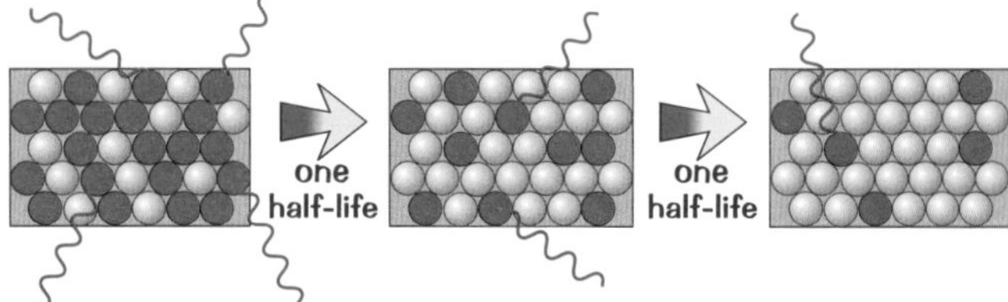

one half-life
one half-life

EXAMPLE:

The activity of a radioactive sample is 640 Bq. Its half-life is 2 hours. What will its activity be after 4 hours?

ANSWER: 4 hours ÷ 2 hours = 2 half-lives.
The activity will halve after each half-life, so:
activity after 1 half-life = 640 Bq ÷ 2 = 320 Bq
activity after 2 half-lives = 320 ÷ 2 = 160 Bq

Half-Life can be shown on a Graph

The half-life of a sample can also be shown on a graph. Relax, this is (almost) fun.

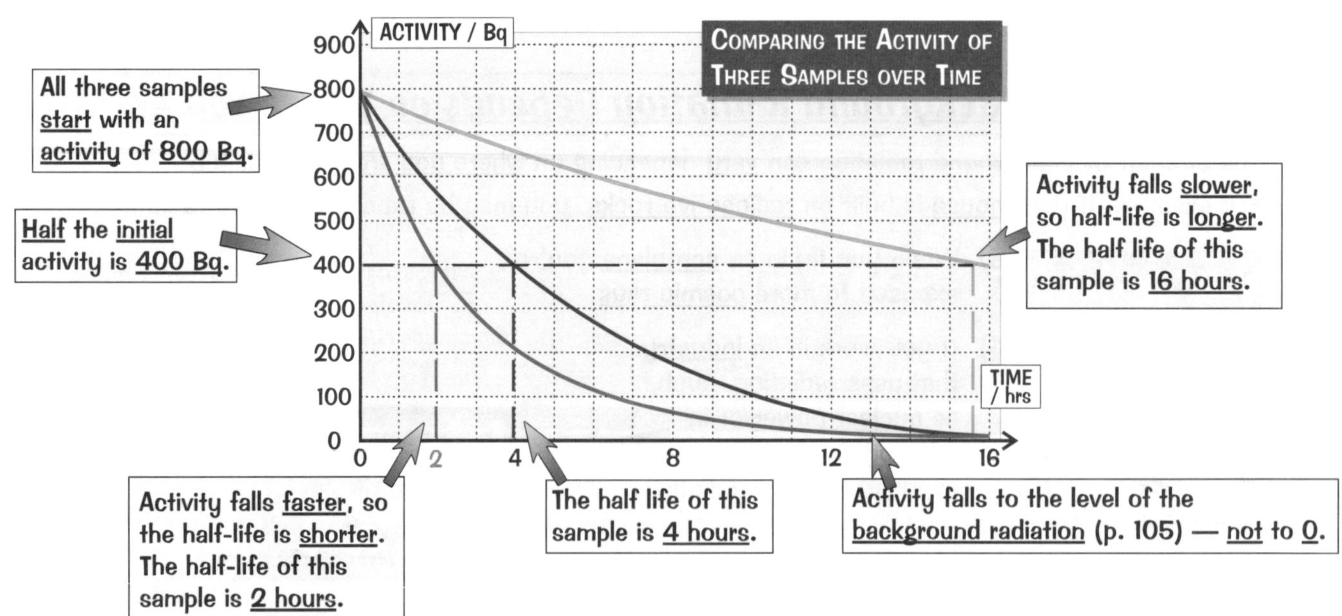

COMPARING THE ACTIVITY OF THREE SAMPLES OVER TIME
ACTIVITY / Bq
900
800
700
600
500
400
300
200
100
0
0
2
4
8
12
16
TIME / hrs
All three samples start with an activity of 800 Bq.
Half the initial activity is 400 Bq.
Activity falls slower, so half-life is longer. The half life of this sample is 16 hours.
Activity falls faster, so the half-life is shorter. The half-life of this sample is 2 hours.
The half life of this sample is 4 hours.
Activity falls to the level of the background radiation (p. 105) — not to 0.

Half-life of a box of chocolates — about five minutes...

To measure half-life, you time how long it takes for the number of decays per second to halve. Simples.

Ionising Radiation

Nuclear radiation (alpha, beta and gamma) and X-rays are ionising. They can damage living cells.

Ionising Radiation Harms Living Cells

1) When ionising radiation meets a molecule it can cause ionisation.
2) This means that the molecule gains or loses electrons.
3) When ionisation happens to molecules within a cell, it can damage the cell.
4) This can cause cancer or kill the cell completely.

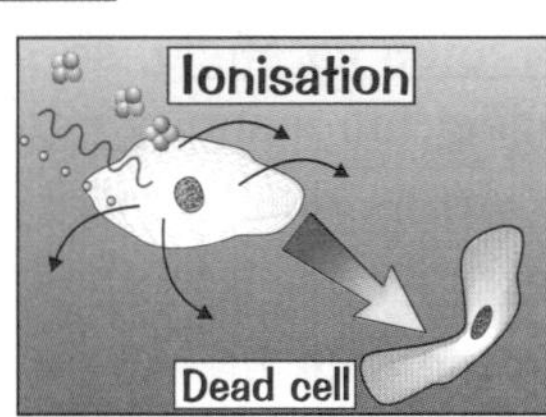

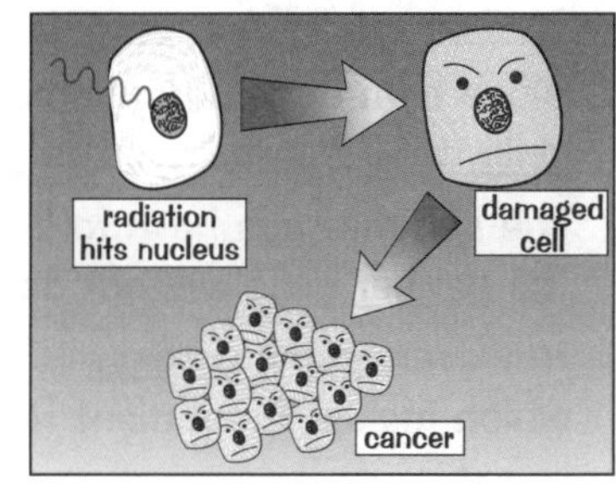

Which Radiation is the Most Dangerous Depends on Where it is

1) Ionising radiation can be absorbed (taken in) by different materials, such as skin.
2) OUTSIDE the body, beta and gamma sources are the most dangerous.
3) This is because beta and gamma can pass through the skin and get to the organs.
4) Alpha is much less dangerous because it can't pass through the skin.
5) INSIDE the body though, alpha is the most dangerous.
6) Beta and gamma mostly pass straight out without doing much damage.

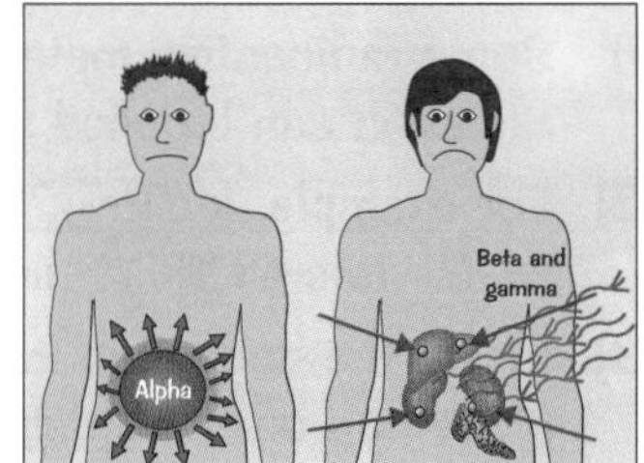

X-rays and Gamma Rays are Electromagnetic Waves

1) X-rays and gamma rays are both ionising electromagnetic waves.
2) They have similar wavelengths, and so have similar properties, but are made in different ways.

X-Rays are Used in Hospitals, but they can be Dangerous

1) Radiographers in hospitals take X-ray images of people to see whether they have any broken bones.
2) X-rays pass easily through flesh, but not so easily through denser material like bones or metal.
3) The thicker or denser the material, the more X-rays that are absorbed.
4) The different amount of radiation absorbed makes an X-ray image.
5) X-rays can cause cancer, so radiographers wear lead aprons, and stand behind a lead screen or leave the room when using X-rays.
6) This helps to keep their exposure to X-rays to a minimum.

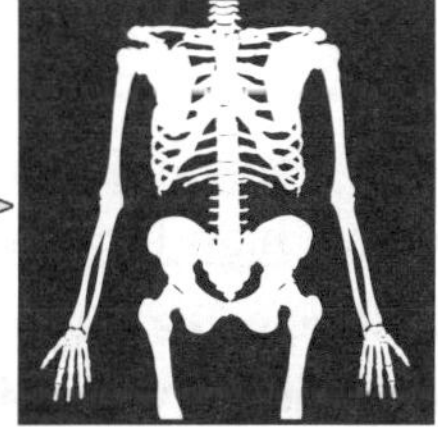

Make no bones about it — this stuff is dangerous...

Alpha particles, beta particles, gamma rays and X-rays can all be harmful if you have too much of them. Easy, right? Well actually this stuff is pretty difficult to get your head around. You're just going to have to get on with learning it.

Medical Uses of Radiation

Ionising radiation has loads of uses in hospitals, and you have to know all about them. Whoop-ti-do.

Radiotherapy — the Treatment of Cancer Using Gamma Rays

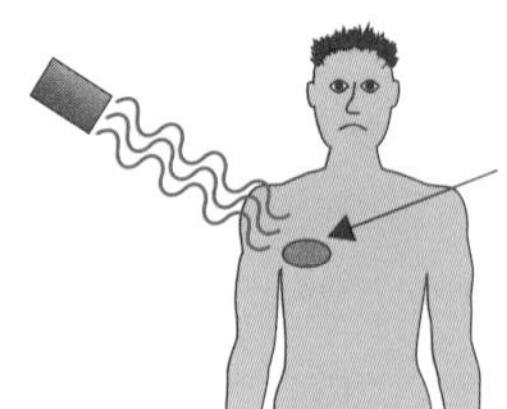

1) Since high doses of gamma rays will kill all living cells, they can be used to treat cancers.
2) The gamma rays have to be directed carefully, so they kill the cancer cells without damaging too many normal cells.
3) However, some damage is done to normal cells, which makes the patient feel very ill.
4) But if the cancer is killed off in the end, then it's worth it.

Tracers in Medicine — Short Half-life Gamma and Beta Emitters

1) Some radioactive materials that give out gamma (and sometimes beta) radiation can be used as tracers in the body to diagnose illnesses.
2) For example, iodine-123 is a radioactive tracer which gets absorbed by the thyroid gland.
3) Inside the body, the tracer gives out radiation which can be picked up on the outside to show where any problems are.
4) All tracers must be GAMMA or BETA (never alpha).
5) This is because gamma and beta radiation can penetrate tissue and so are able to pass out of the body and be detected.
6) Alpha radiation can't penetrate tissue, so you couldn't detect the radiation on the outside of the body.
7) Also alpha is more dangerous inside the body (see previous page).
8) Medical tracers should have a short half-life so they are not active in the body for a long time.
9) This is because radiation can damage cells.

Sterilisation of Medical Equipment Using Gamma Rays

1) Medical equipment can be sterilised by exposing them to a high dose of gamma rays.
2) This works because the gamma rays kill all microbes (germs).
3) Using radiation instead of boiling doesn't involve high temperatures.
4) So things like thermometers and plastic instruments can be sterilised without being damaged by the heat.

Ionising radiation — just what the doctor ordered...

See — ionising radiation isn't all bad. It also kills bad things, like cancer and germs, and helps doctors to diagnose illnesses. Coming up on the next page are even more uses for radiation. Bet you can't wait.

Other Uses of Radiation

Radioactive materials aren't just used in hospitals (see previous page) — you've got to know these uses too.

Tracers in Industry — For Finding Leaks

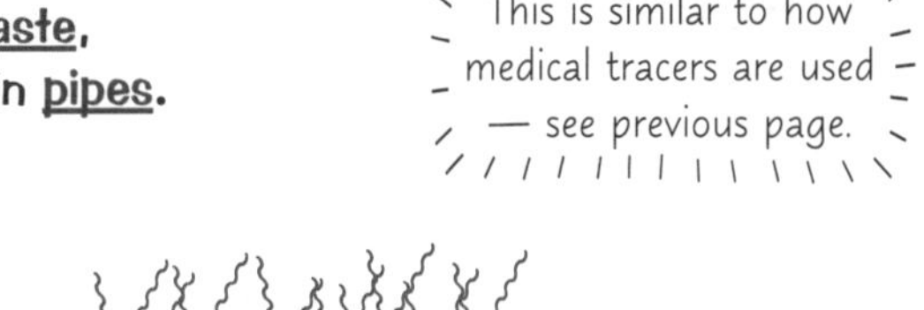

This is similar to how medical tracers are used — see previous page.

1) Radioactive materials can be used to track the movement of waste, find the route of underground pipes or find leaks or blockages in pipes.
2) To check a pipe, you just squirt the radioactive material in, then go along the outside with a detector.
3) If the radioactivity reduces or stops after a certain point, there must be a leak or blockage there.
4) This is really useful for hidden or underground pipes — no need to dig up the road to find the leak.

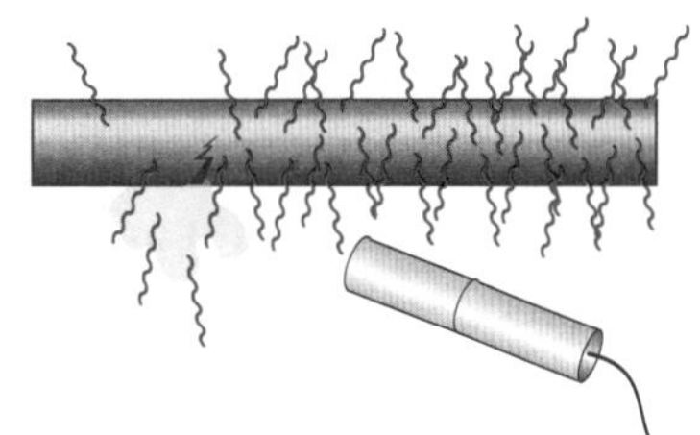

Smoke Detectors — Alpha Radiation

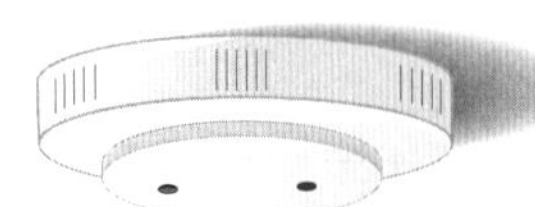

1) A substance that gives out alpha radiation is used in a smoke detector.
2) The alpha radiation causes ionisation of the air particles.
3) The ionisation allows a current to flow inside the detector.
4) If there is a fire, then smoke particles are hit by the alpha particles instead.
5) So there is less ionisation of the air particles.
6) The current is reduced causing the alarm to sound.

Radioactive Dating of Rocks and Old Materials

1) Scientists use radioactivity and half-life to work out the age of some rocks and old materials.
2) The amount of radioactive material left in a sample, and its half-life, tells us how long the thing has been around.

Phil took radioactive dating a bit too far.

Dating Rocks — Relative Proportions Calculations

1) Uranium can have a very long half-life.
2) It decays to produce lead.
3) The ratio of uranium to lead in a sample of rock can tell us how old the rock is, using the known half-life of the uranium (around 4.5 billion years).

Initially	After one half-life	After two half-lives
100% uranium	50% uranium	25% uranium
0% lead	50% lead	75% lead
ratio of 1:0	ratio of 1:1	ratio of 1:3

So if the ratio in a rock is 1:1, we know that the rock is 1 half life old = 4.5 billion years old.

Radioactive Carbon Dating

1) There is a radioactive type of carbon that is found in living things.
2) When living things die, this carbon is trapped inside, and it gradually decays.
3) So the amount of radioactive carbon left in an old material can tell you how old it is.

No need to be alarmed, but there's radiation in your smoke detector...

Nuclear radiation is used for loads more things than tracers and smoke detectors. It can be dangerous if you're not careful with it, but mostly it's really handy. Please don't eat your smoke detector though. Bad idea.

Nuclear Power

One more use for radioactive materials — nuclear power. Keep going, you're nearly at the end of the module.

Nuclear Fission — The Splitting Up of Uranium Atoms

1) Nuclear power stations are powered by nuclear reactors.
2) In a nuclear reactor, uranium atoms split up and release energy in the form of heat.
3) This is a nuclear reaction called nuclear fission.
4) This heat is then used to heat water to produce steam.
5) The steam turns a turbine which drives a generator that produces electricity.

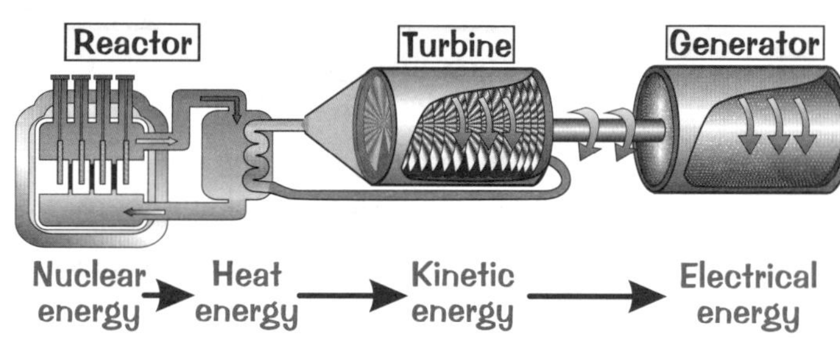

The Splitting of Uranium-235 Needs Neutrons

1) Materials can become radioactive when they absorb extra neutrons.
2) In a nuclear reactor, Uranium-235 (the fuel) absorbs neutrons to create Uranium-236, which is unstable.
3) The Uranium-236 then decays and splits up.
4) This releases loads of energy.
5) It also releases 2 or 3 neutrons which go on to produce a chain reaction.
6) This means that the neutrons get absorbed by more atoms of Uranium-235, which makes more Uranium-236.
7) This then decays to give more energy and more neutrons... And so on...
8) Nuclear bombs are chain reactions that have gone out of control.
9) But in nuclear reactors the chain reaction is kept under control using control rods that absorb extra neutrons.

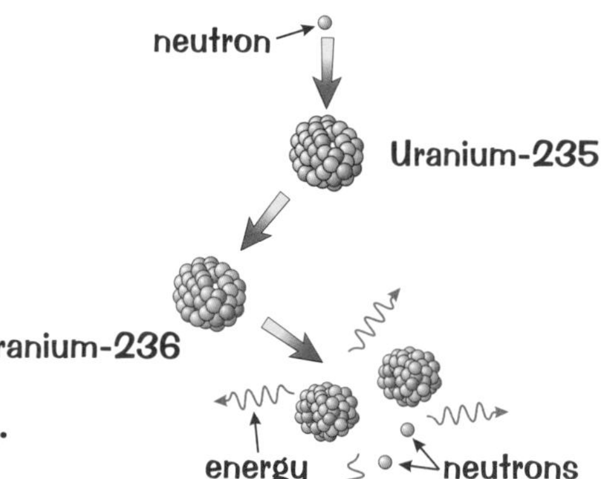

Nuclear Fission creates Radioactive Waste

1) Nuclear fission produces radioactive materials, which can't just be thrown away.
2) Some materials are useful as medical radioisotopes that can be used in hospitals as tracers (p. 108).
3) But some have no use. They are just radioactive waste, which needs to be carefully disposed of.

I know an unstable nucleus — she's always fission for compliments...

Radioactive waste is often put in thick metal boxes and placed in a deep hole, which is then filled with concrete. It's supposed to be safe but some people worry that the materials could leak out and be harmful.

Nuclear Fusion

Loads of energy's released when you break big atoms apart, or when you join small ones together.

Nuclear Fusion — The Joining of Small Atomic Nuclei

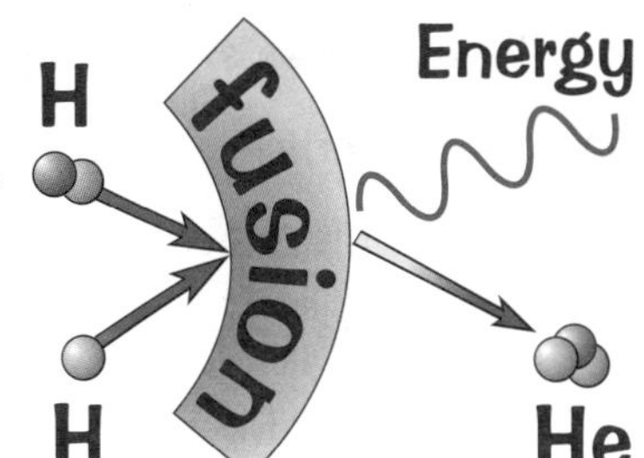

1) Nuclear fusion is the opposite of nuclear fission.
2) In nuclear fusion, two nuclei join together to create a larger nucleus.
3) Fusion releases a lot of heat energy — more than fission.
4) So people are trying to develop fusion reactors to make electricity.
5) The big problem is that fusion only happens at really high temperatures (about 10 000 000 °C).
6) No material can withstand that temperature, so fusion reactors are really hard to build.
7) It's also hard to safely control the high temperatures.

Scientists Work Together on Fusion Research

1) There are a few experimental fusion reactors around at the moment, but none of them are generating electricity yet.
2) It takes more energy to get up to temperature than the reactor can produce.
3) Research into fusion power production is carried out by international groups.
4) This means they can share the costs, expertise, experience and the benefits (when they eventually get it to work reliably).

Cold Fusion — Hoax or Energy of the Future?

1) Cold fusion is nuclear fusion which occurs at around room temperature.
2) In 1989, two scientists reported that they had managed to release energy from cold fusion.
3) This caused a lot of excitement — cold fusion would make lots of electricity, easily and cheaply.
4) The experiments and data were shared with other scientists so they could repeat the experiments.
5) But other scientists did not get the same results when they repeated the experiments.
6) So the method was not accepted and people doubted the claims of the two scientists.

Pity they can't release energy by confusion...*

It'd be great if we could get nuclear fusion to work. There's a load of fuel available and it doesn't create much waste. But at the moment you need more energy to create the right conditions than you can get out. Shame.

*There'd be plenty of physics books to use as fuel.

Revision Summary for Module P4

Some of this stuff can be just learnt and repeated — other parts actually need thinking about. All the information's there, you've just got to sit down and put the effort in. The best thing to do is take it a page at a time, break it down and make sure you've learnt every little thing. If you can answer these questions, you should have no problem with anything the examiners throw at you. You'd better get going.

1) What causes static charge to build up?
2) Which particles move when static charge builds up?
3) Give two examples each of static electricity being: a) a nuisance, b) dangerous.
4) Give three examples of how static electricity can be helpful. Write all the details.
5) Explain what current, voltage and resistance are in an electric circuit.
6) What happens to the current flowing through a circuit if the resistance of a variable resistor is increased?
7)* A resistor in a circuit is supplied with a voltage of 12 V and a current of 2 A. Calculate its resistance.
8) Describe what earthing and double insulated mean.

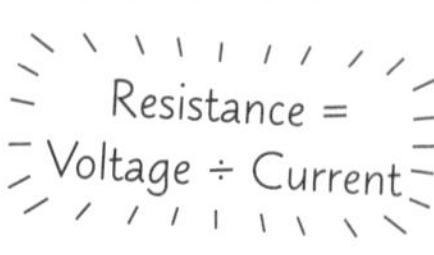

9)* A kettle uses a 230 V mains supply and a current of 10 A.
Calculate its power rating.

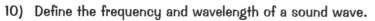

10) Define the frequency and wavelength of a sound wave.
11) Give two examples of how ultrasound can be used in a hospital.
12) What is alpha radiation? What is beta radiation?
13) Give three sources of background radiation.
14) Give a definition of half-life.
15) Briefly describe what ionising radiation does to living cells.
16) Describe the similarities and differences between gamma rays and X-rays.
17) Describe how radioactive materials are used in each of the following:
a) treating cancer, b) as tracers in medicine, c) sterilising equipment.
18) Describe in detail how radioactive sources are used in each of the following:
a) tracers in industry, b) smoke detectors, c) radioactive dating.
19) What type of particle makes uranium-235 unstable in a nuclear reactor?
20) Explain how a chain reaction is created in a nuclear reactor.
21) What is the difference between nuclear fission and nuclear fusion?
22) Briefly explain why it's difficult to produce electricity from nuclear fusion.

* Answers on page 116.

Index

Index

Index

Index

Answers

Revision Summary for Module C3 (page 42)

2) 14 H and 6 C

3)

```
    H   H   H
    |   |   |
H - C - C - C - H
    |   |   |
    H   H   H
```

4) magnesium + oxygen → magnesium oxide

5) $2Na + 2H_2O \rightarrow 2NaOH + H_2$

13) Reaction A has the faster reaction rate.

14) a) 40
b) 108
c) 12 + (16 × 2) = 44
d) 24 + 12 + (16 × 3) = 84
e) 27 + 3 × (16 + 1) = 78
f) 65 + 16 = 81
g) (23 × 2) + 12 + (16 × 3) = 106
h) 23 + 35.5 = 58.5

15) $HCl + NaOH \rightarrow H_2O + NaCl$
73 g + 80 g = 36 g + mass of NaCl
Mass of NaCl = 117 g

Revision Summary for Module P3 (page 59)

1) u = 0 m/s, v = 0.08 m/s, t = 35 s
Distance = (u + v) ÷ 2 × t
= (0 + 0.08) ÷ 2 × 35 = 1.4 m

4) Acceleration = change in speed ÷ time
= (14 − 0) ÷ 0.4 = 35 m/s^2

11) Force = mass × acceleration
= 4 × 7.5 = 30 N

14) Momentum = mass × velocity so,
velocity = momentum ÷ mass = 45 ÷ 6 = 7.5 m/s

18) Power = energy ÷ time = 540 000 ÷ 270
= 2000 W (= 2 kW)

20) G.P.E. = m × g × h = 12 × 10 × 4.5 = 540 J

21) K.E. gained = G.P.E. lost = 150 kJ

Revision Summary for Module B4 (page 82)

4) 80 ants × 4000 m^2
= <u>320 000 ants in the whole car park</u>.

5) (23 × 28) ÷ 4 = 161 woodlice.

Revision Summary for Module C4 (page 98)

12) MgO

18) a) bromine + lithium → lithium bromide
b) chlorine + potassium → potassium chloride
c) iodine + sodium → sodium iodide

Revision Summary for Module P4 (page 112)

7) Resistance = voltage ÷ current
Resistance = 12 V ÷ 2 A = 6 Ω

9) Power = voltage × current
Power = 230 × 10 = 2300 W (2.3 kW)